D1713175

COASTAL ZONE MANAGEMENT:
MULTIPLE USE WITH CONSERVATION

UNIVERSITY OF CALIFORNIA
ENGINEERING AND PHYSICAL
SCIENCES EXTENSION SERIES

Howard Seifert, Editor · Space Technology

Robert L. Pecsok, Editor · Principles and Practice of Gas Chromatography

Howard Seifert and Kenneth Brown, Editors · Ballistic Missile and Space Vehicle Systems

George R. Pitman, Jr., Editor · Inertial Guidance

Kenneth Brown and Lawrence D. Ely, Editors · Space Logistics Engineering

Robert W. Vance and W. M. Duke, Editors · Applied Cryogenic Engineering

Donald P. LeGalley, Editor · Space Science

Robert W. Vance, Editor · Cryogenic Technology

Donald P. LeGalley and Alan Rosen, Editors · Space Physics

Edwin F. Beckenbach, Editor · Applied Combinatorial Mathematics

Alan S. Goldman and T. B. Slattery · Maintainability: A Major Element of System Effectiveness

C. T. Leondes and Robert W. Vance, Editors · Lunar Missions and Exploration

J. E. Hove and W. C. Riley, Editors · Modern Ceramics: Some Principles and Concepts

J. E. Hove and W. C. Riley, Editors · Ceramics for Advanced Technologies

Joseph A. Pask · An Atomistic Approach to the Nature and Properties of Materials

John F. Brahtz, Editor · Ocean Engineering

Edwin F. Beckenbach and Charles B. Tompkins, Editors · Concepts of Communication: Interpersonal, Intrapersonal, and Mathematical

W. D. Hershberger, Editor · Topics for Solid State and Quantum Mechanics

John F. Brahtz, Editor · Coastal Zone Management: Multiple Use with Conservation

COASTAL ZONE MANAGEMENT:

Multiple Use with Conservation

The Authors

LINCOLN D. CATHERS

MARION CLAWSON

J. GORDON HAMMER

FRANCIS J. HORTIG

EDWARD M. MAC CUTCHEON

WILLIAM A. NIERENBERG

ERMAN A. PEARSON

MILNER B. SCHAEFER

NORMAN F. SCHNEIDEWIND

DAVID STERNLIGHT

Editor

J. F. PEEL BRAHTZ

Engineering Consultant,
La Jolla, California

JOHN WILEY AND SONS, INC.
NEW YORK · LONDON · SYDNEY · TORONTO

THE AUTHORS _____

J. F. PEEL BRAHTZ, Engineering Consultant, La Jolla, California

LINCOLN D. CATHERS, Deep Submergence Systems Project, Naval Ship Systems Command, Department of the Navy, Washington, D.C.

MARION CLAWSON, Director, Land Use and Management Program, Resources for the Future, Inc., Washington, D.C.

J. GORDON HAMMER, Head, Civil Engineering Department, U.S. Naval Civil Engineering Laboratory, Port Hueneme, California

FRANCIS J. HORTIG, Executive Officer, California State Lands Commission, Sacramento, California

EDWARD M. MAC CUTCHEON, Director, Systems Development, National Ocean Survey, National Oceanic and Atmospheric Administration, U.S. Department of Commerce, Rockville, Maryland

WILLIAM A. NIERENBERG, Director, Scripps Institution of Oceanography, University of California, San Diego, California

ERMAN A. PEARSON, Chairman, Division of Hydraulic and Sanitary Engineering, Department of Civil Engineering, University of California, Berkeley, California

MILNER B. SCHAEFER (Deceased)

NORMAN F. SCHNEIDEWIND, Professor, Department of Operations Research and Administrative Sciences, U.S. Naval Postgraduate School, Monterey, California

DAVID STERNLIGHT, Director, Economic Planning, Planning and Development Department, Litton Industries, Inc., Beverly Hills, California

PREFACE

The purpose of this book is to indicate a rational approach to regional management of the coastal zone and to describe management's problem. This is supported by three complementary objectives:

1. To describe a rationale for planning that supports innovation by management, provides for optimal utilization of resources, and relates regional plans to national policy.
2. To provide an overview of the structure of the goals for multiple and conservative use of coastal resources.
3. To describe technologies that are applicable in formulating balanced solutions to the management problem of conflicting goals.

Regional planners are required to interpret, evaluate, and coordinate varied inputs from economists, engineers, scientists, and public officials who are concerned with coastal development. I have sought to anticipate their need for a unified approach to managing the coastal zone. Therefore, I have addressed a comprehensive range of technologies and have surveyed a widely diffused problem area to polarize thought in diverse disciplines to classical issues and problems. Furthermore, goals and conflicts are described from the standpoint of public interests represented at the national level. Yet, it is recognized that most planning is implemented properly at local and regional levels. Finally, the selection and classification of topics have been made with careful attention to the requirements of an engineering rationale for planning and design.

The three objectives of this work are singularly addressed in the Introduction, Part 1, and Part 2, respectively. The Introduction offers a first-order resolution of the problem situation. Furthermore, the problem elements are related to a three-phase planning cycle that is depicted schematically. Part 1 includes treatments by specialists in five classical areas of goals and conflicts relating to multiple use of coastal zone resources. Part 2 offers a discussion of technological requirements and resources that are responsive to goals treated in Part 1.

The book is oriented to needs of professional planners and specialists whose disciplines are essential to excellence in coastal zone management. However, I have found the included information to be a useful resource for graduate students in an interdisciplinary seminar on environmental and marine systems.

I acknowledge the guidance and suggestions of members of the *ad hoc* Advisory Committee to the University of California State-wide Lecture Series, "Ocean Engineering and Management of the Coastal Zone." The contributors to this book were previously the lecturers for this series. The members of the Advisory Committee and their affiliations at the time of the University Lecture Series were the following:

Paul D. Arthur, University of California, Irvine

Helen Barry, University of California, Berkeley

F. Gilman Blake, Chevron Research, Los Angeles, California

Joseph E. Bodovitz, San Francisco Bay Conservation and Development Commission, California

J. F. Peel Brahtz, University of California, Los Angeles

Wilbert M. Chapman, Van Camp Seafood Company, Long Beach, California

John P. Craven, Special Projects Office, U.S. Navy, Washington, D.C.

Phillip J. Daniel, Daniel, Mann, Johnson and Mendenhall, Los Angeles, California

Harmer E. Davis, University of California, Berkeley

John C. Dillon, University of California, Los Angeles

Thomas H. Hazlett, University of California, Berkeley

Werner Z. Hirsch, University of California, Los Angeles

John D. Isaacs, Scripps Institution of Oceanography, University of California, San Diego

Russell Keim, National Academy of Engineering, Washington, D.C.

John R. Kiely, Bechtel Corporation, San Francisco, California

Bernice W. Park, University of California, Los Angeles

Erman A. Pearson, University of California, Berkeley

William Pereira, Pereira and Associates, Los Angeles, California

David Potter, General Motors Corporation, Santa Barbara, California

Andreas B. Rechnitzer, North American Rockwell Corporation, Long Beach, California

Milner B. Schaefer, Institute of Marine Resources, University of California, San Diego

H. L. Tallman, University of California, Los Angeles, California

Elmer Wheaton, Lockheed Missile and Space Company, Palo Alto, California

Robert L. Wiegel, University of California, Berkeley

Warren S. Wooster, Scripps Institution of Oceanography, University of California, San Diego

J. F. PEEL BRAHTZ

La Jolla, California
June 1971

CONTENTS _____

Contents

COASTAL ZONE MANAGEMENT:
MULTIPLE USE WITH CONSERVATION

CHAPTER 1

Introduction

J. F. PEEL BRAHTZ

A complex *and diffused* problem situation exists concerning the geographical regions of the coastal zone. Issues and conflicts over environmental protection, urban development, and utilization of resources necessary for the satisfaction of basic human needs are involved. The implications have a social, economic, and technological affect on all levels of the national political structure. Resolution of the problem situation requires a unified management approach, including the advance development planning techniques considered in this work by the authors contributing.

1. THE COASTAL ZONE PROBLEM SITUATION

Public outcry against environmental degradation in the United States is demanding visible and effective governmental response. Precursory utterances in the past by conservationists and other concerned individuals within the professional communities have contributed to the general awakening. Moreover, along with public awareness of the consequences of continuing mismanagement of vital resources, a general appreciation has developed for the scope and complexity of the problem situation.

Government-sponsored studies of major environmental issues and investigations of underlying problems have polarized the need for national policy and regulation to facilitate the evaluation, decision, and implementation processes. Furthermore, where important ecological systems transcend political boundaries, international agreements must be sought. Such policy, to be meaningful, must identify objectives and opportunities and also specify tributary goals and constraints for maintaining acceptable standards of environmental quality and resource conservation.

Recognizing the diffusion of economic, environmental, sociological, and technological factors, investigators have generally called for a well planned and coordinated approach to the major problems. This approach would require policy guidance and at least preliminary implementation of broadly conceived solutions by centralized national authority while seeking the cooperation of responsive regional and local management. Moreover, since the studies and investigations have shown the need for interdisciplinary teams of recognized technologists and professional leaders, a diversity of advanced technical and management skills to resolve the issues and solve the resulting problems of management is needed.

A major sector of the national environment and resources is the coastal zone. This is the staging ground for use of marine resources and constitutes all access to the oceans and the Great Lakes. The coastal zone is particularly recognized by the public as a vital national resource requiring skilled management to solve unique and critical problems. These problems stem from the multiple use of the coastal resources and are sufficiently diffused throughout the national, social, and economic structure to require a unified and integrated resolution similar to that used for national environmental problems.

The coastal zone is a geographical concept. Its predominant physical characteristic is the shoreline where land, sea, and air, or, in geological terms, the lithosphere, hydrosphere, and atmosphere, join to form a triple interface. The coastal zone is a continuum of geographical regions. Each is characterized by its own pattern of economic, social, and political activities, which relate to the distribution and availability of resources. Furthermore, the manner and rate of resource utilization may affect the stability of the constituent geological, biological, and meteorological subsystems interacting and in dynamic balance against their respective environmental requirements. The many and divers human activities involved in the use of the coastal zone constitute imposing, excessive, and competitive demands on the limited resources; consequently they often critically affect regional ecological systems.

The use of natural resources must modify the environment to some degree. It is therefore essential that we sufficiently understand the threatened ecology as to determine what level of man's intervention can be tolerated without destabilizing vital systems. Technology must supply tactical options for pursuing legitimate goals, and the relative consequences of alternatives must be well understood to modulate intelligently our activities in the coastal zone. Furthermore, the need for priority and decision criteria required for proper adjudication of goal conflicts along with the need to conserve resources to protect the natural environment compound and intensify the coastal management problem. Consequently, optimal management of the coastal zone and the best skills and technological capabilities to support this management ideal are required. This implies a broadly conceived systems approach at all levels in the government hierarchy to provide for objectivity and innovation in large-scale conceptual planning with concordant evaluation and implementation of selected strategies.

Excellence in management is an unmistakable requirement for handling the complexities of the coastal zone problem situation.

Features of the coastal zone as a planning consideration

To develop a viable management rationale as part of a master development plan to control man's activities and therefore the extent of his intervention in the coastal environment, the development planner presumes an understanding of interactions between natural and artificial systems. Accordingly, in considering the relevancy of features of the coastal zone to the management function, one must identify relationships between physical characteristics of the environment and purposeful human activities requiring management control.

Often it may not be feasible to relate environmental parameters quantitatively to human operational parameters without intensive analysis considering included geological, meteorological, biological, social, economic, and political factors. However, the development planner will render all problems tractable by acquiring at least a qualitative understanding of the problem elements and their interactions. Generally these problem situations are handled with reasonable credibility when scientific and technical specialists are members of the development planning team.

Geological characteristics. All geologists do not necessarily concur about a universal system for classifying shorelines. In detailed analyses by specialists with singular objectives the classification of coastal phenomena tends to be oriented around their objectives and the special constraints of their disciplines. However, notwithstanding lack of universal acceptance of many generalizations, most geologists recognize that the coastal zone is one of the most dynamically active erosional environments on earth. The eroding forces of wind, waves, streams, and glaciers impinge on the coast to sculpture landforms inherent to the regional geological structures. All coastal landforms can be classified as either *embayed* or *plains coasts*.

On embayed coasts the sea extends inland to form embayments sometimes for long distances. Typical examples are the stream-eroded coastlines of the Bay of Biscay and the glacially modified coasts of Norway, Maine, Scotland, Alaska, and New Zealand. In contrast the plains coasts feature stretches of low-lying sandy islands and sand bars bordering flat coastal lands. Prime examples of this type of landform are the continuous sand bars forming Cape Hatteras on the Carolina coast and similar islands from Long Island, N.Y., around Florida and the Gulf of Mexico, to the southern end of Texas.

The discerning development planner will recognize various environmental features associated with *embayed* and *plains coasts* for their significance to the evolution of economic, political, and social infrastructure. By considering historical examples in regional geography, one gains some understanding of how contrasting landforms have influenced the evolution of economic, social, and political systems. To support conclusions as to the relationships between geological conditions and the systems which man develops to exploit productive resources, one has the tangible evidence of some historical human artifacts, for example, engineering structures still standing which had been placed originally as components of larger systems. Such a retrospective view often may be the most reliable planning premise for formulating new large-scale concepts for the coastal zone. These are likely to include towers, floating airstrips, submerged platforms, and tethered buoyant structures.

Beneficial planning information can be derived from case studies in engineering design. One example is the ill-fated Texas Tower, which was to exploit the outer reaches of the continental shelf off the New England coast for military surveillance to counter the threat of aerial attack against the United States. Although, the concept exploited geological features of that particular coastal region, the design and construction of the installation did not take into account the rigors of the open ocean. Three tower-type structures were erected in 50-foot water depth to accommodate radar equipment and operational personnel on platforms 90 feet above the ocean surface. The platforms were triangular, 200 feet on a side, and supported on 10-foot concrete caissons embedded 50 feet in the ocean floor. One tower collapsed in 1960 because of severe storm damage. The Argus Island Research Station located 30 miles off the coast of Bermuda is a successful example and also involves hundreds of useful offshore oil drilling structures at many locations on the continental shelf. The Argus Island Station is a tower constructed in water depth of 195 feet. The 33-inch-diameter pipe legs are spaced 103 feet square on the bottom and taper to a 60-foot square at the top. The structure withstood exposure to 70-foot surface waves in 1963 with little damage.

The development planner will recognize that large-scale features of the predominant coastal landform are relatively unalterable and represent either opportunity or constraint in structuring a master plan for land use. Conversely, within the limits of technology he may readily modify the small-scale characteristics to achieve planning objectives. The planning concept might provide for the erection of special structures within the surf zone for preventing erosion and transport of beach sand, or it may require dredging of harbor channels to permit access for deep-draft vessels. Regardless of what the engineering and construction objectives are, they must consider the potential impact on the natural environment. Otherwise the activity may ultimately be either useless or counterproductive. Some informational inputs for development planning of this type are knowledge of wave action, sediment transport, and reactions of structures to the forces and physical conditions of the coastal environment.

The engineering community has adopted standard nomenclature for subdivisions of the geological features of the shore zone as indicated in Figure 1.

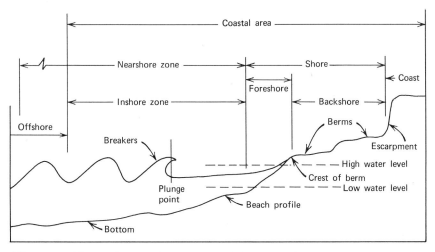

Figure 1. Nomenclature of the physical features of the coastal area.

Biological characteristics. Some aquatic and terrestrial resources are important to the welfare of mankind and depend on certain environments and natural populations of the coastal zone. The ecological systems which contribute to important living resources can be perturbed and inadvertently destabilized by the effects of artificial systems and activities of mankind, including those ancillary to the more basic uses of the coastal zone. Conversely, carefully designed schemes for constructive intervention can improve the living resources involved, particularly those of either recreational or commercial fisheries.

The development planner has to consider his implied mandate to provide for the conservative use and even the preservation of important living resources for future mankind as well as for man's immediate or foreseeable needs. This may indicate subtle requirements in planning and management criteria such as knowledge of the safe minimum levels of conservation which will protect valuable resources against economically irreversible diminution trends. The planner must appreciate that although it is necessary to provide conditions which protect certain species against physical extinction such as caused by the destruction of breeding environments, this is not a sufficient condition for always preserving the economic utility of some extractive resources. Managing the timed extraction of a living resource to maintain the maximum sustainable yield does not necessarily guarantee its ultimate conservation economically. Operating under conditions of sensitive economic balance can fail to provide for the continuance of economic incentives for use in the future.

The estuaries of the coastal zone provide habitats and breeding grounds for many species which comprise important fisheries or are components in the food chain. Also, the flora and fauna near shore areas generally depend on some specific feature of the coastal configuration for either habitat or seasonal refuge. These specified environments can include the bays, estuaries, protected outer coasts, or open rocky coasts, and are not necessarily unique to either of the two classical types of coastal landform, that is, embayed coasts or plains coasts.

Meteorological characteristics. Weather and climate are important planning factors in coastal zone development. Because of effects of climate and weather on resource utility, a development plan must clearly account for these factors.

Usually one of the first questions to be resolved in a specific evaluation of competing coastal resources uses is the degree of compatibility between existing conditions of climate and each of the proposed land uses. Furthermore, the planner may contemplate the feasibility of weather modification or otherwise ameliorating the effects of adverse conditions through available technical options.

The impact of weather and climate appears most significant in recreation, agriculture, and housing development. Outdoor swimming and sun bathing are most enjoyable where prevailing wind intensities and temperatures are mild. Sailboating requires brisk and steady winds distributed over the area of activity. Some agricultural crops require the climatic conditions of the nearshore environment and, therefore, must compete economically for use of premium coastal lands.

Large-scale meteorological characteristics, both cyclical and spatial, are generally considered uncontrollable or independent variables in a planning context. These, as with large-scale geological features, are considered beyond man's reasonable intervention with existing technology. Although large-scale weather and climate modification does not appear feasible in the foreseeable future, techniques for microclimatic control are available for conceptual planning and managing specific situations in coastal development. Research studies are being directed to achieve better understanding of the nature of tsunami, hurricane waves, and the destructive interactions between such disturbances and typical coastal configurations. Also investigations are being conducted on dispelling fog from airport runways and other vehicular transit lanes on the ground including the use of agricultural barriers to both noise and fog. Measures for modifying adverse marine weather conditions include jetties, windbreaks, storm drains, and breakwaters, all of which are included in the development planner's options for resolving conflicts and optimizing the use of coastal resources when meteorological characteristics are germane to the problem.

Uses of the coastal zone and included activities

In associating the needs of mankind with the available resources one must contemplate the feasibility of systems which would transform resource-based inputs into processed outputs designed specifically to serve the defined needs. Concepts for linking resources to man's needs include operational systems which perform functions by incorporating engineering artifice with human activity.

It is in this context that a systems development planner often considers coastal zone problem situations.

Resources of the coastal zone include such consumables as minerals and fish and involve such nonextractive uses as swimming, boating, surfing, waste dumping, sun bathing, and enjoyment of the aesthetic qualities of nature. Some of the significant uses and nearshore activities are classified in Table 1, according to the extractive or nonextractive character of the primary required resource.

TABLE 1

Extractive Use/Activity	Primary Resource
Commercial fishing	Deep ocean fisheries
Aquaculture	Shore zone biota
Surf fishing	Shore zone fauna
Kelp harvesting	Offshore flora
Boat sportfishing	Coastal zone fisheries
Desalination	Ocean chemicals
Mineral production	Marine minerals
Sand/gravel production	Nearshore sediments
Petroleum production	Subsea minerals
Nonextractive Use/Activity	**Primary Resource**
Policing and regulation	Access to coastal areas
Commercial shipping, deep draft	Navigable areas
Commercial shipping, moderate draft	Inshore areas, harbors
Transport right of way	Shoreline
Government reservation	Coastal areas
Underwater parks	Undisturbed sea bed
Housing, real estate development	Shore zone
Swimming, sunbathing, surfing	Unpolluted beaches, water
Waste disposal	Shoreline access to offshore areas
Resorts, parks	Shoreline, beaches
Recreational boating	Protected harbors

In considering the range of uses and included activities involving coastal resources, one realizes that the planning function is motivated by limitations of available resources and constraints on utilization. It is important to discern whether resources are limited by natural supply or accessibility. Moreover, in situations of goal conflict where resource availability is critical, a master development plan may distinguish between mutually exclusive uses and activities and those which can coexist, although competitively.

There is a spectrum of human needs in the many uses and activities in the coastal zone. Some needs are basic and critical to survival of mankind while others are merely desirable options. All, however, have an appropriate place in the economy. The coastal planner should identify resource uses and attendant activities with the urgency and importance of the underlying needs and assign planning priorities accordingly.

Intensification factors. There are factors which intensify the effects of various planning considerations when alternatives are being evaluated or conflicts are being analyzed as part of master plan development. Intensification factors usually can be properly identified and their impact resolved in the context of specific problem situations.

In cases of general or large-scale trends which comprise the coastal planning problem, it is this writer's opinion that by discerning the effect mechanisms of known intensification factors, management has useful leverage for controlling such trends. For example, population growth factors and migration incentives can often be related to distribution of water resources and curbs on environmental pollution, both of which are within the spectrum of management controls.

Worldwide expanding population has a particular impact on coastal zone development. Population migration is probably the most fundamental and pervasive of all planning factors which intensify conflicts and coastal management issues. The density of local populations is directly related to the intensity of the deleterious effects of urbanization on vital signs in the coastal ecology and is often the basis of constraints on coastal resources accessibility. Of the two aspects of population variation, *natural increase* and *migration,* the migration effect is the more complex; however, it is also more amenable to management controls which can be made available to government. Controls that can influence the rate and distribution of population growth may take the form of land-use constraints based on taxation, zoning, and legislative measures which bear on the development of industrial and services infrastructure.

In California air pollution has been analyzed as a factor in the increase of population densities at the outer edges of urban centers, thereby contributing to the sprawl which is threatening the relatively underdeveloped and naturally beautiful central coastline.

However, some planners are visualizing the allotment of future water resources as a potential control mechanism for modulating the growth of population densities along the threatened coastal regions of the state.

Goal conflicts, issues, problems

The issues and problems arising from basic goal conflicts of multiple use of the coastal zone can be resolved most efficiently through a well-ordered master development plan of regional scope. Jurisdictional and legal factors underlying problems of disputed access or control of resources, the economics of profit-oriented competition for access and use of coastal zone resources, sociological and economic factors bearing on issues of environmental degradation and resource conservation, and opportunities for technological innovation are all considerations in the development planning process.

This book addresses a wide range of resource uses, conflicts, and problems of coastal zone management, each from the particular viewpoint of a specialist in one of the classical problem areas. The reader will find it helpful in his approach to the subject to gain an early appreciation of the interdisciplinary perspective which most often characterizes the planning process.

By way of demonstrating the diffused nature of the problems in an interdisciplinary vein of analysis, selected cases of typical goal conflicts, issues, and problems are cited below. Furthermore, these are identified in terms of the coastal zone uses and major planning-management considerations required for resolution.

Mutually exclusive waterfront land uses. Preemptive use of urban waterfront areas by long established manufacturing and distribution industries prevent the development of needed public-oriented commercial uses such as restaurants, motels, and parking lots which would contribute to better balance in a long-term multiple use plan.

Planning-Management Considerations. These involve optimal time-projected apportionment of land resources for multiple use based on life-cycle replacement of facilities and installations; increased intensity of resource use or increased resource availability through technical innovation; and public land acquisition, rezoning, and tax incentives.

Environmental pollution by industrial waste. Waterfront industrial establishments are heavy producers of waste products which tend to pollute the estuaries, harbors, and nearshore waters; this causes administrative reactions from pollution control authorities.

Planning-Management Considerations. These are new technology in waste management systems and rezoning of urban waterfront areas for multiple use compatible with environmental protection and regional resource conservation requirements.

Incremental land use development controlled for local interests in lieu of state or national guidelines. Suitable sites for heavy industries requiring deep water port facilities and back shore accesses are diminishing with respect to increasing national economic need and level of demand. Private ownership of waterfront land is deferring to the pressure of increased property taxes which tends to dispose of holdings by small increments. Local governments are seeking to increase the tax base. Therefore, they do not wish to acquire and hold land without tax benefit for long range future use in the broader interests of nation and state.

Planning-Management Considerations. These are optimal time-projected apportionment of land use; possibility of Federal funding for special lands acquisition in support of integrated master plan development; and possible engineering innovation to provide new systems to anticipate nonavailability of committed land resources (e.g., possible application of civil engineering techniques for floating real estate, runways, and island building).

Wetlands real estate development versus critical wildlife habitats and estuarine breeding grounds as mutually exclusive uses of coastal zone. The demand for private housing increases with population growth. It has been estimated that by the year 2000 three fourths of the population of the United States will be concentrated within the coastal zone and the demand for private waterfront homes will be intensified accordingly. The wetlands and estuarine areas are vulnerable land resources for housing developments as well as sites for commercial complexes. The threat to the environment and the included wildlife is twofold. Critical wildlife habitats have been converted to real estate development and the resulting increase in pollution has damaged estuarine breeding grounds of important marine life species.

Planning-Management Considerations. These include the need for converting specific coastal areas to exclusive commercial or housing development and the impact on biological resources and natural environment; technology of wastes management and pollution control; zoning constraints on critical uses of coastal areas; and evaluation of social and economic factors bearing on mutually exclusive uses of coastal lands.

Public recreation versus private housing as conflicting uses of metropolitan waterfront areas. The need for water-based recreational facilities within metropolitan areas increases with both intensity and extent of urban development. The conflicts between public recreational uses of the coastal zone and private housing or industrial developments is apparent in considering their included activities and accessibility constraints. Private housing restricts public access to swimming beaches; swimming is prevented by industrial waste discharges which pollute the waters; public marinas for pleasure boating are incompatible with commercial fishing docks with the usual cargo waste and fuel spillage. The significant recreational activities are boating, swimming, picnicking, beach strolling, sightseeing, and outdoor sports. These activities require beaches and waterfront parks which are readily accessible (not involving traveling great distances to reach the outer limits of the metropolitan area).

Planning-Management Considerations. These involve acquisition of privately owned lands within metropolitan areas for public recreational uses; public control and restriction of commercial enterprises to recreation-oriented businesses within designated public recreation areas; engineering innovation for creating accessible offshore developments including, marinas, housing concepts, and commercial cargo handling facilities along with new waste management schemes compatible with the nonpollution requirements of metropolitan waterfront.

Commercial fishing and antipollution interests in conflict with offshore petroleum developments. With burgeoning offshore petroleum resource developments, damaging oil spills may exceed tolerance levels for commercial fisheries in many locations. Notwithstanding the overwhelming value of petroleum products to the national economy, commercial fisheries also represent an essential component of the economy and therefore should not inadvertently succumb to competition of use of the coastal zone. Moreover, uncontrolled oil spills as well as continuing low-level pollution from large-scale offshore drilling operations remains intolerable for the aesthetic and recreational qualities of some coastal regions. Considering the serious potential impacts of offshore petroleum development on multiple use of coastal regions, the petroleum industry and the government have initiated significant steps to alleviate the conflict through useful technological innovations.

Planning-Management Considerations.   These are transjurisdictional State-Federal controls with incentives for coordination of otherwise conflicting offshore petroleum and fishery operations; technological innovation to prevent environmental and wildlife damage within estuarine habitats from low-level pollution sources; and engineering concept formulation for integrating petroleum development, fishery, recreation, and aesthetic requirements of the coastal zone.

Incompatibility of local jurisdictions and extensive fishery operations.   The exploitation of commercial fisheries important to the national economy sometimes requires harvesting operations extending to the high seas and coastal waters within different political regimes. Because the natural distribution patterns of certain species of fish transcend artificial political boundaries, the harvesting of important fisheries often is performed under varying legal constraints. Despite the importance of the fishery to the national economy or the need to regulate harvesting operations to provide for the maximum sustainable yield, commercial fishermen are arbitrarily restrained by local and sometimes outdated laws. Such local regulations usually serve special interests, often to the detriment of the natural resource and the national economy.

Planning-Management Considerations.   These involve resource conservation by regulation oriented around natural geographic regions, which transcend local political jurisdiction and serve the national goals.

2. RESOLVING THE COASTAL ZONE PROBLEM SITUATION

Thus far we have considered the nature and scope of the coastal zone management problem. It is necessary to understand the issues, conflicts, and environment within which workable solutions must be developed and implemented to design an appropriate management system and also to perform adequately the included management functions.

In assessing the problem situation, one assumes that the coastal zone is unmistakably a national resource and therefore inescapably is also the nation's business. Adequate planning and management implementation can not take place at the state and regional levels without appropriate national policy guidelines. Furthermore, national authority generally does not have sufficient appreciation and intimate knowledge of regional problem situations to micromanage adequately the local conflicts and environmental resources. Planning and implementing solutions for optimal use of the coastal zone must therefore be cast in a management system that includes the total hierarchy of government from federal to state and local jurisdictions.

The interfaces between hierarchical levels are most appropriately defined in accordance with national policy; however the connectivity and objectivity of the total management system should provide adequately for the unique requirements of each regional and local jurisdiction in its decision-making and implementation function.

Development planning for the coastal zone should be performed with local interests, needs, constraints, and opportunities carefully considered within the framework of national policy and objectives with broad and long-range interests of the nation governing. However, generally national policy should adequately reflect the difficult goal conflicts and unique decision environments for each of the corporate regions. Therefore, it would appear that the essential management functions of planning, implementing, and controlling operations must be provided for in a unified management system linking national, state, and local jurisdictions. The total management system must permit the flow of planning information from the national level down to the local level and feedback from the local level to the national level. The system must process information such that the following sequence of functions are adequately treated and integrated within the planning phase of the planning, implementation, and control sequence:

1. Objectives planning.
   (a) Needs analysis and policy studies.
   (b) Problem definition and system identification.
2. Strategic planning.
   (a) Concept formulation and innovation.

3. Evaluative planning.
   (a) Physical analysis of alternatives.
   (b) Economic evaluation of alternatives.
   (c) Financial evaluation of alternatives.
4. Selection of strategy or problem solution for implementation.

Since a systems approach is unmistakably implied for resolution of the problem situation, we fortunately have the precedence of systems engineering techniques for planning, implementing, and controlling large-scale military systems. Although the coastal zone problem is essentially one of socioeconomic and technoeconomic factors, the experience of military systems will be invaluable in attacking the more socially oriented management problem of the coastal zone.

A development planning rationale for the coastal zone

This book, consisting of the coordinated contributions of the authors, is designed to provide the essential content for rational development planning for the coastal zone. The rationale with which this book is organized is basic to the planning function it purports to serve. This same rationale is basic to the management planning, in accordance with the writer's experience, in research and development of military logistic systems and facilities, including their implementation and control.

Accordingly, it is suggested that the reader consider the possible advantage in approaching the subject of this book, including the respective contributions of the coauthors, employing the same general logic that was used in organizing the subject and its format.

The subject rationale is most directly communicated by the information flow diagram shown in Figure 2 which systems engineers will recognize as fundamental to the general logic they apply in performing planning and design feasibility studies. It is this writer's opinion that the same general model for designing engineering systems can be usefully applied to the accounting of socially oriented resource-utilization systems of the coastal zone. The specific decision criteria remain to be studied and defined for each problem situation.

The reader will note that each step of the planning sequence in Figure 2 is characterized by the repetitive logic working progres-

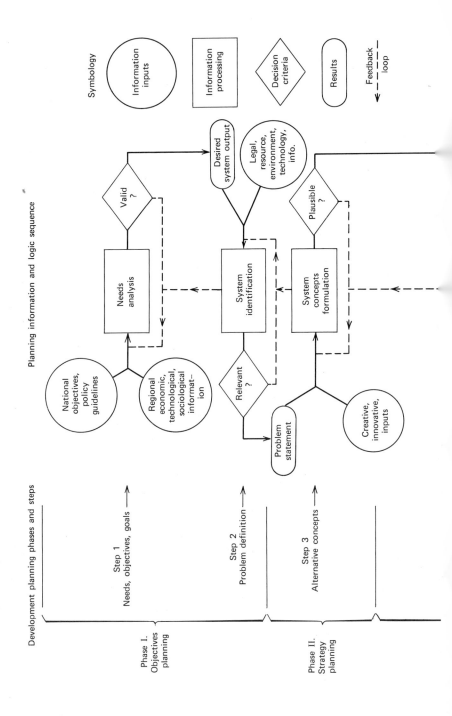

Planning information and logic sequence

Development planning phases and steps

Symbology

Information inputs

Information processing

Decision criteria

Results

Feedback loop

Desired system output

Legal, resource, environment, technology, info.

Valid ?

Plausible ?

Needs analysis

System identification

System concepts formulation

National objectives, policy guidelines

Regional economic, technological, sociological informat- ion

Relevant ?

Problem statement

Creative, innovative, inputs

Step 1
Needs, objectives, goals ⟶

Step 2
Problem definition ⟶

Step 3
Alternative concepts ⟶

Phase I.
Objectives planning

Phase II.
Strategy planning

16

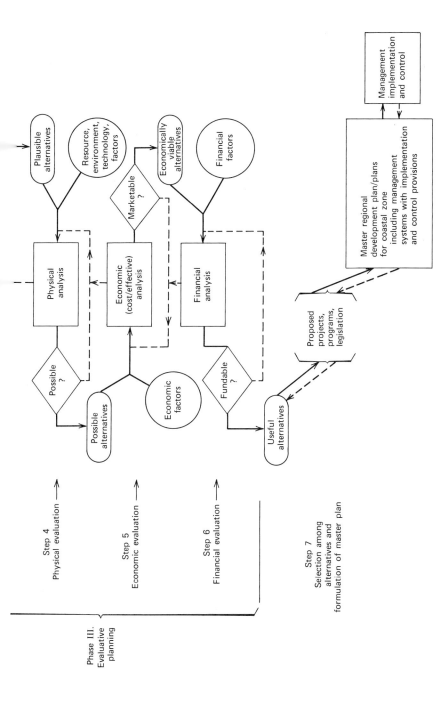

Figure 2. Coastal zone management. State/regional advance development planning cycle.

17

sively to develop useful solutions for defined problems by processing inputs at each decision level in the planning sequence.

The works of the contributing authors are presented to outline the goals, goal conflicts, and management needs, while suggesting the planning resources and technology available to the development planner in performing his essential function for coastal zone management.

PART 1

GOALS AND MULTIPLE-USE CONFLICTS

CHAPTER 2

National Goals, State's Interests, and Jurisdictional Factors

WILLIAM A. NIERENBERG

To many people in the world, the subjects of oceanography and ocean technology are new and exciting and may soon be part of either individual or national goals. This extraordinary rise of interest in these subjects in the last ten years among so many has obscured the history of the subject and in fact has greatly distorted perspectives and unfortunately led to a number of false starts in education, industry, and government. This writer feels that in many areas man must reevaluate what has been done and start over in some areas.

HISTORICAL PERSPECTIVES

Neither oceanography nor ocean technology are new subjects. For example, the laying of the Atlantic cable took place over a hundred years ago. There is no question that this mastery ocean connection between continents was one of the great steps forward in man's technological development. It was a great achievement; cabling equipment that could function adequately over large distances had to be designed. Vessels had to be adapted to the job. A good working knowledge of the topography of the ocean bottom was needed. In addition, there were the engineering difficulties of grappling at 15,000-foot depths, cutting the cable at the bottom as part of the grappling operation, bringing it to the surface and buoying it, grappling for the second half of the cable, bringing it to the surface and buoying it, and finally splicing a section between the two ends. In addition, a cable had to be developed that could withstand the tremendous forces involved in its handling and stand great pressures at depths and the depredation of biota in the ocean. Moreover, the immense hazards to the cable at the continental edge had to be overcome by still additional refinements. In fact, considering the state of technology at the time one wonders if what we have accomplished in the oceans matches this feat.

At even that early date another important lesson was learned. In addition to the ocean technology involved in placing and maintaining the cable, a parallel development in electrical engineering was required to design the cable to allow for the fact that repeaters had to be spaced at approximately 1000 miles. Not only was the practical electrical engineering developed but also a new mathematics evolved to handle this problem and some of the greatest minds of the era worked on it. As can be seen by this problem, ocean engineering, as oceanography itself, is a highly interdisciplinary subject by the very nature of the medium involved. There are the geological, physical oceanography, and air-sea interface problems, as well as electrical engineering and marine biology problems. Even earlier than the laying of the Atlantic cable, Benjamin Franklin recognized the importance of the Gulf Stream and sent an expedition to make physical measurements of it. The subject of oceanography with attendant technology developed at a steady rate in this entire period primarily because of the efforts of scattered individuals and institutions. Until World War II, there were only two or three institutions of any consequence working in the field in the United States. (Of course now there are many more.) Because of its heavy dependence on many other technologies due to its interdisciplinary character, oceanographic development for most of this period had to match the parallel developing technologies. Furthermore, the builders of its basic instrument, the ship, were notoriously conservative. Until recently, the larger faction of the oceanographic fleet was only slightly improved.

In reviewing the preceding brief history, one must mention that one field of oceanography of great technological importance advanced steadily throughout this development. This is biological oceanography; it was represented mainly by the researches conducted by Northern European countries' vessels to optimize fishery returns—particularly that of herring. But here too techniques of physical oceanography were used, in particular the tracking of oceanographic fronts. The question to consider is: what is different today? What has changed? Oceanography and its accompanying technology had an extremely slow development and was pursued by a small number of individuals in a few institutions here and abroad while other sciences and technologies expanded at a very rapid rate. For instance, nuclear physics started just before the turn of the century, considerably after the initial oceanographic investigations, and expanded rapidly both in the basic sciences and in the technology. It is not a question of immediate economic need because today we do not greatly need the vast resources of the ocean nor its potential, despite the importance they may assume in the immediate future. The answer must lie elsewhere and quite clearly must involve human factors. However developed our technology, however well trained our engineers and however formal their approach, it is still true that the practicing engineer depends on intuition based on his personal experience along with his purely formal education in school—his immediate environment colors as much of his thinking. An example of this is the engineer's design criteria for erecting structures that are earthquake resistant. On land he can very easily see the disastrous effect of an earthquake on structures such as frame houses, concrete buildings, and steel bridges, and he designs braces accordingly. However, when he must design structures for the bottom of the ocean basin or at least at reasonably great depths, he often does not consider the very large increase in pressure on such a structure due to the effect of an earthquake. A more complex and insidious natural intervention is a biological one, not unknown on land. The cowcatcher on a steam locomotive was an early necessity but still such intervention is considered newsworthy, such as starlings caught in the intake of a jet engine or squirrels gnawing their way through telephone cables. The ocean, however, is filled with almost every conceivable plant and animal that can chew, bite, whittle, bore, and erode anything. This is certainly a special problem; the ocean engineer must predict the effect of a given animal on a particular substratum. Man always can calculate the tolerance of the oceans to radioactive waste by solving complex, nonlinear hydrodynamic equations to a sufficient degree of approximation, but the solution is not valuable practically in the face of the uncanny ability of some marine species to concentrate particular elements to a fantastic degree. Man has a great store of this kind of knowledge in the engineering problems that are solved on land but as stated earlier this is largely because land is his normal environment and much of this wisdom is accumulated on the basis of the intimate contact with this environment. The oceans, however, represent the most desolate part of the world where man is concerned. At any given time only the smallest fraction of the earth's population is on the ocean and only a small percentage will notice and understand the complex phenomena that take place in the oceans. A very good example is the measure of the state of the surface of the ocean at any given time and place. This measure is called sea state but it has been the almost universal experience of oceanographers that estimates of sea state by experienced oceangoing people such as naval officers, sea captains, and ships' officers are generally unreliable—both in the absolute sense and because they disagree with each other to the point of uselessness. In fact, even this simplest, and one would think elementary, observation of the oceans has been so misleading that serious workers in the field of the wave power spectrum have eschewed the use of "sea state" to abolish completely any reliance on the great volume of old and useless data gathered this way. Pursuing serious technical and scientific work at sea is also very arduous and difficult, often unpleasant, and sometimes quite dangerous—nor is the situation likely to improve rapidly even with the obviously increasing technology applied to the problems of the oceans. Therefore even today such work is reserved to the dedicated few for whom the ocean represents such a challenge that they will undergo these hardships and perhaps even enjoy it. This is also the reason why beyond the lack of a good, intuitive, technological base, the oceans have been largely neglected by the other scientific disciplines. More remarkable is the fact that in the case of meteorology the influence of the oceans on the atmosphere is as important as their interaction with the land surface and undoubtedly more important. However, until recently the actual data from the ocean, 70% of the earth's surface, have been extraordinarily scanty.

Another factor is man's fight for survival on earth. While it never has been easy, it has taken a dramatically different direction in the last decades. The demands and needs of an exploding population are forcing him to a reexamination of the planetary potential. Man's tremendous technological advances have enabled him to make physical changes on the surface of the earth to a degree that has been impossible until recently. Unfortunately we see many examples of adverse effects in California. The effects of large excavation and earth moving construction projects are only too apparent and frightening. Man's solid, liquid, thermal and gaseous wastes are increasing at a rate exceeding population growth with elements of lethality that are reaching threatening proportions. The capital investment generated by this combination of growth and technology becomes more vulnerable, measured in terms of dollars and direct human impact, to acts of nature. Also many people have a psychological need to move to new places. Thus there is an almost universal turning toward the ocean as a significant part of developing global conceptions. Since it is the least known and least understood part, it is in many ways an attractive area for technologists and because of the very bulk of the oceans, it is the natural field of the resource engineer.

GOALS AND FUTURE PROSPECTS

Following the lead of the historians and dividing ocean technology into periods, one can conveniently call the period up to about ten years ago the *early period* and the following period including the present and until about the end of the century the *second*. It is an historical fact that man entered this period last year with an event as significant as the laying of the Atlantic cable. This is the Deep Sea Drilling Project. This project was a major step forward in technology and marked the first profound physical sampling of the great ocean basins. The project was conceived many years ago by the leading oceanographers in the United States and a consortium of institutions proposed to the Federal Government that advancing technology in offshore oil drilling could be adapted to core the sediments of the deep ocean basins and sample the underlying basement rock. After many years of planning, the *Glomar Challenger* went to sea fully equipped to position itself with the aid of satellite navigation at predetermined points on the ocean, remaining within several hundred feet of a fixed point on the ocean surface for several days, lowering a string of drill pipe to the ocean floor, and successfully taking repeatedly 30-foot-long core samples, very often to the bedrock or to the hardest layers they encountered before the bit gave out. The most spectacular results were scientific. Just the preliminary examination of the samples completely confirmed the sea floor spreading hypothesis and the continental drift hypothesis, and also led to the more refined concept of the movement of crustal plates. From the viewpoint of resources, the first definitive information about the possible mineral resources of these great ocean basins was obtained. Because of the size of the oceans, this information is still scanty after only one year of operation but in the course of the next three years a good preliminary forecast should be available. But historically this will probably be best remembered as the first indication of what man can do technologically in this extremely remote environment. But as exciting as this success is, a long period of exploration of the deep ocean basins and at least as long a period of technological development will be required before the necessary tools are available for the economic extraction of this mineral wealth. With this success in mind, it is interesting to guess what the next major breakthroughs will develop in man's ability to live and work at sea. Perhaps the next point will be the successful realization of midocean bases. The demonstrated success of FLIP and its continual and ever expanding use has been a striking indication of the great value of stable platforms. FLIP is a 300-foot towable hull that can be flooded to a vertical position mostly submerged, and in this position it has ridden out major storms with the maximum vertical motion of only a few inches. The parallel technology, of course, is that of the offshore oil rigs, particularly those floated to position on their vertical legs and then moored. These are extremely successful structures in the nearshore zone and much of the technology that was developed for building and handling them can now be applied to the design, construction, and establishment of these bases. They have many uses for both civilian and military and constitute safe ideal structures for operations in midocean. The freedom from motion and safety from storms is a fundamental requirement for all midocean factories and workshops where the personnel are to be selected primarily on the basis of their specialized technical skills and not their relative biological immunity to motion. The next decade will see the construction of the first of these bases and a proliferation of all sizes and shapes in all the oceans of the world.

A necessary corollary to the use of these bases and the more efficient exploitation of the oceans is the high-speed, almost-all-weather boat. Very important advances have been made in developing a class of vessels known as the surface effect vessel (SEV). There are a large variety of ideas and achievements but much remains to be done, particularly about the powerplant to give the vessel the necessary speed and at the same time maintain a useful range. The needed vessel should go at speeds in excess of 100 knots in seas of 5 to 10 feet, with ranges of at least a thousand miles, preferably several thousand. One of the greatest costs of working at sea is the time spent by the personnel going to and from the station; if the station is the middle of the ocean, this is expensive. If the station is the center of a large work area, then real economy will only be achieved when the vessels for high-speed operation in the area as well as a calm midocean harbor are developed. The technical difficulties are formidable but their solution is favorable. The most promising surface effect vessel is the captured air bubble vessel.

It is shaped like a rectangular barge with flexible side curtains fore and aft and on both sides. Air is entrained by the motion of the vessel in the region below the hull and between the curtains, and to guarantee against sudden pulses, a fan is used to supply makeup air. Thus the vessel rides on a bubble of air and the waves that it meets will run through the curtains, the captured air bubble meeting very little resistance. Of course, the desired result is the reduction of wave resistance to a minimum and the elimination of the hump on the power versus speed curve. More important, however, is the ability of the vessel to sustain what would otherwise be the shock of the running sea. Even in the absence of the wave resistance, skin friction is still very high and rises rapidly with speed; therefore a great power source that is light and relatively efficient is required. This has implications for the appropriate propulsion system as well. Again the important problems are the propulsion system and the appropriate material and design of the side curtains.

The submersible in connection with future developments is a very difficult subject. While the submersible will play a very important role in exploration and in routine search and repair missions the numerical proliferation will undoubtedly be in the platforms, high speed vessels, and unmanned devices operating at the bottom of the sea. A great revolution in developments affecting the offshore regions is predicted. The situation today is not comforting. The engineering failures of currently designed and constructed offshore structures are altogether too high to be economically tolerable and are certainly unsatisfactory for an expanding economy. The conflicting goals of a rapidly growing society comprise the serious problems. Man is in danger of losing some of his best coastline—in the West because of the disappearance of sand due to the damming of mountain streams; in the East because of estuarine pollution. Engineering solutions for the design of more marinas and recreation areas presently compound the problem of the loss of beaches; the imagination and engineering required to control the physical and esthetic effects of offshore mining operations, particularly offshore oil production, is not demonstrated. Many imaginative and exciting ideas of the experienced oceanographers have not been employed in these important problems. However, mounting public pressure and concern will force the employment of more ingenuity and technology than has been used up to now.

CONFLICTS AND POLITICAL CONSIDERATIONS

While these developments are taking place on the civilian front, there will of course be corresponding and largely similar developments on the military front. The military will need floating bases for intelligence and tactical warfare and for strategic purposes. They will need the high-speed vessels for the same reasons as civilians do but in addition will need them for the low silhouette for missile radar and satellite radar. The military, however, will have far greater need of submersibles than the civilians and will want to preserve the bottom of the ocean as a base for intelligence purposes. Thus a very serious technological development in the oceans' basins, but still with relatively low human presence, is predicted. The oceans' basins will be a "technological no man's land." This will be a situation unprecedented in world history. Heretofore, sovereignty over a region of the earth could only be established in any practical way by inhabiting the area with sufficient people so their presence and use of the land established a de facto claim. Empty declaration of ownership has never served any sovereign nation. Therefore the political problems that parallel the development of the oceans' basins will be difficult to solve, and man is now in the extremely complex situation of working very hard on the political aspects of the problem because of the unacceptable situation that could arise if proper solutions are not found, but at the same time having insufficient knowledge of the real problems of the nature of this resource and the essential detailed technology required for the framework of such a benevolent philosophy. The situation can become very complicated as foreseen by the number of past experts in this specialized field of diplomacy and by their rapid proliferation. As is of course expected, the problem has become deeply entwined with that of disarmament, the classical problem of fishery rights, and the possibility of using some or all of these resources for the underdeveloped nations.

Before outlining these problems in any detail, it is instructive to study what has happened in one small area and see what conclusions and hopefully what lessons can be applied to the larger ones. This area is that of the freedom of scientific investigation of the ocean. It is strange that the oceanographer finds it necessary to discuss this question. Until relatively recently, there were simply no problems. The oceanographer could investigate freely all the world's oceans outside territorial limits. Also he was an honored guest all over the world. The classic example of this freedom for research on the high seas was shown by the fledgling American Government when it offered water and provisions to Captain Cook on his last voyage of exploration at a time when the new nation was fighting the Revolutionary War with Great Britain. There is a great deal of prehistory in this matter of the diplomacy of the oceans' basins, but we can conveniently begin with the first important action in modern times immediately after World War II when President Truman asserted national jurisdiction over the seabed of the United States continental shelf. This proclamation reaffirmed for the United States its traditional position that the waters above the continental shelf outside its territorial limits are completely open to navigation to all. In retrospect, this was a wise and diplomatic move. It anticipated the important developing technology in the offshore region, that of the continental shelf, and recognized the fact that the nation contiguous to this region is the natural exploiter of that wealth and has the population and resources to cope with it—while at the same time it recognized the status quo of the classical freedom of the seas with regard to navigation and fishing. This move had the great merit of realism. This principle was almost immediately accepted and applied by many other countries of the world. However, some of them went beyond the Truman proclamation and claimed the waters above the continental shelf, and the resources, including the living resources, in them as well, although none offered any obstacles to the right of innocent passage. This series of actions naturally developed into the famous Geneva Conference on the Law of the Sea in 1958, and an important series of conventions were adopted and eventually received the requisite number of ratifications. Perhaps three points should be noted with respect to the Geneva Conventions. The first is that the continental shelf over which natural sovereignty was agreed was defined as extending to the 200-meter depth. However, this provision was diluted by assigning sovereignty to those contiguous slopes and regions that can readily be exploited without, unfortunately, considering the rights of the nonsovereign.

The second point is a negative one; attempts then and subsequently have been made to define more precisely the limits of territorial waters with no real success and in fact there has been a creeping nationalism as country after country defined and redefined the baseline for the calculation of the territorial limits of their own waters—always of course increasing the extent of these waters.

The third point of interest pertains to scientific research. The Conventions of Geneva require the consent of the coastal state before research concerning the region of the continental shelf can be undertaken. The conventions do state that this consent shall be routinely given. However, in the last three or four years, this consent has not been routinely given in several cases. In this author's opinion the Treaty states exactly that the permission will be routinely granted, and that the spirit of the Treaty was that the same freedom that oceanographers have enjoyed for nearly a century was to be continued. Presently the more the international organizations have entered the field to help the oceanographers to become more international, the less international they have become. Perhaps these feelings of being hemmed in by this creeping nationalism can be compared to those of the cattlemen of the Old West who felt their freedom slipping away with the encroachment of the nesters and their barbed wire fences.

How this actually affects oceanographic research on the high seas is discussed in the following. That part of the effort which represents routine surveys, for example, bathymetric, which must be planned long in advance, the necessary delays and bureaucratic obstacles can undoubtedly be overcome. But for that part involving forward-looking vital research programs, already existing difficulties are further compounded. At least in the United States, funding a long voyage to a remote area is very complex and takes altogether too much time. The available funds rarely come from one source but must be pieced together for the ship operations from a variety of agencies. This can require a lead time of a year or more in the planning of a program on research that a good investigator would feel should be done more quickly and flexibly. But because of the vagaries of the financing, the final geographic lines may not be determined before 6 to 3 months before the expedition starts. After this planning, the difficulties imposed on the chief scientist if the necessary permission for work on the continental shelf in a given area is denied him at the last moment are immense and waste and confusion unnecessarily take place.

Considering the larger question of the orderly development of the resources of the oceans and the ocean basins in terms of current experience in the research area, the working oceanographer is, of course, nervous about the prospects.

Perhaps the subject can be approached more positively by asking what, if any, definite actions will nations take to dispel some of the uncertainty. One seems certain. The United States and Russia are negotiating a treaty directed toward the disarmament of the ocean bottom. There are many possibilities but probably they will be successful in jointly outlawing the emplacement of weapons of mass destruction in the deep ocean basins. This is very much in accord with treaties now in existence outlawing the use of space as a base for such weapons. There is little opposition to the proposed treaty and, clearly, if implemented it would remove the possibility of a serious obstacle to the development of these same basins. Necessarily, a nation that has made a large investment in bottom-mounted weapons would not be enthusiastic about allowing complete freedom of action within a considerable distance from such emplacements. However, it is not probable that any treaty would restrict other military uses of the ocean bottom—most likely that of listening posts for intelligence and other military operations. These are benign, at least compared to the possibilities of modern weaponry. But such installations would necessarily conflict to some degree with other uses and pose certain problems with regard to the security of these installations. The question as to the military use that a nation may put its own continental shelf to will probably be open for some time to come. This is purely a disarmament question since the continental shelf and the corresponding subsoil is now by international agreement assigned to the contiguous nation. The rest of the question is open to difference of opinion both within countries and outside as to the timetable needed for executing the appropriate arrangements. As is well known, the Government of Malta in the year 1967 introduced a resolution before the assembly of the United Nations proposing the total internationalization of the seabed beyond sovereign limits with the noble purpose of reserving the fruits of the exploitation for the underdeveloped nations of the world via the United Nations or some specialized agency of the United Nations. This resolution, the Maltese Resolution, brought out into the open, perhaps prematurely, the discussion of this complex problem that has been going on for many years within the more sober and quite specialized agencies and tribunals of the international world. As stated earlier pressures generally balance each other. On one hand, it is almost universally felt that we should come as quickly as possible to a diplomatic resolution of the problems of ownership and the character of the exploitation of these vast ocean basins. Perhaps we can make wise decisions at this early stage that could help resolve potential future conflicts and provide for a more orderly and efficient framework of utilization. There is also the related specter that has not yet formed an impor-

tant basis for these discussions—an ocean that will be ruined by
pollution before the nations can wage an effective joint campaign.
On the other hand our knowledge of the ocean basins is minimal
from the viewpoint of their exploitability, particularly their mineral exploitability, and despite the initial success of the *Glomar
Challenger* it will be many years before an adequate picture of the
geology and its mineral content is available. How to write rules
and regulations, construct the framework of operations, and allocate the presumed profits of this exploitation is certainly difficult
to specify in view of the actual uncertainties; a real concern has
been expressed that premature regulation and unwise procedures
can do more to stifle a development program of the magnitude
envisaged than any other single factor. The responsibility of those
preparing positions in this field is not enviable. The differences of
opinion that exist within the United States are about as extreme
as those found in the international sphere. The average citizen
would not intuitively realize that the military wants to see as much
of the ocean bottom internationalized as is possible and remain
outside the domain of any single nation's jurisdiction. Of course
this closely follows the traditional concept of freedom of the seas
that the military has always cherished. On the other hand, the
more territorially concerned agencies of government prefer to see
national ownership extend as far out to the middle of the oceans'
basins as possible because it is their classical view that territories
should be under sovereign ownership and subject to license and
exploitation by the sovereign. It is amusing though to remark that
while this glorious debate is taking place, the Treasury Department
has quietly ruled that any minerals brought back from beyond the
territorial limits from the ocean basins shall be subject to tariff
as if they came from another country.

One interesting aspect of this discussion of the role of the oceanic
resources in world affairs is the position being taken by many of
the developing nations, particularly South America. Whereas the
larger nations seem to move favorably in the direction of maintaining the international aspect of the ocean basins, these developing
nations are generally opposed and are the ones primarily responsible
for the specific actions that run counter to this philosophy. This
viewpoint on a historical basis is understandable because most of
these nations started as colonies—used primarily as sources of raw
materials for the mother country—and were left without the development to use these materials in their own manufacturing or
were completely stranded when the market shifted from this one

commodity. Thus they are hesitant about a world policy that may control the raw material wealth of an ocean basin that they intuitively feel is in some respect theirs because of its relative geographic proximity. Since the technology necessary to exploit this wealth belongs largely to the developed nations, they feel that they may be economically in the same position as when they were colonies albeit via a more benign and complex route. The inconsistency of this position is that the exploitation technology is closely coupled to the necessary exploration and development technology and these resources can never be well identified nor initial pilot operations commenced unless a suitable regime is established for orderly economic development. It also denotes a lack of confidence on the part of these nations in the United Nations' ability to carry out that part of the Maltese Resolution which would reserve the proceeds of internationalization for the underdeveloped nations. Unfortunately, these two groups of nations are roughly the same as the former colonial-colony groupings, which tends only to sharpen the difference. Of course, one of the problems involved is the varying conception of what the nature of the international operation will be. One extreme would be a corporation or corporations formed under the aegis of the United Nations. This would be a totally new concept, and because it is radically new, such a proposal might assuage the fears of the smaller nations. A more conservative approach is to depend on the expertise of the existing larger national corporations who have apparently learned to operate fairly effectively in an international environment and with whom the smaller nations have found a considerable degree of accommodation. In fact, these large corporations are just in the initial stages of their international activities and may grow into the role needed for developing ocean resources on a global basis.

There remains the important question of how the oceans relate to the growing concern for quality of life on this planet. The oceans, of course, as with the atmosphere, are thoroughly international. Some local problems will be treated nationally, such as estuarine pollution and the loss of beach sand. There are other problems—and they are growing in importance—that affect the oceans in the larger sense. These are, for example, organic pollution due to DDT and diphenyls from plastics, metals such as zinc and copper from sewage plants, and petroleum products from ships and wells. Some of these pollutants have known serious ecological effects; other are of concern because they are being introduced at a rate approaching the natural insertion and intuitively this is felt to be a danger signal. Increased development of the ocean basins can only aggravate the situation. Clearly, international action on a grand scale is called for. It would have been significant if the Maltese Resolution had made specific recognition of this problem. This author proposes that if significant international action is taken in the economic development of the ocean basins, the first proceeds be used to foster programs to counter the pollution of the oceans.

BIBLIOGRAPHY

Brahtz, J. F. (Ed.), *Ocean Engineering*, Wiley, New York, 1968.

Commission on Marine Science Engineering and Resources, *Our Nation and the Sea*, Superintendent of Documents, U.S. Government Printing Office, Washington, D.C., January 1969.

Committee on Oceanography, *Oceanography 1966, Achievements and Opportunities*, National Academy of Sciences—National Research Council, Publ. 1492, 1967.

Committee on Oceanography and Committee on Ocean Engineering, *An Oceanic Quest*, National Academy of Sciences, Publ. 1709, 1969.

Institute of Marine Resources, *California and Use of the Ocean;* A Planning Study of Marine Resources, prepared for the State Office of Planning, University of California, Institute of Marine Resources, La Jolla, Calif. IMR. Ref No. 65-21, 1965.

SESOC Advisory Committee of Commerce Technical Advisory Board, *Surface Effect Ships for Ocean Commerce*, Superintendent of Documents, U.S. Government.

U.N. General Assembly, "United Nations Conference on the Law of the Sea," Official Records A/Conf. 13/38, 7 volumes, 1958.

CHAPTER 3

Conservation of Biological Resources of the Coastal Zone

MILNER B. SCHAEFER*

The land and ocean in the vicinity of the triple interface of land, sea, and atmosphere, which may be referred to as the coastal zone, constitute one of the most valuable features of our nation because of the many different ways man uses this region and its resources, and because so much of the population lives, works, and plays in it or near it. This multiplicity of uses, by increasing numbers of users, has generated important issues, even hot controversies, at local, state, national, and even international levels. Many of the uses of the coastal zone, and a large share of the issues and problems, involve the biological resources, which are the topic of this chapter.

From the biological viewpoint, as from other viewpoints, we cannot define the coastal zone precisely. Yet it is desirable to keep in mind some idea of what we mean by the term. It is, roughly, the sea and land adjacent to the interface, encompassing that region where terrestrial activities importantly impinge on the marine environment, marine resources, and marine activities, and where marine activities importantly impinge on the environment, resources, and activities of the land. Obviously, no precise boundaries can be given, since the intensity of this interaction is greatest at the water's edge and slowly fades out as one moves away from the

* Deceased. Dr. Milner B. Schaefer returned to his post as Director, Institute of Marine Resources, University of California in February 1969 after completing an eighteen month assignment as Science Adviser to Secretary of Interior, Stuart Udall. A long time advocate for intelligent use of marine resources benefitting mankind, Milner Schaefer considered his work for this book to be in the vein of public service.   Ed.

interface in either direction. What I have in mind is the region of most intense interaction, from a few miles back of the beach to perhaps 10 or 15 miles offshore. From a biological viewpoint, we cannot regard this zone as isolated from other regions of either the land or the sea because of the migratory nature of many of its organisms, as well as because of the influences on the biota in this zone of natural processes, and man's activities, even more remote in space, both on land and sea. For example, numerous species of fish that inhabit the coastal zone are highly migratory, just as are many species of land and sea birds that are, in part, dependent on it. Also, in the case of the marine organisms, some that at their adult stages are peculiar to the coastal zone, such as the spiny lobster of California and points south, and have larval and juvenile stages that are pelagic, living in the open sea for many months before becoming members of the bottom community of the inshore zone. Conversely, some marine species that as adults live well offshore inhabit the inshore zone during their early juvenile stages, for example, menhaden and peneid shrimp.

However, the coastal zone is biologically unique and of special importance in several ways. In the first place, it is a region of very high biological productivity due to a number of physical processes. Nutrient chemicals, such as phosphates, nitrates, and biologically important trace elements, reach the inshore margin of the sea from the land by rivers and other forms of runoff. Coastal upwelling is also an important means by which the plant nutrients in the photosynthetic upper layer of the sea are regenerated in the coastal zone, and also to some considerable distance in the open sea beyond. Coastal upwelling occurs in such regions as the California Current where, due to the direction and force of the winds and the rotation of the earth, the surface water of the ocean moves offshore and is replaced by upwelled water from a few hundred meters depth. This upwelled water is laden with the nutritive mineral elements, such as nitrates and phosphates, that have been regenerated in the deep sea by bacterial decomposition of the feces and remains of organisms that have fallen out from the upper layer of the ocean. In areas along the coast where these nutrient rich waters are upwelled to the sunlit, photosynthetic zone there ensues a rich bloom of plants, both the attached plants along the shore and the tiny floating phytoplankton offshore, upon which all life in the sea depends. We should remember that it is only in the upper hundred meters, or less, of the ocean where light is sufficient to support photosynthesis. Thus the replacement of the fertilizers in this upper sunlit layer, both by terrestrial runoff and by coastal upwelling, is of fundamental importance to the high biological productivity of the coastal zone of the sea. Finally, because the coastal zone is shallow, the remains of the dead plants and animals that fall to the bottom are not lost from the near-surface layer as they are in the offshore ocean over the abyss. These remains provide food for many species of benthic organisms, and the mineral nutrients regenerated by bacterial and biochemical action are brought back from shallow bottoms into the sunlit zone by wind stirring and other shallow mixing processes. The high biological productivity of this region, as well as the ready accessibility of its resources to fishermen, is reflected in the fact that a major share of the harvest by our commercial fisheries, and recreational fisheries, is taken from the coastal zone or the immediately adjacent high seas. The National Commission on Marine Science, Engineering and Resources [1] has estimated that 70% of present United States commercial fishing effort is exerted in coastal waters.

Another aspect of the coastal zone of great biological significance is the existence of unique habitats. These include river estuaries, where there is an intermixing of fresh and saltwaters, semi-enclosed embayments, salt marshes, littoral and sublittoral mud flats, and tide pools. In each of these habitats exist communities of plants and animals that are peculiar thereto, some of the species members of which live only in these particular environments. Because of this richness and diversity of habitats, the coastal zone has an extremely varied, and in many respects unique, biota. In some cases, also, these habitats of the coastal zone are obligate environments of high seas, pelagic organisms at certain stages of their life histories, as already mentioned.

It is perhaps useful to give some examples of the unique and varied biota of the coastal zone:

This is the unique habitat of the large attached algae, such as the giant kelps that occur along our coasts, because it is only along the coast that the bottom, to which these algae are attached, is sufficiently near the sea surface to be within the range of photosynthetically effective quantities of sunlight. Associated with the kelp beds is a whole community of marine invertebrates, fishes, and mammals.

Only in the coastal zone occur the salt marshes, where a wide variety of halophitic higher plants grow, and again particular biological communities are associated with these plants. In addition to the permanent inhabitants of the kelp communities and the salt marsh communities, these are important locations for some migratory organisms. For example, in the case of the kelp beds, such fish as yellowtail and seabass visit them for food and perhaps shelter; and in the case of the marshes, migratory birds visit them for food, shelter, and breeding purposes.

Characteristic of the coastal zone are the abundant benthic invertebrate organisms that subsist not only on benthic algae and phytoplankton, but also on organic detritus and bacteria associated with the seabed. These include such delicious food organisms as oysters, clams, mussels, abalone, and some varieties of crabs.

A very important aspect of the marsh and estuarine portions of the coastal zone is as obligate habitats for the young stages of a number of commercially and recreationally important marine species of the high seas. For example, the peneid shrimps, which live as adults and spawn offshore, spend a critical share of their juvenile lives in the inshore marshy and estuarine areas. Similarly, menhaden, shad, striped bass, and a good many other important fish species either spawn in the estuarine regions or use these regions as critically important nursery grounds for their young. This is particularly important on the Gulf and South Atlantic coasts of the United States where there is much estuarine habitat, and numerous commercially and recreationally important species that depend on it.

As a last example, the truly anadromous species, such as the Pacific salmons, and some of the seagoing trout species, spawn in freshwater streams or lakes, although they pass their adult stages largely in the open sea. These species not only transit the inshore zone in the course of their migrations between the sea and freshwater, but also the estuarine and nearshore oceanic waters constitute important nursery grounds for the young of many of them.

1. ORIGIN AND NATURE OF THE PROBLEMS

The rapid growth of the human population in, and immediately adjacent to, the coastal zone is well known, and the concomitant urbanization of long stretches of the shore is self-evident. In 1968 in another paper, this author stated that the California population was expected to grow from a current level of about 18 million (it is now over 20 million) to about 30 million by 1980 [2]. This population is, and will certainly continue to be, heavily concentrated in the coastal zone. It is obvious that we will soon have a great megalopolis, "Sanlosdiego," extending from Santa Barbara through Los Angeles and San Diego to the Mexican border. A similar development of almost continuous urbanization along the coastline is, of course, occurring on the east coast of the United States with the burgeoning, interstate megalopolis of "Bosnywash" extending from Boston through New York to Washington, D.C. Indeed, about 30% of the total population of the United States lives within a 50-mile belt along our coastlines, representing only about 8% of the total land area. Due to immigration, the population of this coastal strip is growing more rapidly than the total population of the United States.

Not only is the population of the coastal zone and the immediately adjacent hinterland increasing in numbers, but also, with growing affluence, each inhabitant demands more and more goods, services, and amenities.

Because of the speedy advance of technology, people no longer need work such long hours as formerly, so that there is also, on the average, greatly increasing leisure time. The 5-day week is almost universal; a 4-day week is not uncommon; and there has been considerable speculation to the effect that, in order to achieve full employment, we may, in the future, have to go to a 3-day week, or take much longer vacations. For people living within the 50-mile belt along the coastline, and especially for those in the urban concentrations on the coast, much of the leisure time is expended in recreation involving the use of the sea and its living resources. With increased leisure time, and especially longer and more frequent vacations, increasing numbers of people from the more remote parts of the United States are also visiting the seashore for rest and recreation.

The multiplicity of human activities in the coastal zone, for the production of food and industrial goods, services, and recreation and other amenities, as well as for disposal of waste materials of our urban-industrial civilization, affect the organisms of the sea and shore in multiple ways. To put it simply, man is a new, and potentially violently disruptive, element in the ecological regime of the coastal zone.

Thus with the increasing human activity in the coastal zone, it is not possible completely to preserve the preexisting ecological regime. With the injection of large numbers of human beings into various coastal-zone habitats, there must be some adjustment, and revision, of the ecological regime. The central problem, then, is to decide what ecological revisions and adjustments are desirable, from the standpoint of the long-range welfare of mankind, and how they can be attained.

The main purpose of this chapter is to examine significant relationships of man and the living organisms of the coastal zone to show something of the importance of these living resources to man and to expose some of the author's biases as to the directions that man might take toward a socially desirable solution of the central ecological problem.

The term "conservation" is used in the title of this chapter. In its ecological context, the term "conservation" was deliberately chosen by Gifford Pinchot in 1907 as the name for a popular movement to curtail the profligate, heedless use of this nation's forests and other natural resources that had characterized the rapid agricultural and industrial development of the West. It is still used in that sense, as well as in many others. One current use of the term is the undisturbed preservation of selected wilderness areas and some other habitats. It also often refers to refraining from present use of nonrenewable resources, such as petroleum, in order to preserve them for the future. Again, it is common to see conservation defined as "wise use" or "the greatest good for the greatest number"; these definitions are not very useful because of lack of precision and objectivity.

The sense in which the term conservation relates to the problems of the coastal zone and their possible solutions is similar to that of Professor S. V. Ciriacy-Wantrup, discussed at length in his book on resource conservation [3]. Professor Wantrup considers "conservation" a useful term for the reallocation of rates of use of resources toward the future, as contrasted with "depletion" which is reallocation of rates of use of the resources toward the present. This merely describes a process and is neutral in relation to choice of the rate of use. But we are concerned with selecting some desirable rate of use, or "state of conservation."

In seeking this desirable "state of conservation," we must consider the nature of the resources of concern. For one category of flow resources, that is resources that are continuously renewed, the rate of renewal is not affected by human action or by rate of use; this includes such things as solar radiation, tides, winds, and rainfall (at least to a first approximation). For other flow resources, however, man can and does significantly affect the stock of the resource and its rate of renewal. A most important category of resources thus affected by human action consists of those where the resource can be driven down to a level, a critical level or zone, where recovery of the resource is physically, economically, or socially impossible. The living resources of the sea are notably in this last category. For them, the rate of renewal of the resource is dependent upon the quantity of the stock left to perpetuate itself, and there exists for each such resource, some level below which the population cannot recover. However, in the case of many species, at least, the "state of conservation" is reversible over a very wide range of stock size and rates of use. For associations of species of organisms, such as ecological communities, the concept of the critical zone, that is, a changed condition of the ecological community that is irreversible, is, perhaps, even more pertinent. As Ciriacy-Wantrup has pointed out, a *minimum standard of conservation* is the preservation of resources of this category in such a state that the effects of utilization of the resource remain reversible [3]. This, of course, makes it possible for us to preserve all of the options, not only for ourselves but also for succeeding generations of men. For example, it implies preservation of all species from being driven to extinction. It also requires that ecological habitats and communities be preserved, so that future options as to desirable compositions of communities and ecological balances are not foreclosed.

It is to be noted, however, that the *desirable* state of conservation may well be, and often is, at some level of resource abundance and a corresponding rate of resource use that is well above the minimum standard of conservation. We seek to establish some desirable levels of this sort.

Thus use of "conservation" in this chapter refers to (1) maintaining the living resources in that state where they are well above the critical zone, avoiding irreversibilities, and (2) establishing some acceptable state of conservation of ecosystems, and of each of their living components, within that boundary condition.

It is to be noted that the second criterion does not rule out seeking some optimum state of conservation. However, the difficulties in treatment of natural resources conservation as an extremum problem are well known. While we should obviously strive for an optimum state of conservation, I am not convinced that we yet know how even to determine what it is, let alone how to achieve it. Difficulties in selecting optimum use rates of natural resources have been discussed by Ciriacy-Wantrup [3]; by Hirshleifer, De-Haven, and Milliman [4]; by Landsberg, Fischman, and Fisher [5]; and others. The obvious definition of an optimum, of course, from the strict economic standpoint, is the time distribution of use rates that maximizes the present value of the flow of net revenues. More broadly, from a welfare or social standpoint, one could aim at maximization of the social net revenues, that is, the balance of social benefits over social costs. As Ciriacy-Wantrup has pointed out, however, this creates some difficulty regarding criteria for distribution of social net benefits over time. Furthermore, many of the uses of the living resources of the sea involve social benefits that are difficult to quantify, because their acquisition does not involve the market economy. In addition, since the living marine resources are very largely common property, not subject to ownership, we get heavily involved in "spillover" effects, where important indirect effects, beneficial or adverse, fall to the public rather than the private sector. I am not too sanguine, therefore, that we can arrive at any appropriate means of dealing with the optimization problem.

2. WAYS IN WHICH LIVING RESOURCES ARE INVOLVED WITH THE USES OF THE COASTAL ZONE

With the foregoing background for orientation, we may now usefully proceed to more specific considerations.

As indicated earlier, the biota are involved with man's uses of the coastal zone in many ways. In these circumstances, some classification of man's uses of the coastal zone will be helpful in considering in an orderly manner the ways in which they affect, or are affected by, the biota, the conflicts that may arise, and the specific nature of the conservation problems. In this context, the following classification may be useful:

1. Direct uses of living resources.
    - Extractive use for food and other marine products (i.e., commercial fisheries and aquaculture).
    - Extractive use for recreation (sportfishing and hunting).
    - Nonextractive uses: observation for recreation; observation for science and education.
2. Other uses of the coastal zone that importantly depend on the biota.
    - Waste disposal—biodegradable wastes.
    - Biological extraction of inorganic materials.
3. Human activities that incidentally affect, or are affected by, the biota.
    - Uses of marginal lands.

- Solid waste disposal and sanitary fill.
- Building sites.
- Airports.
- Harbor construction.
- Modification of shoreline for recreation.
- Beach erosion and maintenance.
- Waste disposal—nonbiodegradable wastes.
- Ocean shipping.
- Other forms of transportation (pipelines etc.).
- Power generation.
- Ocean mining.
  - Hard minerals and construction materials.
  - Petroleum and natural gas.
- Shoreside recreation (picnicking, swimming, surfing, etc.).
- Communications.
- Military defense.

3. DIRECT USE OF THE LIVING RESOURCES

Direct use of the living resources is an important activity in the coastal zone, both as a source of supply of food and other marine products and as a source of recreation. There are two kinds of recreative use of the living resources: first, extraction by sport-fishing and hunting (the latter applying only to a few kinds of water-associated birds, such as ducks and geese), and second, recreation through observation of the wild animals in their natural habitats. Observation for scientific and educational purposes is, of course, operationally rather closely related to the nonextractive use for recreation. All of these uses of the living resources of the coastal zone are of importance to many people, and there are certain conflicts among them, both real and imagined, as well as conflicts between these various uses of the living resources and other activities in the coastal zone.

Extraction for food and other marine products

So far as the use of living resources for food and other marine products is concerned, an important distinction must be made between the exploitation and management of the wild stocks and the husbandry or aquaculture of certain organisms in captivity, both because of the nature of the activity itself and because of the nature of the property rights in the two cases. In the case of aquaculture, an owner usually has property rights both to the organisms cultured and to the area in which the activity is carried out (in some cases he may have only a temporary leasehold or right of access), whereas the exploitation of the wild stocks is normally not subject to individual property rights either in the resource or in the sea space or seabed where it occurs.

It is often asserted that the people of the United States are not a fish-consuming people, and the statistic of some 11 pounds per year per capita of edible marine products is cited in support of that. What is ignored, however, is that the United States has one of the highest per capita levels of total fish consumption in the world—over 80 pounds per capita in 1968 (live-weight basis), considering all fishery products [6]. A large share of this fish appears on the consumer's plate as chicken, pork chops, or beefsteak, since the use of fishmeal as an animal-protein supplement to feedstuffs for poultry, cattle and swine is the largest, and the most rapidly growing, use of fish in the United States. Furthermore, it is important to note that the United States is the major world market for certain high-priced marine products, including the lobster and shrimp that come from coastal zones. It is also of interest that the annual potential fisheries yield in areas of present United States fisheries, according to a recent symposium of experts on the subject [7], is about 22 million tons per year, compared to a present production of only about $\frac{1}{10}$ of this amount. A large share of this potential harvest is available in waters in, or closely adjacent to, the coastal zone on the Pacific, South Atlantic, and Gulf of Mexico coasts of the United States. Thus although important problems of conservation for some commercial species exist, that is, problems of maintaining the populations in a condition to support sustained high production, there are major problems of fisheries development for other, much underutilized species. California provides an important example, where, although we do have problems of conservation with respect to sardines, mackerel, lobster, shrimp, and some other species, we have also some much underutilized stocks near our shores. The most notable example of the latter is the anchovy, of which the present stock is about 5 million tons in coastal waters off California. It probably could sustain a harvest of a million tons a year. It is essentially unutilized, with a current catch limit for the manufacture of fishmeal of 75,000 tons per year.

Aquaculture is receiving a great deal of attention today, not only from marine biologists and other scientists, but also from industrialists and politicians as well. Although I am not as enthusiastic as some of my colleagues concerning the potentiality of aquaculture for producing large quantities of inexpensive animal protein as a partial solution to the world food problem, this is undoubtedly an excellent way of increasing the limited supplies of oysters, clams, shrimp, and other coastal-zone organisms of high unit value, to the considerable profit of the aquaculturists. But enthusiasts for aquaculture as a means of producing vast quantities of foodstuffs sometimes tend to ignore the realities of the sea. One notable example concerns the culture of oysters, mussels, and similar filter-feeding molluscs. Aquaculture enthusiasts cite the yield from culture of mussels in Taranto, Italy, as some 60 tons per acre per year, or in Spain, some 120 tons per acre per year, or the growing of oysters by hanging culture in Japan, some 24 tons per acre per year, greatly exceeding the yields of the best farmlands. They go on to infer that, by developing much larger areas along the seacoasts for this kind of farming, vast production could be achieved. This is misleading, because the production of mussels or oysters over a given acre of the seabed does not much depend upon production of organic matter in the water immediately above that acre, but is more dependent on the flow of water past the molluscs, enabling them to strain out of it the feed produced in a vastly larger area. Since the feed can only be removed once, increasing the area of culture does not proportionately increase the total production. This is not only obvious from theory but has been practically demonstrated in areas such as Willapa Bay in the state of Washington and elsewhere.

In addition to the purely scientific and technological problems of improving the efficiency and effectiveness of aquaculture, the principal handicaps to the fuller development of this sort of enterprise in the coastal zone seem to be the institutional handicaps which beset its more rapid development, which are discussed further below.

Extraction for sport

The second important direct use of living marine resources is for sportfishing (and hunting of a few kinds of marine birds). Sportfishing is especially popular near highly populated areas, such as southern California. It is attractive because it provides an opportunity both to get away from the urban environment, and at the same time to pursue an emotionally satisfying activity. Although, as shown elsewhere [8], the size of the sportfish catch in California, with the exception of a few species, is much smaller than the commercial catch, recreational fishing is of considerable economic importance, because of the expenditures by the sportfishermen in pursuing their recreation, estimated in California to be something over 100 million dollars per year. There is considerable argument among economists, as well as technologists, as to what share of such expenditures should be attributed to the utilization of the fish resource itself to make it economically comparable with the commercial fishery. In any case, several hundred thousands of California's citizens engage in ocean sportfishing, so a significant share of the population is directly involved, generating a high degree of political interest, whatever the economic values may be.

Nonextractive uses (recreation, research, and education)

A third category of direct users of the living resources are those who derive pleasure from observing them. We have no good measurements of the extent of this use, but several hundred thousand people per year have been recorded as whale watchers at the Cabrillo Monument in San Diego, and thousands of people pay fares each year on whale-watching boats from San Diego and Mission Bay, as do those patronizing the glass-bottomed fish-watching boats at Catalina Island [8]. The numbers of Scuba divers and skin divers in California are in the tens of thousands. There is also a large, but unrecorded, number of marine birdwatchers.

In addition to the recreational observation of the living resources, observation of the undisturbed biota in the natural environment is also essential for scientific and educational purposes; a number of marine preserves have been set aside for these purposes in California, and yet others have been recommended.

Important conflicts exist among the various users of the living resources, as well as conflicts between them and other users of the coastal zone. With respect to conservation objectives, I believe that all categories of users of living resources agree on the necessity for the minimum standard of conservation, that is preserving from irreversible change all of the species and important ecological communities. Beyond this, however, there are considerable, sometimes violent, differences of opinion as to what is the desirable level of populations of the exploited organisms and of their rates of use. The nonextractive users are, in general, most concerned with the preservation of all the various species and the various kinds of habitats and are less concerned with the magnitudes of the populations above the safe-survival level, so long as they are sufficient for aesthetic satisfaction through their observation, including adequate preserves set aside for science and education. However, for certain categories of organisms, including birds, whales, sea otters, seals and sea lions, a good many of our citizens are greatly opposed to *any* extractive utilization, finding the "slaughter" of these mammals and birds emotionally repugnant, even though it may present no danger to the survival of the species or their sustainable harvest.

Both commercial fishermen and sportfishermen agree that it is desirable to have *some* use of the living resources, but the appropriate level of the populations and the rates of extraction are subject to disagreements. Although it is difficult to generalize, I believe that it may be fairly said that most commercial fishermen are concerned with maintaining the populations in a condition to provide maximum utility to themselves. A great many approve of a slightly different criterion, the maximum sustainable harvest, and some will go along with the criterion suggested by some economists —the maximum net economic yield, discounted to present time. I believe that most sportfishermen desire that each kind of sportfish be maintained at a level where they will catch satisfying numbers and sizes of fish. This may very closely coincide with any of the possible optima suggested for the commercial fishery. However, there seems to be less conflict between these two groups of users over the desirable state of conservation than over the allocation of the allowable catch from those living resources for which the allowed catch must be limited. There also exists considerable difference of opinion between commercial fishermen and at least some sportfishermen concerning the effects of the commercial fishery on species that are, or may be, the food of the recreational carnivores. The most interesting example in California is the anchovy, of which there is a very large stock, as I have mentioned, that is much underutilized. Many recreational fishermen have opposed permitting any significant utilization of the California anchovy because of fears that the commercial fishery would not be properly regulated and would cause the "disappearance of the anchovy just like the sardine," and because they believe that any sizable reduction of abundance of the anchovy would diminish the populations of the carnivores that eat them, among other prey, and that are pursued by the recreational fishermen.

These matters are not discussed in great detail here. They are more thoroughly discussed in a planning study that the Institute of Marine Resources completed a few years ago for the State Office of Planning [8]. The California Advisory Commission on Marine and Coastal Resources, which is advisory to both the Legislative and Executive branches of the California State Government, has also thoroughly reviewed these problems and has made firm policy recommendations, designed to accommodate the legitimate requirements of both the recreational and the commercial fishermen, while maintaining all of the fish populations at levels where they are capable of providing maximum sustainable harvests, as determined on the basis of adequate, objective scientific findings [9].

The situation of aquaculture presents a somewhat unique case of conflict among users of living resources, at least in California. It is forbidden to culture native species, although it is permitted to utilize exotic species. For example, one can culture abalones from southern California in northern California but cannot culture abalones native to southern California in southern California. I am not entirely sure about the rationale of this legal requirement, but perhaps it arises from fear that the aquaculturist would preempt the habitat of wild stocks for his farm and would thus interfere with users of the wild, common-property resource.

There are, of course, important conflicts between the use of the living resources of the sea and other uses of the coastal zone. These fall in three categories: (1) uses of the coastal zone that diminish the living resources because of elimination or other irreversible modification of habitat; (2) activities in the coastal zone that increase the mortality or decrease the reproduction of the living resources, thus diminishing their potential for the direct users; and (3) physical interference between the users of the living resources and the other users of the coastal zone. Most of these conflicts can most appropriately be discussed later, as the various other uses of the coastal zone are considered.

However, it is convenient here to mention the specific problem of aquaculture as a case of physical interference among users. Aquaculture differs somewhat from other direct uses of the living resources because, as noted earlier, it requires that a certain area of seabed, and in some cases a portion of the overlying waters, be preempted for that particular use. In the case of aquaculture involving floating rafts or cages or the erection of trellises or other objects on the seabed, it can also interfere with transiting vessels and can modify the seascape of local inhabitants and other frequenters of the shore. Each of these reasons has caused objections to specific aquacultural projects. This is a good illustration of the problem of arriving at the proper socially desirable mixture, or choice, among multiple uses.

4. OTHER USES OF THE COASTAL ZONE THAT IMPORTANTLY DEPEND ON THE BIOTA

Biodegradable wastes

The most important activity in this category is the disposal of biodegradable wastes. As indicated earlier, one of the important attributes of the ocean with relation to our urban, industrial civilization is that it is a very convenient and economical place to dispose of some of the wastes (which, particularly in the case of the urban complex, have to be put *somewhere*, in order to achieve a mass balance, that is to prevent the city from being eventually buried under its own dejecta). This is because the ocean is a very large hole, filled with seawater, that mixes itself quite rapidly and thus can dilute the wastes; and it also contains bacteria and other organisms that feed on some of the waste materials and thus dispose of them by degradation. For example, the biota of the sea rapidly oxidize organic waste, such as domestic sewage, reducing it to carbon dioxide, water, and its mineral constituents. It is, however, possible, especially in restricted areas of the sea, such as in bays and estuaries, but also even along open coasts in near-surface waters, to run so much of this material into the environment, so rapidly, that the capacity of the sea to dilute it, and the marine biota to assimilate it, are overwhelmed.

Two outstanding problems with domestic sewage are its population of pathogenic organisms, and the high content of organic matter, with its concomitant biological oxygen demand (i.e., the amount of oxygen required for its oxidation through biological processes). Adequate dilution is helpful in dealing with both of these problems. Dilution can decrease the concentration of pathogenic organisms to a level where they are no public health hazard, and, of course, these organisms eventually die in seawater. It is to be noted, however, that some marine food organisms, such as clams and oysters, tend to concentrate and retain microorganisms. Thus oysters, clams, and others can be important vectors for hepatitis and other human diseases in polluted areas. Dilution, where practicable, is also a convenient way of dealing with the biological

oxygen demand, since adequate dilution prevents the rate of oxidation of the organic matter reducing the oxygen in the environment
to a level which is adverse to fish and other marine organisms.

It is frequently desirable, before the effluent is put into the ocean,
to reduce the pathogenic organisms and the biological oxygen
demand of the sewage by treatment in sewage-treatment plants.
This is particularly true in the case where an urban complex is
located on an estuary or embayment with restricted exchange with
the open sea, but it also may be true in some situations along the
open coast. It is, in large part, a matter of engineering and economics to determine which is the more effective way to deal with
the material—to put it through a secondary treatment plant, or to
put it deeper and farther offshore to attain greater dispersion and
dilution.

However, a sewage treatment plant, with secondary treatment
involving digestion of the organic wastes in controlled ponds, does
not get rid of all problems. The effluent from such a treatment plant,
after the secondary treatment, is rich in plant nutrients (phosphates and nitrates) resulting from the bacterial oxidation of the
organic wastes. These nutrients, when introduced into a restricted
environment, can be a great nuisance, because they stimulate the
growth of plants, often producing blooms of phytoplankton that
are undesirable. It is interesting to note that, while, on the one
hand, some biologists investigate means of fertilizing the coastal
zone by adding inorganic fertilizers through artificial upwelling
and other means, others are concerned with the adverse effects of
these same kinds of nutrients from waste disposal. It seems that
the difference between the beneficial addition of nutrients, called
"fertilization," and the problem of "eutrophication," due to nutrient
addition, is, essentially, that in the case of fertilization we get
increased crops of something we want, and in the case of eutrophication we get increased crops of something we do not want.
Obviously, we need to learn a great deal more about the food-chain
dynamics of the coastal zone to forecast and control the results of
various modes of intervention through addition of plant nutrients.

Other than learning how to manage the wastes from secondary
sewage treatment better, so they will become fertilizers rather than
sources of eutrophication, this material can, again, be dealt with
by adequate dispersion and dilution. It can also be handled by
tertiary treatment, that is, treatment to remove some or all of the
plant nutrients. An important aspect in designing efficient tertiary
treatment is the determination of just which nutrients, in a given

circumstance, need to be removed to prevent the undesirable blooms. Interestingly enough, a great deal of effort is being put into the effective removal of phosphates, which are critically important nutrients in many freshwaters and perhaps in some bays and estuaries. In the open ocean along the Pacific coast, however, it appears that phosphorus is not the critical limiting element, whereas the nitrogen compounds are limiting.

Biodegradation is also an important property for ocean disposal of other types of wastes. One of the best known examples, although it is, indeed, mostly a problem in restricted freshwaters rather than in the sea, is that of detergents. Some years ago, the most commonly used detergents in this country were alkylbenzene sulfonates, highly resistant to biological degradation. These were both a very great nuisance, because of their foaming action but were also somewhat toxic to aquatic organisms. By replacing them with more easily biodegradable detergents, linear alkylate sulfonates, the problem has largely been solved. Another group of wastes where biodegradation is an important consideration are pesticides. At the present time, as is well known, agriculturists and home gardeners have found it convenient to use considerable quantities of chlorinated organic pesticides, including DDT, dieldrin, heptachlor, and such. One of the reasons that agriculturists find these convenient is that they are not biodegradable, hence have long-lasting effects in the field. However, they reach the sea both by rivers and other runoff, and through the air, as aerosols, and are building up in the marine environment in important quantities. Since they tend to be concentrated through the food chain in the sea, they can become particularly deleterious to organisms high in the food chain. The best known example is the lethal effect on several species of fish-eating birds, through interference with their reproductive mechanisms. An obvious solution is to switch from these chlorinated hydrocarbons to other existing and more easily biodegradable compounds, such as botanicals, carbamates, and some organophosphorous compounds, and to develop even better ones.

Another aspect of waste disposal and pollution involving biodegradable materials is pollution of the sea by oil. This has for many years been somewhat of a nuisance to people along the shore, because ships are wont to pump their bilges, and tankers to clean their tanks, at sea, putting the oily waste overboard. Since petroleum is floatable, it tends to concentrate at the sea surface, where it can further be transported by currents and winds to arrive at the land-sea interface, where it interferes with recreational enjoyment of the beaches and spoils pleasure craft, fishing craft, and fishing gear. Recently, however, a source of much greater pollution of the sea by oil has been accidents to large tankers transporting the material, which is an almost inevitable consequence of the increased movement of great quantities of petroleum by sea, in larger and larger craft. The *Torrey Canyon* incident, where that tanker went aground off the south coast of England, liberating about 100,000 tons of Kuwait petroleum, is a well-known example.

Production of petroleum from beneath the sea by the drilling of wells on the continental shelf and prospectively in even deeper water is another important source of catastrophic liberation of large quantities of petroleum through blowouts. In early 1969, a blowout of a well in the Santa Barbara Channel, California, resulted in the liberation of some 7000 tons of petroleum in the nearshore waters during the first couple of weeks, and a total of 10,000 to 12,000 tons during a period of 3 months. In both the *Torrey Canyon* and the Santa Barbara incidents, these large quantities of oil resulted in much contamination of the beaches, creating a great public nuisance. In both cases, a good many sea birds were coated by the floating oil and died. These highly visible phenomena attracted great public attention, both through local observation and the press.

In addition to the effects on birds, petroleum is damaging to marine organisms in two ways. First, large quantities in the intertidal zone can coat benthic marine organisms sufficiently thickly to interfere seriously with their respiration and feeding. Second, the lighter fractions of the petroleum, especially the volatile aeromatics and the phenolic compounds such as naptholenic acids are directly toxic to marine organisms. Thus fresh natural petroleum, depending on its content of these compounds, can be dangerous to marine biota in concentrations of 1% or less. However, the toxicity of spilled petroleum declines very rapidly in the first few hours, or days, after its liberation into the marine environment, because the aeromatics are volatile and the phenolics, being water soluble, rapidly become diluted. Also, marine bacteria metabolize the lighter petroleum fractions quite rapidly. Bacteria also metabolize, although more slowly, the heavier fractions, so that oil introduced into the sea is eventually all chewed up by these organisms. Following the early evaporation of the lighter fractions, evaporation continues at a diminishing rate for some weeks, during which the material is further eroded by photooxidation and bacterial degradation. After about 3 months at sea, there apparently remains a persistent asphaltic residue, that represents about 15% of the original volume in the case of oil such as the Kuwait petroleum that was lost from the *Torrey Canyon*. The resulting black, tarry lumps that came ashore are familiar to most of us who frequent beaches. Although not toxic to organisms, they are a great nuisance on the beach.

From experience of the *Torrey Canyon* event, the Santa Barbara event, and other experiences and experiments, it appears that natural petroleum, even in fairly substantial quantities, especially after disappearance of the toxic light portions, is not very harmful to most marine biota. In consequence, as has been stated by the biologists of the Marine Biological Association of the United Kingdom who studied the *Torrey Canyon* event in considerable detail [10], "Floating oil is not a serious hazard in the open sea save in the case of birds. . . . Oil deposited on the coast is, however, severely damaging to coastal amenities, and may affect shore animals by smothering them." These scientists and others have also found that on shores left untreated by detergents the oil is removed by organisms as well as other natural agencies. In the case of the Santa Barbara spill, quite extensive observations were conducted commencing almost immediately after the blowout began. It has been shown that there was very little effect on organisms other than those in the littoral zone, with the exception of the unfortunate seabirds. Effects on organisms in the littoral and sublittoral zones were slight and transient. There appears to have been no significant disturbance of the ecological regime in the Santa Barbara channel area.

On the other hand, more adverse effects were observed after the grounding of a small Japanese tanker, the *Tampico Maru*, at the entrance of a small cove in Baja, California, in 1957, that resulted in the liberation in this small cove (the circulation of which to the open sea was partially blocked by the wreck) of about a third of its cargo of 59,000 barrels of dark diesel oil at the time of the accident and the leakage of the remainder during the following 8 months. In this case, there was quite heavy mortality of benthic animals shortly after the shipwreck, although effects on plant species were much less. In consequence of the reduction of plant grazers, an extensive bloom of attached vegetation developed, but after 9 months many of the animals had reappeared. It took about two to four years for nearly full restoration of the ecological community [11].

It appears that cleanup measures can be more damaging to the marine biota than the petroleum itself. In the case of the *Torrey Canyon*, emulsifiers used to clean the beaches on the British coast were apparently much more damaging to the biota than the crude oil itself [10]. On the other hand, it appears possible to improve greatly on the chemical products employed in that case. A dispersant called "Corexit," that is, a proprietary product developed by one of the affiliates of the Standard Oil Company of New Jersey, shows considerable promise in being much less toxic than the detergents used after the *Torrey Canyon* accident. The use of dispersants that break the petroleum into fine droplets dispersed through the seawater, in addition to cleaning up the shoreline so that it is aesthetically more pleasing, has a potential advantage that, by breaking the petroleum into small droplets with a large total surface area, it may be more readily attacked by the marine bacteria, accelerating biological degradation. On the contrary, however, there is some concern about a possible disadvantage that, in breaking the material into small droplets, one also provides a larger surface area for the toxic light petroleum fractions to interact with the marine biota that may ingest them or otherwise come into contact with them.

In connection with this source of contamination of the sea we need assiduously to pursue preventive measures, such as the separation of oil from the water when pumping bilges, load-on-top techniques for retaining tanker washings for disposal ashore, more stringent safety regulations on drilling of oil wells under the sea, and improved blowout-prevention equipment. It is important to remember, however, that in the case of such catastrophic events as collisions of tankers or blowouts of petroleum wells, no matter how careful we are, the catastrophic event of small probability is bound to happen, sooner or later. It is thus important that we know how to deal with it, and be prepared to act promptly, when it happens.

Organisms for extraction of inorganic materials from seawater

Another use of the coastal zone, although it is more potential than present, which depends importantly on living elements, is enlisting the aid of marine organisms for the extraction of inorganic materials from seawater. At one time, of course, this was an important source of iodine and potash, which were extracted from kelp and other seaweeds, which concentrate both of these elements from seawater. That sort of industry has, in most parts of the world, been long replaced by other techniques. It has been recently suggested, however, that it may be possible to develop strains of bacteria, or other organisms, that can be employed industrially in the extraction from seawater of such important trace elements as uranium and vanadium.

5. HUMAN ACTIVITIES THAT INCIDENTALLY AFFECT THE LIVING RESOURCES OR ARE AFFECTED BY THEM

Numerous activities in the coastal zone are in this category, where the activity is not primarily concerned with the biota of the sea but is importantly affected by the biota or has important effects on the biota or their utilization.

Activities affected by marine organisms

Of the items listed in the outline above, those that are particularly affected *by* the biota of the sea, are ocean shipping, some other forms of transportation (such as pipelines), some aspects of power generation, certain types of harbor construction and maintenance, some aspects of military defense, communications by underwater sound, and some shoreside recreation, especially swimming. Where nonrecreational swimmers are involved in scientific or industrial activities, such as scientific observation and collecting, underwater construction, maintenance of subsea oil, and gas wells, and such, they, too, are subject to hazards from marine biota.

The effects of the biota that need to be taken into account in respect of these several activities may be conveniently considered in four categories: (1) fouling organisms that interfere with the operation of equipment, (2) organisms that destroy structures or equipment, (3) direct hazards to man from organisms, and (4) interference by organisms with communications.

Fouling organisms. Several varieties of plants and numerous kinds of animals that foul the bottoms of ships significantly reduce their speed and can also change their stability characteristics; man's battle against these fouling organisms, and also the boring organisms mentioned later, is as old as marine navigation [12]. These same kinds of organisms also grow on fixed structures in the coastal zone. Fouling growths on pilings and docks generally present no important problems, but when they grow in pipelines carrying seawater to power plants for cooling purposes, they foul the interior of such lines diminishing the flow; this requires such countermeasures as constructing the plants so as to reverse the flow periodically in the intake and outlet lines, so as to use the hot waste water to destroy the fouling organisms. In the case of plants using seawater for desalination, or for extraction of dissolved chemicals, where quantities of waste heat are not available, other countermeasures need to be taken.

Another way that the biota of the coastal zone interfere with the operation of seawater intakes is the presence, under some circumstances, of large quantities of the larger vegetation, such as kelps and other seaweeds, that have been torn from the bottom and are loose in the sea. These can interfere with the operation of the plant if they enter it and therefore must be separated either by suitable screening devices on the pipeline intakes, or by some sort of settling and removal process between the intake and the plant.

A further adverse effect of fouling organisms is the alteration of the buoyancy of floating structures. This can be important to marker buoys and other aids to navigation, and also to buoys supporting instruments for oceanographic or meteorological observations.

Effects on buoyancy may also be significant in the case of floating pipelines. A notable example is a submarine pipeline being considered as a possible means of bringing freshwater from northern to southern California, as a plausible economic alternative to terrestrial routes.

With increasing use of unattended automatic equipments, such as instruments for measuring ocean currents, television monitors, automatic equipment for controlling submarine oil wells, and so forth, the role of fouling organisms in interfering with their operation is becoming of increasing importance. Indeed, any kind of equipment that operates under the sea for extended periods of time needs to be designed bearing in mind the possible effects of fouling organisms, as well as the purely chemical and physical effects within the sea.

Destructive organisms. The best known example of organisms that actually destroy materials and equipment put into the sea are the teredos, gribbles, and boring clams that attack wooden structures, such as ships and docks. Despite our increased sophistication in dealing with these creatures, they represent a significantly important factor in the coastal zone in many parts of the world. Great economic loss continues to result from destruction of wooden ships and other wooden structures such as docks and barges by these organisms. Their prevention by chemical or other means is not inexpensive, hence continues to be an important subject of scientific inquiry and engineering development.

In addition to the organisms that attack wooden structures, there are some species of molluscs (clams and mussels) that bore into rocks and concrete, by either mechanical or chemical means, and can, in consequence, be deleterious to concrete structures under some circumstances.

An unusual, but interesting, example of destruction of equipment by marine organisms is the propensity of sharks to bite into the plastic lines used for taut anchorage of buoys employed to support current meters and other instruments, and the conductor cables that transmit data from the depths to the surface elements. The Woods Hole Oceanographic Institution has suffered rather considerable losses of instrumental buoys from this source, and it has also been a source of difficulty to the buoy operators at the Scripps Institution of Oceanography, and elsewhere, as well. In addition to destroying the anchorages of such buoys, thus cutting them adrift, sharks also sometimes cripple them by biting through the insulation of conductor cables leading from deep instruments to recording packages in the surface buoys. I believe this phenomenon is observed only in the pelagic realm and is not really of great concern in the coastal zone, but it does illustrate the kind of adverse activities of marine organisms against which the engineer must continually be on guard.

Direct hazards to man from organisms. Organisms of the coastal zone can also be a considerable nuisance to certain kinds of shoreside recreation. In addition to the sand fleas and other insects that are a minor annoyance to picnickers and sunbathers, jellyfish and other coelenterates with powerful nematocysts provide painful experiences, and in some cases real hazards, to unprotected swimmers. A recent infestation of Chesapeake Bay by a horde of stinging jellyfish is a typical example of great annoyance. Some other coelenterates, such as the Portuguese-man-of-war, can be more hazardous. This species has been known to incapacitate swimmers.

The most fearsome hazards to recreational swimmers and to men in the sea engaged in scientific and industrial pursuits by Scuba diving are sharks. Although the number of shark attacks are few, these great fishes present a real hazard in some tropical and subtropical localities and are the source of great apprehension in many other localities. Much research has been done toward developing chemical repellents, or physical repellents, for these creatures, with little success. In some locations they can be fenced away from heavily frequented bathing beaches, and an intensive fishery is probably one of the more effective ways of keeping down their abundance.

In addition to sharks, barracuda, moray eels, and sea snakes present minor hazards to swimmers in some localities.

Interference with communications. Marine organisms in the coastal zone, as elsewhere in the ocean, can interfere with communications by underwater sound, especially high-frequency underwater sound. Although our naval defense forces are concerned with all of the many ways in which organisms can affect their ships, equipment, and operations, the interference of organisms with underwater sound has been of special importance in connection with submarine and antisubmarine warfare. Organisms in the sea can present false targets to sonar equipments, and can, by scattering sound, limit their range and add to the background noise hampering signal recognition. In consequence, such biological effects on underwater sound are an important subject for study by scientists and engineers developing submarine detection equipments, and also those developing means for submarines to avoid the detection equipments of opposing forces. Organisms in the sea, especially shoals of zooplankton, shrimps, fish, and so forth, can likewise interfere with the use of underwater sound for echo sounding to determine the depth of water below ships, both military and commercial, and thus interfere with navigation.

This entire category of biological phenomena that affect other human activities in the coastal zone is, of course, a bit far afield in the context of conservation of the living marine resources, because, indeed, most of the things under this topic are not adverse to the biota themselves, and indeed some may be beneficial to the living resources and to some of the people that use them. For example, buoys, platforms, docks, and other structures covered with fouling organisms provide enhanced food and shelter for fish that are pursued by recreational fishermen. Indeed, recreational fishermen find that oil-well platforms have enhanced the abundance and availability of several species of sportfish. As mentioned later, in connection with solid-waste disposal, California and other states are actually in the business of building artificial reefs using solid waste materials, cement blocks, or quarry rock, to increase this type of habitat to improve recreational fishing. However, these phenomena are all elements of the total environment of the coastal zone, as modified by man's activities, and need to be taken into account in striking the balance sheet, when attempting to move toward whatever may be the social optimum in the multiple use of the coastal zone. Furthermore, we need to take into account possible adverse effects on other marine organisms of new countermeasures against these particular adverse effects of marine biota. For instance, in controlling the jellyfish in Chesapeake Bay, one should avoid damage to the other recreationally and commercially important living resources of that estuary.

Activities that affect the living resources

Let us now turn to the consideration of human activities in the coastal zone that are not directly concerned with the living resources but have important effects on them. Of the human activities that incidentally affect or are affected by the biota (p. 42), the most significant are various uses of the marginal lands, disposal of non-biodegradable wastes, and ocean mining. Each of these categories are treated individually.

Use of marginal lands. In order to accommodate many urban and industrial demands, man is prone to rearrange rather extensively the shoreline and the adjacent uplands in a variety of ways.

The locations of most coastal cities were initially determined by opportunities for marine commerce, but the natural harbors or roadsteads seldom continue to be adequate, in consequence of which much dredging, filling, construction of breakwaters, and so forth, is undertaken to expand and improve them.

In our modern age of air transportation, extensive areas are required for the landing and takeoff of airplanes, and these require large, level sites. Coastal cities that are not blessed with an abundance of closely adjacent level land often find it economical to construct it by filling in marshlands, shallow water embayments, or estuaries along the coast. San Diego provides an example in California. In other cases, where level shoreside sites were initially available for airports without much modification of the marine environment, subsequent need to extend the airports to accommodate more traffic or larger airplanes results in extensive dredging and filling activities. New York and San Francisco are examples.

Cities also must dispose of tremendous quantities of wastes, because, as Professor Norman Brooks [13], of the California Institute of Technology has emphasized, there is a large importation of materials *into* the city and, to obtain a mass balance, they have to be exported *out* to somewhere, land or sea. One of the most popular ways of getting rid of large quantities of solid wastes, such as construction materials, worn-out machinery, and nonburnable garbage and trash, is to put them in depressions in the earth near, or in, the city and cover them over with soil. This gets rid of the waste and provides additional usable land. Garbage, including not only the solid materials, but also organic wastes, are often similarly disposed of in so-called sanitary fill, whereby these materials also are put in depressions and covered over with earth. Many city developers have regarded marshlands and shallow coastal waters as ideal for these purposes, because they are convenient for disposing of the waste materials, and the operation provides additional level land near the sea for industrial sites, home sites, parks, golf courses, and so forth.

It has also been popular specifically to create construction sites by filling in marshes and shallow waters, either carving off hillsides to provide the fill, as has been extensively done in locations near San Francisco Bay, or by dredging material from the seabed, of which much of Miami provides a well-known example.

Another motive for rearranging the shoreline is to provide for additional recreation. Dredging and filling are employed to scallop the margin of the sea to provide more beaches for swimmers, sunbathers, and picnickers, and also to provide a greater expanse of sheltered waters for small boat harbors, water skiing, and so on. The extensive rearrangement of Mission Bay in San Diego, and the construction of two new peninsulas in San Diego Bay from dredging spoil provided in the course of deepening the channel, are examples of this sort of thing.

Construction of breakwaters to provide sheltered harbors or to improve channels also has significant effects on the sandy beaches, because these structures modify the transport of sand by alongshore currents, as has been explained in detail, for example, by Douglas Inman [8]. Inman has also shown that flood control activities in the hinterland have markedly diminished the supply of new sand to the beaches of southern California, and, since this material is being continuously lost to the deep sea through the submarine canyons, the long-term effects on the sand-beach environment can be of considerable importance. In attempts to offset the effects of these kinds of engineering activities, still further engineering is done to retard the movement of the beach sands or to rearrange them by further dredging and pumping.

It is to be noted that man's activities in modifying the river runoff in the hinterland also affect the habitat of living resources in the coastal zone by changing the environment in other, more subtle, ways, by modifying the supply of freshwater. This can have important biological effects on creatures of the marshlands and estuaries.

From the viewpoint of the conservation of the living resources of the coastal zone, these modifications of the margin of the sea have two important consequences: the elimination of habitats for living aquatic resources, and the modification of such habitats.

Probably the most serious and critical problem we face in the coastal zone is the complete elimination of the habitats of certain aquatic communities, by covering them over to make land, or by extirpating the habitat by digging a hole, so that the shallow water is replaced by deeper water, or by completely changing the substrate. This sort of activity is extremely critical, because it violates the important minimum standard of conservation, which consists of avoiding irreversibilities, at least for local marine biological communities, and, in some cases, for entire species or subspecies of limited geographical distribution. Most of this kind of modification of the margin of the sea is physically irreversible, because once a marsh or a piece of estuary is filled in or dredged out, it is not possible ever to restore it. Of course, one might argue that, given sufficient funds, and providing that the species concerned were not driven to extinction because of their maintenance in other refuges, it would, in principle, be physically possible to restore the habitat and the biological community. However, even if this were true, such modification is certainly at least economically and socially irreversible. Because of such considerations, the planning study *California and Use of the Ocean* [8] published in 1965 made the following recommendation:

In certain portions of the coastal zone, such as bays and estuaries, irreversible modifications are being made at a rapid rate. Pending completion of the detailed inventory . . . to provide the basis for a master plan, it is recommended that each proposal for modification of the critical areas be reviewed by the State Government. Modifications which are irreversible and which will preclude other beneficial future uses might well be held in abeyance pending the development of a master plan.

The Governor's Advisory Commission on Ocean Resources, reviewing this study the following year, emphasized the importance of this particular recommendation. In 1967, the California legislature passed the Marine Resources Conservation and Development Act that established the California Advisory Commission on Marine and Coastal Resources; in its first annual report [9] this commission, among its primary recommendations for immediate action, recommended that "pending completion of the inventory of coastal lands and the development of a master plan, state agencies concerned with marine affairs should be empowered by the legislature to temporarily prohibit irreversible modification to the coastal zone."

One alternative to continued modification of the shoreline to provide for airports, plant-sites, recreational areas, and such, is to build offshore structures—either islands or large floating platforms. Both seem to be feasible, and in at least some cases economic, from an engineering viewpoint. The proposed Metropolitan Water District nuclear power and desalination plant near Los Angeles was designed to be built in an offshore, man-made island. Offshore floating airports are under serious consideration at Los Angeles, New York, and Chicago.

In addition to direct, purposive physical modifications of the coastal zone, which eliminate habitats of important marine biota, the kinds of activities discussed can have almost equally serious effects in the modification of habitats in ways that may not have been foreseen. For example, the construction of harbor works, jetties, and so forth, not only modify the beaches through their effects on the flow of sand moved by alongshore currents, but also, through modification of current patterns, can have extensive effects in other ways, such as modifying sediment distributions in the sublittoral zone, with important effects on the benthic biota requiring certain sediment types. Again, harbor works that eliminate or diminish surf can seriously affect specialized organisms, such as certain kinds of clams that require the turbulent, strongly aerated, waters of the surf zone. As already mentioned, changes of freshwater flows to the ocean can also damage the biota of the coastal zone. To give just one example, that has received a good deal of national publicity, the modification of the freshwater flow into the Everglades in Florida, for purposes of flood control and control of saltwater intrusions, is apparently having extremely serious effects in that extensive marshland. Such effects can be important not only to the regular inhabitants of such environments but also can have serious repercussions on offshore species that inhabit them during part of their life history. In the case of the Everglades, a notable example is the peneid shrimps of the Gulf of Mexico, some important populations of which spend their larval stages in the Everglades.

Ocean disposal of nonbiodegradable wastes. Included in this category is the disposal in the nearshore portion of the ocean of solid and liquid wastes, of a nonbiodegradable nature, that arise from activities on the land. Wastes that arise from ocean-based activities, particularly ocean mining, are discussed separately.

Nonbiodegradable wastes arise from a multiplicity of terrestrial activities and their effects in the ocean are likewise highly varied. Some of the effects are beneficial, whereas others are harmful, and the same waste, handled in different ways, can be beneficial or harmful depending on when, where, and how it is introduced into the marine environment.

Solid Wastes. Solid, nonbiodegradable wastes are produced in the urban industrial complex by many activities, and the total quantity to be somewhere disposed of is tremendous. One large component is construction materials—the waste concrete, metal, and so forth, from demolition of structures and from construction by-products. Another large component includes junked automobiles, streetcars, buses, and other vehicles and machinery. Since it is often not economical to recycle the material back into industrial uses, it becomes solid junk, to be gotten rid of. A third large source is all of the miscellaneous refuse, organic and inorganic, from household and commercial activities, typically some 2 pounds per capita per day, of which about half a pound is garbage. This trash can be disposed of at sea, in which case the organic fraction has much the same effects and problems as other kinds of organic sewage already discussed. Organic garbage and trash can, however, also be incinerated, and the solid residues of metal, glass, and ash added to the volume of other nonbiodegradable material to be disposed of on land or at sea. The foregoing types of wastes are all normally collected by the municipal waste-disposal services. Total wastes currently collected amount to 5.3 pounds per capita, per day, expected to increase to 8 pounds by 1980 [14]. Another kind of solid waste is the spoil from terrestrial excavation or marine dredging, which may be removed from a given site and placed in the ocean in the coastal zone to get rid of it.

The principal biological effect of these solid, nonbiodegradable wastes put in the sea is to modify the seabed habitat, although the finer components, such as silt from dredging or incinerator ash, can be directly deleterious to marine invertebrates by covering them so that they may be deprived of oxygen or food, and to marine plants by the light-depriving effects of increased turbidity. These, in turn, can affect the animals that feed on the plants and benthic invertebrates.

Modification of habitat by solid waste is not necessarily undesirable. The larger chunks, such as construction materials, old automobiles, and so forth, can be used for the construction of artificial reefs, mentioned earlier, providing improved and expanded habitat for benthic organisms that are food for desirable varieties of fishes, and also providing refuges and breeding places for such fishes. Indeed, as already noted, such materials have been used in California, Florida, and elsewhere. In California, at least, however, it turns out to be more economical to use quarry rock than any of these materials, because of the greater convenience in handling and transporting the rock, and because of the fact that old automobiles and other metallic wastes rapidly corrode and go into solution in seawater. From an overall systems viewpoint it might still be more economical to society to use these junk materials for building artificial reefs, if the cost of waste disposal by alternative means were cranked into the calculation. That is, the equivalent of the disposal cost by other means might profitably be provided as a subsidy to the people building the artificial reefs, to induce them to use the waste materials rather than cement blocks, or quarry rock that, in the absence of such an arrangement, cost less to the reef builder.

Even in circumstances where the solid, nonbiodegradable wastes cannot be employed in the ocean in beneficial ways, it may still be quite a good place to dispose of them. Because a small area of ocean bottom can accommodate a large quantity of such wastes, and their disposal need have no deleterious effects on adjacent areas if properly handled, it is quite legitimate to continue to set aside limited, carefully patrolled dumping grounds for such disposal. But each such area should be selected and its use controlled so as to minimize damage to the biota.

One category of solid wastes that I have not yet mentioned are radioactive materials. Disposal of solid radioactive wastes in the coastal zone is only practical for very low-level solid wastes, such as laboratory and hospital trash. Several studies have shown that this kind of material, especially when packaged in concrete to immobilize it, can safely be deposited in carefully selected dumping grounds in the shallow coastal zone and, indeed, such dumping grounds were established at several locations off the Atlantic coast, where deep water is not available anywhere near to shore. At the present time, however, no such materials are being thus disposed of in the United States, because terrestrial disposal grounds have turned out to be preferable. But ocean disposal may be necessary, or desirable, for other countries having more limited land area, and can be accommodated without appreciable deleterious effects on the living resources of the sea, or man's use of them, if done carefully in selected, limited areas of the seabed.

Liquid Wastes. Nonbiodegradable liquid wastes that affect the living marine resources also arise from a great many scientific, industrial, and domestic activities. For illustration, take the following few examples: acid wastes from wood pulp mills, containing biologically refractory lignin fractions of the wood and various inorganic chemicals; soluble metallic salts and other metallic compounds in solution or fine suspension, arising from numerous industrial processes (e.g., mercury compounds from various chemical syntheses; lead compounds from mining, smelting, preparation of paints, and other processes; zinc wastes from mining, smelting, and industrial uses such as galvanizing; chromium compounds from manufacturing processes or from chromium-treated cooling waters; cyanides, sulfides, and fluorides from various chemical and industrial processes). A more extensive list appears in a recent report of the Committee on Water Quality Criteria of the Federal Water Pollution Control Administration [15].

Nearly all of these waterborne wastes find their ultimate sink in the ocean, and this is a perfectly good place to dispose of them, providing that it is properly and carefully done. The problem, of course, is in designing the input into the ocean in such a way as to ensure sufficiently rapid dilution so that the toxic material is never in high enough concentration to be harmful to marine organisms or to man, either directly or through accumulation and transfer via the marine food chain.

Low-level radioactive wastes from reactor cooling water, nuclear fuel reprocessing plants, start-up water from nuclear marine power plants, and other sources constitute a category of liquid wastes that have received a great deal of attention from the scientific and engineering community. These wastes are potentially dangerous to man either by direct exposure, in some instances, or, more frequently, by concentration and return to him through marine food products. There has also been some concern about possible adverse effects on the marine biota themselves. A great deal of research, both fundamental and applied, in respect to these problems has been supported by the Atomic Energy Commission in the United States, and by similar agencies in other countries, as well as by the International Atomic Energy Agency. On this basis, considerable quantities of such materials continue to be introduced into the ocean, under careful monitoring, without hazard either to the marine biota or to man. The largest input of this sort into the sea in the United States is, of course, the Columbia River where the operation of the reactors at Hanford, Washington, produces a considerable volume of waterborne radioactive materials, arising from neutron irradiation of metals in the cooling water of the reactors, and some contamination through leakage from fuel elements. Although the flow into the sea has been as high as 2000 curies per day, the environment—terrestrial, lacustrine and marine—is carefully monitored, and it is clear that this radioactivity has presented no hazard. Indeed, the effects of waste heat in the Columbia River on some of the more sensitive fishes appears to be more of a potential problem than the radioactivity.

We can draw an important lesson from our experience in dealing with radioactive waste materials, both in the terrestrial and marine environments. The cautious approach to the disposal of this category of wastes, based on extensive scientific and engineering investigation, offers a model of how we ought to be dealing with many other categories of wastes that, while not so fearsome, may be potentially equally, or even more, hazardous to man directly and through damage to his biological environment.

A waterborne waste of growing concern because of its biological effects is waste heat. The problem of thermal pollution, of both water and air, as has been pointed out by Norman Brooks [13] and others, is one of the more difficult and rapidly growing problems of the urban industrial complex. Our use of increasing quantities of energy, in various forms, is accompanied by the generation of a great deal of heat that goes into the atmosphere or the waters. For example, steam power plants are no more than 40% efficient, regardless of whether they use fossil fuel or nuclear fuel. In order to operate a power generating plant efficiently, one requires a low-temperature heat sink, and this can be obtained by using large quantities of cooling water, at as low a temperature as possible. For urban coastal communities, seawater is the sink of choice.

In arid coastal regions such as southern California, freshwater for industrial and domestic purposes, and for local agriculture, at least for selected high-value crops, must be imported from elsewhere (e.g., from the Colorado River and soon from the Feather River in southern California) or extracted from the sea. Desalination of seawater is already of some importance in these applications and is expected soon to be economically competitive with imports. The combination of desalination and production of power for other industrial purposes, using nuclear fission as the heat source, is especially attractive. This is, of course, another source of waste heat, as well as of saline water (a desalination plant returns to the sea waste water of double or triple the original salinity), which has to be disposed of in the marine environment.

Large quantities of waste heat introduced into a limited volume of water can raise the temperature to levels deleterious to many aquatic organisms. This problem of thermal pollution is already acute in some rivers and lakes and is becoming so in estuaries and other restricted marine waters. The open, oceanic waters of the coastal zone, however, can accommodate very large quantities of waste heat, because of their large volume and extensive mixing, with very little increase in temperature and, consequently, no hazard to the ecology of the coastal zone, *if* the effluent cooling water is introduced in such a manner as to obtain sufficiently rapid dilution by mixing. In order to ensure this, it is customary for the governing authority, when issuing a permit for construction of a coastal power plant using seawater for cooling to specify the maximum increase in temperature that will be permitted at various distances from the outfall. An important engineering challenge is the efficient design of the disposal systems to meet these criteria for preventing damage to the biota of the coastal zone. But an even more interesting challenge is to devise means for using at least some portion of the waste heat in beneficial ways. For example, the waste heat may be used in connection with breeding of oysters in captivity, to extend their spawning seasons; this is already being done in a few places. Scientists in the United Kingdom are also experimenting with using waste heat to enhance the growth rate of plaice, an expensive flatfish, that is commencing to be grown in captivity. In the vicinity of some of the outfalls of cooling water of power plants in California, some of the subtropical fishes, such as bonito that are summer visitors, stay around all winter, which is much appreciated by sportfishermen; perhaps we might apply this effect in a purposive fashion. It has also been suggested that a clever engineer might design a system by which warm water could be kept in a narrow strip along a beach, providing comfortable swimming in northern California, and even in southern California in the wintertime. I believe we would be willing to accept some modifications of the marine biota along a few beaches for the sake of this amenity.

Ocean mining. With increasing demands, decreasing grades of ores from terrestrial sources, and advances in marine technology, we are rapidly extending our mining activities from the dry land to the submerged portion of the continent. In the coastal zone, the submerged portion of which is essentially submerged continental material, the mineral resources are of the same kinds as those on dry land, with the exception of a few things, such as magnesium metal, bromine, and other dissolved materials obtained from solution in seawater. Note, however, that many of the dissolved materials that we obtain from the sea are also available from salt brines on the land. The recent growth of marine mining of various kinds may be seen from Table 1.

From the seabed, interestingly enough, one of the more important categories of materials presently being mined is sand and gravel

TABLE 1
Values of Mineral Production (by Source) from Oceans
Bordering the United States, 1960–1967
(in Millions of Dollars)

Year	Magnesium Metal and Compounds, Salt, and Bromine[a]	From Wells: Petroleum, Natural gas, and Sulfur[b]	Sand and Gravel, Zircon, Feldspar, Cement Rock, and Limestone[c]	Combined
1960	69.0	423.6	46.8	539.4
1961	73.0	496.6	46.2	615.8
1962	89.1	620.7	44.3	754.1
1963	84.6	730.8	42.5	857.9
1964	94.5	820.3	43.6	958.4
1965	102.6	933.3	51.4	1087.3
1966	117.0	1177.7	51.6	1346.3
1967	145.4	1404.8	55.9	1606.1
Total:	775.2	6607.8	382.3	7765.3

Source. National Council on Marine Resources and Engineering Develment [16].

[a] Seawater.
[b] Ocean subfloors.
[c] Beaches and seafloors.

for construction purposes. In addition, rather considerable quantities of oyster shell are dredged in such places as Galveston Bay and San Francisco Bay, as a source of calcium carbonate. Small quantities of zircon, feldspar, cement rock, and other materials are being mined in shallow waters. Placer deposits of gold and other materials are known to exist in drowned beaches, off Alaska for example, and are expected shortly to come into production. Phosphorite precipitates on the seabed off southern California, and in some other localities, offer promise for eventual production of fertilizer materials.

The most rapidly growing sector of marine mining in the United States is production of petroleum, natural gas, and some sulfur, from wells drilled into the seabed on the continental shelf, the value of this production having grown from 424 million dollars to 1405 million dollars from 1960 to 1967. It is rapidly becoming both technically and economically feasible to drill production wells in deeper water, on the upper part of the continental slope.

Extraction of dissolved materials from seawater, primarily magnesium, bromine, and various components of sea salt, is a specialized industry carried on in only a few favorable localities. It is the principal source of magnesium metal in the United States, and that is the single most valuable dissolved material mined from seawater, followed by bromine. The winning of magnesium from seawater depends not only upon the seawater itself, but on a large, low-cost supply of calcium carbonate and low-cost power. Because of this, preferred locations are on the Gulf Coast where abundant oyster shell may be dredged as the source of the calcium carbonate, and where low-cost power is available.

With respect of ocean mining, we need to take account of four categories of effects that can have important impact on the living resources of the sea: (1) effects of geophysical prospecting; (2) direct damage to benthic organisms by mining operations; (3) effects of deposition of mining spoil and other waste materials arising from the mining process; and (4) pollution from beneficiation and processing at sea.

Prospecting for petroleum and natural gas, and to some extent for other deposits, involves determining the deep geological structures of the underlying seabed through geophysical methods, including seismic reflection and refraction methods, measurements of gravity fields, and measurements of magnetic fields. The first of these presents some hazard to fish in the coastal zone because the use of explosives can kill fish in the near vicinity of the shots. In consequence, where explosives are used, it is important to establish appropriate controls on the quantities and kinds of explosives to be used and means of monitoring the operations so that explosive charges are not set off in the near vicinity of large concentrations of fish. Such controls have been in operation in California for some years. Fortunately, with the development of nonexplosive energy sources, which do not produce the sharp shock waves generated by explosives that are so damaging to fish, much of this kind of prospecting can be done with little hazard to the biota.

Such surficial mining activities as the dredging of sand and gravel, fossil oyster shell, or phosphorite nodules, and other kinds of dredging or excavation, are harmful to the benthic biota inhabiting the dredged areas and will also preempt fishing at the same time the mining occurs. Since the actual mining occupies, generally, only a relatively small part of the sea bottom, however, it should result in only minor biological damage, except in especially critical habitats. Selection of areas where such mining activity is to be permitted requires, of course, rather careful evaluation of the relative values of the damage to the biota and of the gain to society from the mining operation. To give just one example of an important recent conflict of this sort, there has been a sharp controversy over the effects of dredging of fossil shell in Galveston Bay on the living oyster reefs, and effects on the fishes of the superjacent waters as well, the latter being due to allegations that the dredging not only interferes with the food of the fishes, but also, due to silt put into the water, is directly deleterious to them.

Direct damage to the biota in the area actually being excavated is not the only possible deleterious biological effect. Material that is removed to uncover ores or gangue that is removed with the ores and separated, is returned to the seabed. This material can smother benthic biota and can also, in the case of fine silt that remains suspended in the water for considerable time, interfere with the photosynthesis of plants by increasing turbidity and may be deleterious to the fishes of the overlying waters, as has been claimed in the case of the oyster-shell dredging in Galveston Bay. It is, therefore, necessary carefully to control such mining operations, so that the spoil is replaced on the bottom in very restricted areas, and carefully, in order to minimize the pollution hazard. In the case of suction dredges, such as have been proposed for the harvesting of phosphorite nodules, whereby the nodules would be separated from other materials on the dredging vessel at the surface, rather sophisticated methods are required to put the separated material back down on the bottom, with minimum contamination of the water column and of the seabed.

Related to the foregoing, is the problem of disposal of wastes that can arise from the beneficiation or processing of ores at sea. The phosphorite nodules off California, for example, are low grade ores of phosphorite, containing much extraneous material [17] so that they need to be beneficiated before marketing [8]. This may very well be done at sea to save the transportation of the unwanted material. Another example is the possible processing at sea of ferromanganese nodules. Although these occur in the deep sea, rather far from the coastal zone, they offer at least a useful analogy. These ferromanganese nodules, although they contain considerable quantities of iron and manganese, are probably most valuable as low grade ores of nickel, copper, and cobalt, the iron certainly being noncompetitive with other sources and the manganese more probably so in most localities. If one could develop an economical and efficient means of removing at sea the valuable metals, which occur in concentrations of only a few percent of the mass of the ore, leaving the rest of the material in the ocean, there are obvious advantages in lowering transportation and handling costs. But processing at sea can result in waste materials, both from the unwanted parts of the nodules and from chemicals used in the processing, which may be deleterious to the biota either of the sea-floor or of the water column. This must be taken into account in developing such at-sea processing schemes.

Physical interference with the use of living resources. An important aspect of ocean mining operations, and of other activities, such as emplacement of military installations on the seabed, creation of dumping areas for solid waste disposal, establishment of military testing ranges, or designation of safety zones for submarines, is that all such activities represent a physical interference with the *use* of the living resources by commercial or recreational fishermen. This sort of interference comes about in two ways, first by preemption of the space for other than fishing purposes, and second, by erection of structures that interfere with the fishermen's activities.

Where a mining operation or some other preemptive activity is going on, a fishing operation cannot be conducted in the identical space. At least equally important in preempting fishing space is the establishment of safety zones around the actual sites of such activities. The setting aside of sea areas for military purposes, from which fishermen are excluded, has in some instances considerably handicapped them. Even more conflict will arise in the future. As has been pointed out by John Craven [18], with more widespread use of man-in-the-sea techniques, that it is going to be necessary to establish some new maritime law to give priority and protection to the vulnerable man in the sea in emergencies; this will require additional temporal and spatial restrictions of other operations, including fishing.

Physical interference of structures with fishing gear has most frequently occurred in connection with oil wells, pipelines, and submarine cables. It is a common practice, and compulsory on at least the outer continental shelf, when abandoning an oil well, to cut off the casing at or below the seafloor. Stubs may be subsequently revealed by current erosion and present a hazard to nets and trawls. Unburied pipelines present a similar hazard, as do other structures on the seabed. On occasion, trawl gear has fouled submarine cables used for transoceanic communications, with consequent damage both to the cable and to the fisherman's gear.

Unmarked and uncharted structures are most hazardous. Showing these obstacles on charts is of some advantage, but, in view of the present lack of precision of navigational methods available to fishermen, this, by itself, does not enable safe operation near to such obstacles. A superior method is to mark these obstacles, so that they can be directly located by the fishermen.

Potential hazard from submarine structures is undoubtedly going to increase, because of the objection of citizens to above-water structures that disturb their enjoyment of the seascape. For example, the major objection of citizens of Santa Barbara to the leasing of submarine lands for petroleum production offshore from that city was to seeing platforms, or islands, for the drilling of oil wells even as far away as 5 miles off the beach. In consequence of such demands to eliminate surface structures, there is currently considerable scientific and engineering effort directed to development of techniques for carrying on mining and petroleum-producing operations entirely under the sea. Indeed, John Craven [18, 19] and others have asserted that methods of operating entirely under the sea may prove eventually to be cheaper than operating from the surface, because of the advantages of getting away from the well-known handicaps of the air-sea interface.

6. SOME ASPECTS OF PLANNING AND DECISION-MAKING

It should be evident from the foregoing review, which is by no means a complete catalogue of the multiple interactions of man with the biota of the coastal zone, that living resources are of indispensable importance for many of our activities there, and that additional important uses of the coastal zone affect the living resources, beneficially or adversely, in multiple ways. In consequence, conservation of the living resources, in the sense of maintaining the minimum standard of conservation, as earlier defined, and moving toward an optimum state of conservation involves planning and decision-making in the context of the total ecology of this region. To do this successfully, we must know enough about the living resources, their interactions among themselves and with their abiotic environment, and the effects of man's activities, to enable the manipulation of the resources and the environment in a predictable, purposeful fashion. Although this degree of understanding is a necessary condition for conservation of the living resources of the coastal zone, for the benefit of mankind, it is by no means a sufficient condition. The capacity to manipulate the world does not necessarily ensure that it will be manipulated to the net benefit of society, because our mechanisms for planning and decision-making are not yet so well adapted to the purpose. It would not be appropriate to attempt here any full elucidation of this topic. However, a few brief remarks concerning the nature of the difficulties, and possible contributions to a solution, are in order.

Most fundamental, perhaps, is the fact, previously pointed out by others [20], that the anthropocentric Judeo-Christian philosophy is not well attuned to the need for man to consider himself as a part of nature, to adapt himself to it rather than to try to master it by force. There is a tendency, in consequence, to approach the ecological problem by dominating nature, rather than by preserving it, and by adapting our needs and desires to the imperatives of the total ecological environment, evolved over eons, in which we find ourselves.

On a more pragmatic level, there is the problem, peculiar to certain classes of natural resources of which the living marine resources are a notable example, of the lack of ownership of these resources by any single social group. The effects of this have been called by Garrett Hardin [21] "the tragedy of the commons." What is the common property of everyone is the responsibility of no one. Or in economic terms, many of the economies and diseconomies are external to the user, falling to society as a whole. Those natural resources that are the common property of all society tend, therefore, to get short shrift in contrast with the things that are the property of particular individuals or groups, because each man is more interested in his own welfare than that of the whole community.

There are, of course, both modern and ancient examples of good management of common property resources by governmental institutions. Examples are modern forest management in parts of Europe and North America, or the ancient system of management of nearshore fishery resources in Polynesia before the advent of European civilization. Such is, however, the exception in the modern world. But the solution to this problem is not necessarily the reduction of all resources to restricted ownerships. It is, we hope, possible to perfect modern institutions for effective management of common property resources.

An important aspect of the problem of the commons is that both the legislative and executive branches of our government, being composed of people and not of gods, carry on much of their business by reacting to special interests and pressure groups. Despite the early efforts of Gifford Pinchot, Theodore Roosevelt, and their disciples and heirs, it is only recently that a significant pressure group has developed to bring strongly to the attention of governmental agencies, both the legislative and executive, the important concept of conserving the elements of our natural environment, even though this involves other values than the economist's standard of maximizing the net economic yield discounted to present time.

Another source of difficulty in achieving a total environmental approach to problems of the coastal zone is that local, state, and national governments are organized according to a different taxonomy. Rather than having governmental units concerned with all of the environmental elements in a given geographical unit, ideally a geographical unit that also corresponds moderately well to a natural ecological unit, we organize our governments basically according to various functions. Thus we have separate divisions of government for those activities that create problems in the environment, such as agriculture, mining, commerce, housing and urban development, highway construction, and military actions, while the activities involved with taking care of the problems thus created are in yet other divisions, such as public health and welfare, pollution control, parks and recreation, or fish and game.

One solution, which has worked moderately well in at least some circumstances, is to create some sort of regional authorities that cut across, coordinate, and, where necessary, supersede the individual authorities dealing with the various functions, or fragments of ecological units, in the coastal zone. I cite, for example, the San Diego Port Authority, dealing broadly with the integrated development of San Diego Bay. The San Francisco Bay Conservation and Development Commission seems also to be making admirable progress.

At the state level, it became evident some years ago when our State Office of Planning was putting together a California Development Plan [22] that there needed to be an appraisal of the ocean, its resources, and its problems, especially in the coastal zone, which cut across all of the individual functions and activities according to which the plan was being organized. In consequence, and I believe it was somewhat of a pioneering effort, a study [8] was made, referred to several times already in this paper, which formed an important part of the input to California's consideration of these matters extending up to the present time. Recently, the State Government has established an Interagency Council on Ocean Resources (ICOR) chaired by the Lieutenant Governor, the members of which are the heads of the various agencies and departments concerned in various ways with the coastal zone and also the more distant ocean. This group has the responsibility of devising the California Comprehensive Ocean Area Plan to provide a comprehensive framework for the proper consideration of all of the multiple uses of the sea. To replace a Governor's Advisory Commission on Ocean Resources originally appointed by Governor Brown and reappointed by Governor Reagan, the California Legislature in 1967 established a California Advisory Commission on Marine and Coastal Resources, which is an advisory group of nongovernment experts, drawn from many sectors, including the universities, industry, and the several pertinent professions, to advise broadly on marine affairs, providing input to ICOR and the legislature. Among other duties, it is charged with reviewing the Ocean Area Plan. Hopefully from these efforts will develop some kind of statewide, or regional, authorities responsible for the comprehensive, long-range planning of the multiple use of the coastal zone that, I am convinced, is the road to a livable marine environment for the people of the coastal megalopolis.

Studies at the national level have arrived at similar conclusions. The report of the National Commission on Marine Science, Engineering and Resources [1], "Our Nation and the Sea," has concluded the following:

The key to more effective use of our coastline is the introduction of a management system permitting conscious and informed choices among development alternatives, providing for proper planning, and encouraging recognition of the long-term importance of maintaining the quality of this productive region in order to insure both its enjoyment and the sound utilization of its resources. The benefits and the problems of achieving rational management are apparent. The present federal, state, and local machinery is inadequate. Something must be done.

This National Commission has recommended that the Federal Government adopt a Coastal Management Act to provide policy objectives for the coastal zone and to authorize Federal grants-in-aid to facilitate the establishment of state coastal zone authorities, empowered to manage the coastal waters and adjacent lands. The Commission's report goes on to indicate the functions and powers that should be vested in the coastal zone authorities.

The National Council on Marine Resources and Engineering Development has likewise given great attention to the problems of the coastal zone and to possible avenues toward their solution. Like other groups that have studied the problem intensively, the Council [23] has "noted the uniqueness of marine science affairs of the coastal zone—resulting from intense, varied human uses superimposed on an intricate, delicate ecology, and involving an array of governmental entities to manage the zone. This severe administrative fragmentation, as well as the confrontation between different interests, suggests the need for unifying concepts by which we can deal with these problems." The Council has indicated that it believes much can be accomplished by using existing capabilities and existing authorities, but that some sort of regional authorities, similar in makeup to the existing River Basin Commissions, may be needed.

Recently the Subcommittee on Oceanography of the Committee on Merchant Marine and Fisheries of the House of Representatives, holding hearings on the recommendations of the Commission on Marine Science, Engineering and Resources, has put much of its attention on the problems of the coastal zone, and means to their solution [24].

Senators Magnusson and Hart introduced, on August 8, 1969, a bill [25] "Coastal Zone Management Act of 1969" to authorize and encourage states to establish coastal authorities, including interstate coastal authorities when desirable. Funding, on a matching basis, would be provided by the Federal Government, and the programs of the coastal authorities would be subject to Federal review and approval. The responsible Federal agency under this bill would be the National Council on Marine Resources and Engineering Development. It is anticipated that members of the House of Representatives' Committee on Merchant Marine and Fisheries will introduce a similar bill, but designating an existing department as the responsible Federal agency.

It does, therefore, appear hopeful that we may, in the not distant future, see the establishment of necessary regional authorities for the management of the coastal zone, according to realistic geographic units, whereby the total ecology of these units may be taken into account in the decision-making process. However, just as the existence of knowledge concerning the ecology of the coastal zone is of little use without the appropriate kind of planning and decision-making authorities, the converse is also true. Unfortunately, we have yet a great deal to learn about the living resources, their interactions among themselves and with their environment, and the effects of our manipulations—knowledge that even the best designed authority will require if it is to achieve adequate conservation of the living resources. It is the urgent task of scientists and engineers to provide this knowledge.

REFERENCES

1. Commission on Marine Science, Engineering and Resources, *Our Nation and the Sea—A Plan for National Action*, U.S. Government Printing Office, Washington, D.C., 305 pp., 1969.
2. M. B. Schaefer, "Economic and Social Needs for Marine Resources," in *Ocean Engineering*, J. F. Brahtz (Ed.), Wiley, New York, pp. 6–37, 1968.
3. S. V. Ciriacy-Wantrup, *Resource Conservation—Economics and Politics*, revised edition, University of California, Division of Agricultural Sciences, 1963, 395 pp.
4. J. Hirshleifer, J. C. DeHaven, and J. W. Milliman, *Water Supply—Economics, Technology and Policy*, University of Chicago Press, 1960, 378 pp.
5. H. H. Landsberg, L. L. Fischman, and J. L. Fisher, *Resources in America's Future*, Resources for the Future Inc., Johns Hopkins Press, 1963, 1017 pp.
6. U.S. Bureau of Commercial Fisheries, *Fisheries of the United States— 1968*, C.F.S. 5000, 1969, 83 pp.
7. Dewitt Gilbert (Ed.), *The Future of the Fishing Industry of the United States*, Vol. 4, University of Washington Publ. in Fisheries, N.S., 1968, 346 pp.
8. Institute of Marine Resources, *California and Use of the Ocean*, a Plan-

ning Study of Marine Resources, prepared for the State Office of Planning, University of California, Institute of Marine Resources, La Jolla, Calif., IMR Ref. No. 65–21, 1965.

9. California Advisory Commission on Marine and Coastal Resources, *Defining the California Public Interest in the Marine Environment*, First Annual Report of the Commission, Sacramento, Calif., January, 1969, 71 pp.

10. J. E. Smith (Ed.), *"Torrey Canyon" Pollution and Marine Life*, Marine Biological Association of the United Kingdom, Cambridge University Press, 1968, 196 pp.

11. W. J. North, M. Neushul, and K. A. Clendenning, "Successive Biological Changes Observed in a Marine Cove Exposed to a Large Spillage of Mineral Oil," *Proceedings of the Symposium Sur Polutions Marines Par Les Microorganismes Produits Et Les Petroliers* (Monaco), pp. 335–354, 1964.

12. D. L. Ray (Ed.), *Marine Boring and Fouling Organisms*, University of Washington Press, Seattle, Wash., 1959, 536 pp.

13. N. H. Brooks, "Man, Water and Waste," in *The Next Ninety Years, Proceedings of a Conference at California Institute of Technology*, March 1967, pp. 91–112, 1967.

14. Anon., "Why the U.S. Is in Danger of Being Engulfed by Its Trash," *U.S. News and World Report*, September 8, 1969, pp. 64–65.

15. Federal Water Pollution Control Administration, *Water Quality Criteria —Report of the National Technical Advisory Committee to the Secretary of Interior*, U.S. Government Printing Office, Washington, D.C., 1968, 234 pp.

16. National Council on Marine Resources and Engineering Development, *Marine Science Affairs—A Year of Broadened Participation, Third Report of the President to the Congress on Marine Resources and Engineering Development*, U.S. Government Printing Office, Washington, D.C., 1969, 251 pp.

17. J. L. Mero, *The Mineral Resources of the Sea*, Elsevier, New York, 1965, 312 pp.

18. J. Craven, "Technology and Law of the Sea," *Ohio State University Conference on Law, Organization and Security in the Use of the Ocean*, Vol. 2 (March 17–18, 1967), pp. 1–37.

19. J. Craven, "Res Nullius de Facto—The Limits of Technology," *Symposium on the International Regime of the Sea-Bed*, Istituto Affari Internazionali, Rome, 1969 (In Press).

20. Lynn White, "The Historical Roots of Our Ecological Crisis," *Science*, Vol. 155 (1967), pp. 1203–1207.

21. Garrett Hardin, "The Tragedy of the Commons," *Science*, Vol. 162 (1968), pp. 1243–1248.

22. California State Office of Planning, *California State Development Plan Program*, Sacramento, Calif., 1968, 363 pp.

23. National Council on Marine Resources and Engineering Development, *Marine Science Affairs—A Year of Plans and Progress; Second Report of the President to the Congress on Marine Resources and Engineering Development*, U.S. Government Printing Office, Washington, D.C., 1968, 228 pp.

24. Subcommittee on Oceanography of the Committee on Merchant Marine and Fisheries of the House of Representatives, 91st Congress, 1st Session, *National Oceanographic Program—1969*, Part I, Serial No. 91-5, U.S. Government Printing Office, Washington, D.C., 1969, 511 pp.
25. S.2802., "Coastal Zone Management Act of 1969," 91st Congress, 1st Session (introduced in the Senate August 8, 1969 and referred to the Committee on Commerce).

CHAPTER 4

Social Needs and the Urban-Marine Environment

MARION CLAWSON

A growing population, higher real incomes per capita, and a changing American life style all make new demands on all natural resources, including marine resources and those of the water's edge.

A number of economic and social changes are occurring simultaneously in the United States. It is difficult to isolate the effect of any single changing force; a likely hypothesis is that they are all closely interrelated, and that the effect of each largely depends upon the presence of others. As a simple expository necessity, we must describe several, one at a time, but their interrelatedness should be constantly borne in mind in the discussion which follows.

At the outset, it is necessary to assert also that these socioeconomic changes are producing new demands on natural resources, but demands which are by no means unmanageable, if the thought and effort to cope with them is exerted. The old Malthusian approach to natural resources is far from dead, among the "viewers-with-alarm"; its opposite, an easy optimism that science and technology can readily deal with every problem, hence there is no real problem, is perhaps more popularly accepted today. This author's position is intermediate: new demands bring new problems, but not unmanageable ones; we can have an environment which in large part meets our desires, but we cannot expect it without effort on our part. For better or worse, we live in an age when the "natural" environment is largely what we make it; we can attain most of what we want, if we really try; and if we fail the fault is ours.

1. SOCIOECONOMIC TRENDS

At the risk of telling the reader what he already knows, let me review the postwar socioeconomic trends which, in my judgment, have most affected natural resource demands and use generally.

First of all, population has risen rather rapidly in these postwar years [1]. We sometimes forget, and indeed younger people never know from personal experience, that the specter of a constant or even a declining population haunted the economic literature of the 1930s. Birth rates had fallen over a long preceding period, until they were approaching the declining death rates, and it was easy to make demographic projections that resulted in a population ceiling, followed by a population decline, all to occur in the two decades or more through which we have just now passed. Economic analyses were based on this type of demographic stagnation, with warnings that economic stagnation would follow unless appropriate economic policies were followed.

The war upsurge in birth rates ended all that—although many demographic analyses continued to project a population ceiling long after the evidence was clear that a major change had occurred. Long declines in birth rates have occurred in many Western societies and are now beginning to appear in some Oriental ones, but the experience of the United States of a major and continued reversal in this trend was a relatively unique experience in world history. The war upsurge in birth rates continued in the postwar decades, and a new demographic orthodoxy of relatively high continued natural increase in population arose. Many striking arithmetic calculations, each based upon a constant percentage population increase, engaged popular attention. But, in the past half dozen years, birth rates have fallen again, and now are at about pre-World War II levels.

In the total population picture, death rates (at least until now) have been statistically dependable—slightly declining from year to year, but stable. However, birth rates have been variable and, to a considerable extent, unpredictable. The human animal varies his reproductive rates, not only as to numbers of children but as to timing within the marriage cycle, in ways that are not always predictable or even obvious after the fact. Demographic projections still predict almost unanimously continued increases in population, but at slower rates than projections made a decade ago. Perhaps the most significant fact is that increases today and in the future take place from a much larger population base; a 1.5% annual increase from our present base of 200 million is a net increase of 3 million people—almost as many people as the first census found in 1790 in the whole United States. My own intuitive judgment is that our demographic projections are less reliable than we usually assume as we make our economic projections, but my research and analysis of future resource problems are based on the assumption of a moderately rising total population.

Perhaps even more striking than the changes in national total population have been the changes in its geographic distribution. People migrate freely within the United States, and some sections of the nation have grown much more rapidly than others. In a typical California group, at least half were born in some other state; at one time, the proportion of Californians born in other states was fully two-thirds. Arizona, Nevada, and Florida have experienced immigrations of similar proportions. But most large urban complexes have also gained from net migration. Americans have been engaged since the war in a vast exodus in rural areas; more than half of all counties in the United States lost population in the decade of the 1950s, some of them had been losing before that, and most of these and some others will show further losses in the 1960s. The situation is much more extreme than these simple facts suggest. In many counties which did not lose population, it was only the growth of the county seat or other larger towns which maintained total population; the truly rural areas and smaller towns lost population in those counties. But population migration is always selective—migrants are never a random cross-section of the whole population. While many sociologists believe but may have difficulty proving that migration selects certain personality types, there is no question but that migration is selective as to ages—it has always been the young and the relatively footloose who moved first and most easily. That was true in the California gold rush more than 100 years ago and has been true ever since. Migration out of rural areas has been age selective; farmers and small town people who do not migrate are getting old, and as the present older population dies, the population changes will be even more drastic than those of the past two decades.

A new demographic phenomenon, and a very striking one, has emerged in the past decade for a substantial number of primarily rural counties—annual deaths now exceed annual births [2]. The numbers of young adults, in the child-bearing ages, in such counties has fallen so low as a result of out migration that, in spite of approximately average reproductive rates for the young adults who have remained, the number of babies born annually is less in recent years than the total deaths of the old people. Future population changes in such counties may be depressing to contemplate and experience.

The population movement toward the urban complexes has been one of concentration, on a national scale; but there has been an accompanying outward movement of people from the older city centers [3]. Many cities did not gain population during the 1950s, and some lost; many of the readily available data for this and for earlier decades are quite misleading, because they were based upon "cities" which have constantly expanded in area. That is, many a city as originally defined, sometimes more than a century ago, has lost population for many decades; but the city boundaries were pushed out from time to time, so that statistics for the enlarged city showed a population increase. This redefinition of cities is still going on, although the pace of physical expansion has slowed down in the past two or three decades. In spite of these misleading statistics, the fact is that urban population growth has taken place overwhelmingly at the suburban margin, at population densities much lower than those existent in the older city centers. Population has moved outward, as cities grew, for many decades; the rate has been faster since the war. Nowhere in the United States is this visually more obvious, more impressive, and, I would say, more depressing than in some parts of California.

This centrifugal movement of people within each urban complex has also been selective, as to age, race, income, occupation, and social class. The young married adults with small children have typified the suburban migration; while some people of other ages or other stages in the life cycle have also migrated, the migration has indeed been proportionately high in young adults with children. The older cities have had a major in migration of previously rural Negroes, until today many of our larger cities or major parts of them have had more Negroes than whites; whites have migrated to the suburbs, many of which have been, de facto, closed to Negroes. This racial differential population movement is obvious to even the most casual observer; not quite so obvious, but perhaps equally important, has been the differentiation by income, occupation, and social class, within each racial group. More and more of our urban residential areas are relatively homogeneous for such large distances that residents in them are effectively isolated from other economic, social, and racial classes.

The postwar years have seen major economic advances also; the Great Depression of the 1930s is a vivid memory to those of us who experienced it, but a vague one to more than half of the total population today. Some part of the real economic advance in recent decades is obscured by the rather persistent price inflation of the postwar years, but the material well-being of the total population has clearly improved [4]. Gross national product has increased, sometimes more rapidly than at other times; in recent years, the annual increment in United States output has been as great as the total output of some quite important countries of the world. The United States economy *is* an enormously productive one, and this opens up great possibilities to us as a nation. We may all be critical or regretful that so much wealth has gone into foreign adventures, or we may criticize priorities in national expenditures; but we have not faced a real pinch, in terms of reduced levels of living —we may not have advanced as much as we would like, or would otherwise be possible, but no real case can be made that a decline has occurred.

The simple statistics have a dramatic quality, at least to an economist. In current prices, average per capita personal income has risen from about $1500 in 1950 to about $3100 in 1967 or more than doubled in 17 years; in constant (1958) prices, the change has been from $1800 to over $2700 or a 50% increase. A doubling of personal income since the end of the war, from a level which was already high by world and by historical standards, is a truly major accomplishment.

The resultant increase in family income of typical or average families has underlaid many of the changes in life style which are discussed later and has been a major factor in the increased demand for natural resources, especially for recreation and other direct consumption purposes.

As personal incomes rise, the use made of them changes. Engel's law related to the slowly rising expenditures for food in the family budget, as family income rose; but other "necessities" such as rent tend to show a similar relationship. As income rises, more expensive types of food are purchased, so that even food is not a constant. But the really dramatic changes take place in the area of "discretionary" spending, and nowhere is this more marked than for recreation. Our data on recreation expenditures are seriously deficient, in part because national income data are by categories of goods and services, not by purpose of expenditure; thus most sports clothing is classified as clothing, most vacation housing as housing, most automobile expenditures as transportation, and so on, in spite of the fact that each was for the purpose of outdoor recreation [5]. As nearly as can be estimated, the proportion of total disposable income used for all kinds of recreation has been slowly but irregularly rising since the war; and the proportion of the recreation expenditures used for outdoor types of recreation has also risen irregularly but considerably.

The United States today has a disgracefully large amount of poverty, but it is poverty at a level which is considered luxury in some parts of the world; too many of our citizens are held down, in their search for personal achievement, by prejudice and unfriendly action, yet our society is one where personal ability counts for more, in comparison with inherited position, than in almost any other. Most of us are still constrained, in our life styles, by limited personal income; but the ability of a large proportion of the total population to consume what once were luxury goods of the rich is enormously impressive, at least to this author.

The outlook is for continued increased real incomes per capita; there is a very high degree of consensus among economists, both on this conclusion and even as to the rate of increase. A continued increase in real income per capita in the general magnitude of 2% annually will double such incomes in a generation. If the median family income in the United States today is about $8000, then by the year 2000 or shortly thereafter it should reach $16,000 in terms of the same general price level. There may be few people then below the present poverty income line—indeed, there is no reason why there should be any. But there is likely still to be "poor" people then, if we mean by "poor" that their incomes will be less than half of the national average.

As incomes have risen, the importance of time has increased [6]. Part of the real increase in income has taken the form of more leisure—longer paid vacations, more years of youth before entering the labor force, more years in retirement, as well as more nearly universal 5-day work weeks and 8-hour work days. Working people have some daily leisure, some weekend or other leisure on a weekly basis, and some at less frequent intervals of a vacation nature. But young people have more time free of both school and work, old people have more free time, and other forms of leisure are more varied than once was the case. Many people today can afford the money for activities for which they cannot afford the time, and I think that this relationship will become intensified as time goes on. Among professional people, it is often harder to find the time for an activity or a diversion than it is to find the money.

I think there will be a further rise in average leisure per capita in the United States but much less than the anticipated rise in per capita real incomes. Average leisure per capita is affected by numbers of persons not in the labor force because too young or too old or because they choose not to work, as well as by average work hours per week. In recent years, we have seen the emergence of truly extended vacations—perhaps "sabbaticals" is a better term—for working people. Now there is a large scale effort to reduce the typical work week from 40 hours to 35 or 30, either by shortening the workday or by shortening the work week; also a steady increase in amount of paid vacation is taking place. It seems unlikely, however, that the average per capita annual leisure can increase more than about 13% over the next generation, while the projection is for an approximate doubling in real income per capita in the same period. This alone will considerably shift the balance between income and time, as constraints upon individual action.

Many other socioeconomic changes of the postwar period might be mentioned, but I shall discuss only one: the increase in production and in distribution of knowledge. Research—pure, applied, and developmental—has added greatly to the sum total of human knowledge in recent years. The mass of information is now so great, in some fields, that finding what has been done already may be more costly than discovering it anew, and this in spite of ingenious information retrieval systems—it may be easier to make a new needle than to find the one in the haystack. But the spread of information, by informal education, news media, and so on, has been equally impressive. Universities are in the information business, broadly defined.

The increase in knowledge has had its impacts, good and bad, upon natural resources. We invented detergents, which reduced the demand for the raw materials which would otherwise have been required for soap; the "hard" detergents polluted our waters in ways that were obvious and distasteful to the general public, and the industry developed a "soft" or degradable detergent to avoid legislation which would have abolished the hard detergents. Synthetic plastics have replaced metals to a substantial degree, thus reducing the demand on natural mineral deposits; but most of these plastics decay very slowly, and we are building up enormous accumulations of discarded plastic containers, which will pollute our environment for centuries. Improved transportation has both increased the supply of land and water available for recreation use and the usage of such land and water, until today there are few sheltered spots left in the United States. And so it goes, in a rapidly changing technological society, where new problems and new opportunities arise continuously.

2. CHANGING LIFE STYLE

These varied aspects of modern life may be summarized by saying that Americans are developing a contemporary life style which differs considerably from that of their parents and grandparents [7]. The most significant aspects of that life style are the hardest to measure—differing ideas and concepts of what life should offer and of how one should manage his own personal affairs. As one of the older generation, this writer is constantly amazed at how young people today take for granted consumption patterns and personal freedoms that a few years ago were unthinkable; yet, thoughtfully reflecting upon their attitudes and upon the actual situation today, they are reasonable in their views. Why should anyone today accept without protest poverty, bad living conditions, social discrimination, lack of opportunity, or a number of other unsatisfactory aspects of life? We hear much about the revolution of rising expectations in the economically less developed parts of the world; perhaps the revolution of rising expectations is more vigorous within the United States.

But these attitudinal dimensions of the new life style are less easily measured and are more debatable than some quantitative aspects of present-day living. While there has been much exaggeration on the subject, yet it is true that in the United States we are developing what can well be called a suburban life style. This is based on a single-family dwelling, home ownership (with a large mortgage, typically), attendance at reasonably good schools by the children—at least through high school and usually through college, family participation in community activities, and the like. While many millions of people in the United States do indeed live in this way today, other millions live in apartments or other high density forms of living, some of which are physically superb, others mediocre, and a disgracefully large proportion decadent, dilapidated, and substandard by any reasonable definition. Moreover, there are still many millions of people in very small towns and rural surroundings, and poverty is relatively more prevalent there than in the cities [8]. But it is the new suburb which characterizes contemporary America; and, surely, nowhere is this more evident than in California.

Another but closely related objective measure of the changing life style is the volume of consumption gadgets. The present might equally well be called a gadget society as to be called a suburban society. Radio, television, hi-fi or other phonographs, dishwashers, clothes washers, clothes driers, vacuum cleaners, toasters, grills, disposals, hair dryers, and dozens of other gadgets are now commonplace, if not universal. One need only read the advertisements in any daily newspaper or look around in any middle class home to see the variety and number of such gadgets. It is noteworthy, and probably significant, that much decadent housing in the United States is more nearly up-to-date in its gadgets than in its structure. The owner or tenant apparently values the gadgets more than he does the structure; gadgets can be added incrementally more easily than can home improvements; they can be moved when the owner moves elsewhere; and they have been available—indeed, pushed by aggressive advertising—on relatively long-term credit which is often quite costly in conventional terms of interest rate. The old definition of an indestructible child's toy was one that lasted 3 days; the new definition of a durable household gadget is one that lasts as long as the installment payments on it.

Consumption gadgets have been particularly noticeable in outdoor recreation in recent years. Water sports have undergone a revolution since World War II. Boats have improved greatly and are easier to maintain, and trailers have made them more mobile, hence usable on any water body within a very wide radius from home. Boat motors, especially outboard motors, have improved greatly; horsepower has increased by several times, without commensurate increases in motor cost; many motors today can pull the owner's boat at speeds which make water skiing possible, when once this was a rarity. Water skiing, scuba diving, and numerous other water-based recreation activities have boomed in the postwar years. An equal revolution has occurred with camping; new materials and styles of tents, many new forms of trailers and camper units, and many smaller gadgets have both stimulated camping and served the demands of the increasing army of campers. Snowmobiles have opened up winter outdoor recreation to those unwilling or unable to undergo the physical effort of older forms of winter sports such as skiing; the latter, too, have boomed as they have become mass activities. Jeeps and other special vehicles have opened up much previously inaccessible territory, often to the serious damage of the areas concerned.

The increased education, both formal and continuing, previously mentioned, is another manifestation of the changing life style.

Education has always been both an investment in the productivity of the individual and a form of consumption, and so it remains with perhaps the consumption side increasing in importance. Many young people are going to college today, with or without completing degree requirements, for whom the education may prove to be a dubious production investment. For instance, it is highly doubtful in my mind that many subprofessional career goals are sufficiently benefitted by college training to warrant the cost. Yet I surely welcome their opportunity to obtain formal education which may make them better citizens and more fully developed individuals. However, other forms of cultural activities have increased greatly also. The great boom in phonograph records and television sets may seem a dubious cultural advance to critics, but surely it has brought a new level of cultural consumption to millions of persons. Concerts, art museums, and many other activities have all shown growth rates in the postwar years, with more or less equally impressive proportions.

Still another objective measure of the changing life style has been a great increase in travel. Automobile ownership and automobile travel increased greatly in the interwar years, and highway quality (more than highway mileage) increased at the same time. Americans were well on the way to becoming an automobile-oriented people by the time of World War II. But the postwar years have seen great expansion in automobile ownership too; today, many families have two, three, or more cars. The suburban style of living requires automobiles; for instance, a suburban family would be unable to obtain even groceries, were it not for the transportation provided by their car. The employed members of the family usually need a car to get to work and often a different car for each worker; the woman of the household needs a car to chauffeur her children about and for her own needs. The interstate highway is increasing the utility of the family car for long distance travel, especially travel for recreation. However, the airplane has also opened up distance travel to increasing numbers of people, both for business and for pleasure. One can fly from Washington to Chicago, have a productive conference, and fly back again, not only in the same day but within the normal working hours of the day. Transcontinental travel and international travel today is enormously quicker and more pleasant than in this author's younger working days. The number of young men and women, of college age, who fly from the Midwest to the Rockies for a weekend of skiing in the winter is impressive. By compressing space, we have stretched time; but our demands for time have increased more than proportionately; everyone boasts of how busy he is.

It is wrong to call this new American life style a leisure society, although leisure is highly important in it and often gives a purpose or direction to the lives of many persons. There has been a great increase in leisure and in leisure time activities, and these do dominate many aspects of life, at least for many people. But it is also a hard-working society; many who have lived and worked in some foreign countries are impressed at how much harder and more intensively the average American worker works, than does his foreign counterpart. The contemporary American society is still one which puts high stress on personal accomplishment and achievement, not only financial but professional. Economic success is still valued highly, by the great majority of persons. The new American life style is different than that of other countries today, or than that of our own country in earlier times, in a great many complex and sometimes subtle ways; increased leisure and increased leisure activities are part of that life style, but only a part of it.

3. RESOURCE AVAILABILITY AND RESOURCE QUALITY

The rising affluence of the American people naturally leads to the question: are our natural resources, generous though our endowment is, adequate for the demands? The answer, in brief, is that the quantity is enough, but quality poses more serious problems [4, 9].

The increasing output of goods and services makes an increasing demand upon natural resources, but not as much so as one would think. Technology is resource-conserving, to a substantial degree. Plastics, made of common materials, replace metals that are scarcer and are not renewable in the ordinary sense of the term. Improved methods of generating electricity require vastly less coal and oil today, for our present output of electricity, than did the methods of a generation ago. Many products of today are much more highly processed than were the industrial products of earlier generations. One need only compare the modern interspace rockets with the steel rail of a century ago, to have a dramatic contrast in degree of refinement of basic raw materials. In these and other ways, modern technology gets a greater economic output from a given tonnage of raw materials than was possible in an earlier day.

At the same time, an increasing proportion of our total economic output is made up of services, which require much less raw material input than do consumption goods of various kinds. The services component is likely to continue to grow in relative importance; in most advanced economic societies, it is relatively high and rising.

In spite of these reasons why the raw material component of gross national product is rising less rapidly than the total output, it still remains true that an advancing economic output requires more raw materials. Will they be available, in the volume needed and at reasonable prices? Without going into this subject in depth, the research conducted at Resources for the Future has shown that the welfare of the American people for a generation or two ahead will *not* be hampered by either absolute scarcity or rising real costs of basic raw materials. There may be problems in getting enough supplies of some materials at some times, but they will be manageable problems. The old fear of an absolute shortage of basic raw materials seems unwarranted.

Two qualifications must immediately be made: the situation may be worse in some other parts of the world, and the quality of resources available may not be as high as we will want. Some other parts of the world now have, and others may have, a population pressure on natural resources that will be serious, if indeed not unbearable. Modern agricultural science has opened up enormous potentials for increased output, and the problem of food alone is nowhere near as serious today as we thought it was a decade ago. But modern man, to live, as contrasted to mere existing, requires a lot more than food. For instance, I have recently helped to make some studies of agricultural possibilities in the Middle East; the Nile Valley can be made to yield double its present agricultural output, but it is much more difficult to see how Egypt, with 30 million people on 7 million acres of arable land and with limited other natural resources, lacking in man-made capital, can attain a modern level of living for a constantly rising population. Many other countries seem to be in equally bad situations. Our relative complacency about the United States natural resource situation should not obscure bad situations elsewhere in the world.

However, even in the United States, the matter of resource quality is less satisfactory. There may be enough water, but how badly polluted; plenty of air, but how smog-laden; enough land, but how badly disfigured? The research program at Resources for the Future is putting growing emphasis on this matter of resource quality, or quality of environment or of living. A family that earns enough to eat and has adequate shelter and clothing turns to the amenities of life, to beauty, and to objects and activities for mental and emotional nourishment instead of merely to physical well-being. This is true also in a nation. There has been a real awakening in the United States, about natural beauty, quality of the environment, and—their opposite—pollution. California surely experienced a dramatic example recently, with the offshore oil leak and the pollution of beaches. Very few, if any, voices were raised then to say that the country needed oil from submerged areas more than it needed the absence of pollution on its beaches. There was a time when most cities welcomed smoke belching from factory smokestacks, for this meant jobs; today, the same city may want jobs but it feels that the pollution is unnecessary.

I would not argue that everyone everywhere today values beauty more than dollars, or that everyone everywhere is consistent in his statements and actions about resource use and resource conservation. At one level of thought and action, a person may condemn air pollution or landscape degradation, and at another level of action may buy products which have been made only as a result of that pollution. One might drive to a meeting to help pass a resolution condemning offshore exploration for oil, while using gasoline that came from such offshore exploration. However, consistency of thought and action is not universal outside of the natural resource field, and there is no reason to expect it here. I do argue that there is a rising tide of national interest in resource conservation, natural beauty, wilderness preservation, and associated matters, and that many an industry will feel a degree of popular wrath in the years and decades ahead, if it ignores these popular attitudes.

When this author studied economics in college, air and water were two examples of free economic goods. Everyone needed them, but they were too common to have value. There are still as much water and air as ever, but air and water of desired purity are becoming scarcer and more valuable. Today, the environment as a whole takes on characteristics of common economic property—it belongs to everyone, everyone uses it, no one is in a position to deny it to others, and no one is in a position to capture the increased value of an improved total natural environment. One of our problems of social engineering for the future is to devise efficient ways in which the interests and activities of many individuals can be harnessed to improve the natural environment that affects everyone.

4. OUTDOOR RECREATION AS AN EXPRESSION OF LIFE STYLE

Since outdoor recreation is both a major form of expression of the emerging life style and a chief claimant for natural resources, including marine resources, a closer look at it is desirable. Outdoor recreation is a broad term, including many activities appealing to persons of different interests and ages, calling for participation at various times, and making differing demands on natural resources. For some purposes, it is accurate and useful to speak of outdoor recreation as if it were a single entity, in the same way one speaks of food; but, for other purposes, one must distinguish among the many kinds of outdoor recreation, just as one must distinguish among kinds of food.

Outdoor recreation activities can be grouped into broad categories. The Outdoor Recreation Resources Review Commission made one such classification, based largely upon management criteria [10]. It divided outdoor recreation into six categories: (1) high-density recreation, intensively developed and managed for mass use; (2) general outdoor recreation areas, subject to substantial development for a wide variety of specific recreation uses; (3) natural environment areas, suitable for recreation in a natural environment, usually in combination with other uses; (4) unique natural areas, of outstanding scenic splendor, natural wonder, or scientific importance; (5) primitive areas, undisturbed roadless areas, characterized by natural, wild conditions, including "wilderness areas"; and (6) historic and cultural sites, of major historic or cultural significance, either local, regional, or national.

A different grouping of activities may be more useful for economic analysis and includes three broad categories [11]. There is user-oriented outdoor recreation whose distinguishing characteristic is its ready location with respect to where users live. This type of activity occurs mainly after school or after work, although some people may engage in it during the middle of week days or on weekends. Playgrounds, playing fields, neighborhood parks, tennis courts, golf courses, swimming pools, zoos, and other types of areas are involved. Individual areas are often relatively small, as little as an acre, but generally under 100 acres each. Many such areas are provided by city and county governments; some are private. The natural resource qualities of such areas can be modest—space, not too steep, not too wet, will often do. Wherever Americans live, they will develop some outdoor recreation areas of this type nearby. The number and facilities of user-oriented recreation areas are disgracefully deficient in the poorer districts of our cities, and yet there are some—the streets often serve as a substitute.

At the other end of the scale are resource-based outdoor recreation areas, whose distinguishing characteristic is their superb natural resources. National parks are an excellent example of this type. Mountains, forests, lakes, swamps, seashores, and other physical resources are included in this group. Such areas are where you find them, and, as a matter of fact, most are located some distance from where most people live. As a result, most visits to them take place during vacations or long weekends. For example, a visit to a national park may be part of a vacation trip. Resource-based outdoor recreation areas tend to be large—up to a million acres or more for large national parks, and rarely as small as 100 acres. Many are federally owned, although some state parks and considerable private acreage also qualify.

In between are the intermediate recreation areas—intermediate in location, resource quality, size, and time of use. They are typically the all-day or weekend areas. Preferably located within an hour's driving time from users' homes, generally within 2 hours time and on the most attractive sites that can be found or developed. Such areas usually exceed 40 acres in size and may range up to several hundred or a few thousand acres. Many are built around a small body of water, either natural or man-made. Many such areas are state parks, but some federal reservoirs, some county parks, and increasing numbers of privately owned areas fall into this category. The intermediate type areas may provide the locus for a major share of the increased outdoor recreation of the future. Natural resources suitable for them are vastly more common than the natural resources required for the resource-based type; more flexibility in location removes them from some of the restrictions of the user-oriented type. Ingenuity and modest inputs of management skill, capital, and labor can make quite attractive recreation areas out of some rather ordinary-appearing land. The urge for the outdoors can be satisfied here, for many millions of Americans.

Regardless of how one classifies outdoor recreation areas, there is both a continuum of types and a system of areas. There are areas typical of user-oriented and of intermediate types, as described previously; but there are also some areas with some characteristics of each of these groups—for instance, a large city park, on the edge of the city or outside of it, which is used primarily on weekends and includes such activities as camping. Other examples of borderline cases can be cited. There are few clearcut and sharp boundaries in this continuum, nevertheless dominant characteristics of modal types do exist and can be recognized.

The system aspect grows out of the outdoor recreation activities of users; few people want, or are able, to spend all their leisure on a single outdoor recreation activity. Instead, they seek a variety of activities, and this requires a variety of areas. Their use of intermediate areas on weekends is related to their use of resource-based areas during vacation, and similarly for other pairings of major types and for specific activities within each major type. If a major new park is added to a system, then its presence leads to its use, and the use of every other unit in the system is to some degree affected. Likewise, if a new suburb or a new housing development is built, a new recreation demand is created locally, and its effect is felt on parks in surrounding areas. The strength of the effect in each case diminishes with distance; nearby parks are affected more, distant ones less. An outdoor recreation system, with its points of demand and of supply, is similar to an electric power distribution system with its generators and its load centers. The addition of a new generator to such an electric system affects the use of every existing generator in the system, at least to some degree.

In considering outdoor recreation, it is necessary to describe and define the unit of analysis. Most available statistics use "visit" as the unit of measurement; a visit is like an admission to the movies —each person is counted each time; hence it is possible to have more visits to state parks or to federal reservoirs than there are residents. But this is a rather misleading statistic, because it implies that an outdoor recreation experience takes place wholly at the recreation site.

The whole outdoor recreation experience is a useful unit of analysis [11]. It consists of the following five essential parts:

1. Planning or anticipation, when the individual, family, or other group considers what it wants to do, where it wants to go, how much time it will take, what equipment or supplies it wants to take, and how much money it wishes to spend or must spend is necessary. This phase usually takes place in the home, or at least in the home town. At this stage, the individual or group is uncommitted, and more open to information and advice. According to this author, more than half of all the expenditures for outdoor recreation are made during this phase—most equipment, including the car, is bought here, along with much of the gasoline and food.

2. Travel from home to the recreation site is necessary. Often this requires more time and more expense than will the later activities at the site. Some people apparently travel for the pleasure of the travel itself—"sightseeing" is given as the reason for a great deal of travel. But many people find the travel more boring than

stimulating—necessary and unavoidable, but with negative or low positive value to the whole experience. Road conditions, such as traffic congestion, and character of scenes from the moving car can affect enjoyment of travel. The overwhelming proportion of recreation travel is by private car; planes, busses, boats, and other modes of transportation play a much more limited role.

3. Activities on-site are the basic purpose of the whole recreation experience. These include a wide variety of specific activities; the more popular recreation areas have something for every member of the family, and each person may seek more than one activity during a visit. For instance, a swim in the lake may be followed by a picnic. The psychological motivations and satisfactions of specific activities vary also—release of tensions, rest and recuperation, discharge of physical and nervous energy, sheer fun, pleasure from association with friends or family, learning through play, and many others.

4. Travel from the site back home is necessary. This may follow the same route as travel to the site. The recreationist may well be in a different mood, now that his vacation is largely over. He may be tired, broke, and discouraged about returning to work, when he had been fresh and eager as he went toward the site. We know very little about the attitudes and satisfactions of travelers, regardless of the direction of their travel; but, drawing on my own experiences, I judge there is at least some difference between the going and the returning phases of travel for recreation.

5. The final stage is recollection. After the recreationist returns home, he recalls at intervals the earlier parts of the recreation experience. He may relate his experience to friends, neighbors, and fellow workers—sometimes beyond the point of their maximum interest. His memory may be buttressed with color slides, souvenirs, and other artifacts. The recollection may bear little resemblance to the event—bigger fish are caught in the living room and office than on the lake—and the discrepancy may widen as time goes on. But this is a major part of the whole recreation experience; perhaps half of the total satisfactions of the whole experience arises in this last phase. From the recollections of earlier experiences are likely to come the anticipations and plans for the next one.

The whole recreation experience is a package deal; all phases are necessary, and the participant will balance up all the costs against all the benefits. Costs are not merely in monetary terms, but include inconveniences, discomforts, and negative reactions of various kinds. For example, the dirty restroom may create a negative impression which the good food at the restaurant hardly offsets. Planners, park administrators, and other public officials must consider the whole experience as a package deal also; it is not enough to consider what the recreationist will do, or wants to do, at the site. Consideration must be given to how he will get from home to the recreation site, and back again—as anyone who has ever experienced a holiday traffic jam knows very well. I think public officials must also consider how to help the recreationist in the planning or anticipation stage, so that he can make more informed choices with more likelihood that the results will match his expectations. Also recreationists might acquire more satisfying souvenirs for the recollection stage.

The whole recreation experience must be the unit of economic analysis also. The money a recreationist spends at the recreation site is only a small part of his total expenditure; travel costs, equipment costs, and other expenditures are predominantly in other phases than the on-site part of the whole experience. But the reactions of the recreationist to other parts of the experience, notably to the travel phases, may affect his willingness to pay for the satisfactions he gets at the site. There is reason to suspect that many park visitors evaluate the travel phases negatively.

A brief look at the historical record of outdoor recreation in the United States may be informative. City parks really began on a significant scale in the late 1800s, as did city playgrounds. The number of areas, their total acreage, numbers of employees, and other measures of capacity or management have risen steadily over the decades, although there was a cut back in the depression years of the 1930s. National parks began with the establishment of Yellowstone in 1872, and their number, acreage, and facilities have also expanded over the decades, at varying rates. Other kinds of units, such as national monuments and national seashores, have been added to the national park system. National forests were established under an act passed in 1891; their total area expanded greatly in the early years of this century, so that by 1910 it was almost as great as today. Some boundary changes have eliminated some areas and added others since then. Although there were some notable exceptions, state parks really got their major impetus during the 1930s; federal public works programs provided manpower and money to improve such areas, and the states responded by establishing them. This same decade saw the beginning of TVA and the enlargement of the Corps of Engineers and other water management agencies, which have built many reservoirs in the intervening years, at which water-based recreation has been highly popular.

Attendance records at these various types of areas began at different times. There have never been inclusive attendance figures for city parks; too many of them are too easily accessible to the public to measure attendance easily, and too many are unmanned most of the time, so that counts or estimates of visitors are impossible. However, other indirect measures strongly suggest a steadily rising public participation in activities at city park and recreation areas, perhaps of the general order of 5% annually. Recreation attendance figures at national parks began before 1910, and at national forests in 1924. Attendance at each dropped by nearly two-thirds in World War II, as gasoline and tire rationing sharply cut into recreation travel. In other years, attendance has mounted steadily, averaging between 8% and 10% annual increases for most periods. At this rate, total attendance doubles each 8 to 10 years. Some attendance data for state parks began before World War II; attendance at them apparently also dropped sharply during the war but since then has risen at about the same rate as in national parks and national forests. At the federal reservoirs, attendance data began at various dates but became really meaningful only after the war. The addition of many new reservoirs and the technological revolution in water-based recreation have combined to give such areas an extremely rapid growth in outdoor recreation—something of the general order of 25% annually for reservoirs built by the Corps of Engineers.

Several aspects of this historical record of attendance at public outdoor recreation areas require special notice. First, the rate has been relatively constant on a percentage basis. The higher the absolute level of the attendance, the greater has been the increased numbers each year—the more people engage in outdoor recreation, the more they want it. The doubling of attendance each 8 to 10 years has continued as attendance has mounted to higher levels. Second, there has been no clear evidence *yet* of a slowing down in rate of annual growth. The percentage increases in recent years have been just as large as in earlier years. Third, some slackening off in growth rates is inevitable some day—past and present growth rates would lead to impossible results, if long continued. For instance, extending past growth in attendance at Corps of Engineers reservoirs to the year 2000 would require that every man, woman, and child spend 2500 days annually at a Corps

reservoir! Some day there must come a slackening and then a level-
ling in growth in use of public outdoor recreation areas—but when
and at what level?

We know very little about what is behind these recreation attendance data. It seems fairly certain that much of the increase is
due to more people using such areas, but some is due to more
visits annually per user—but how much to each? It also seems clear
that a good many people never visit a publicly owned outdoor
recreation area of any kind, not even a city park or playground.
However, we do not know how this proportion has changed in the
past. The statistics on visits to public recreation areas are outdated
and somewhat unrevealing. The enormous increases in use of such
areas can only mean a changing life style, one with far greater
emphasis on the outdoors.

5. OUTDOOR RECREATION IN CALIFORNIA

The foregoing description of outdoor recreation nationally applies to California as well. California is larger than many nations,
and it contains a wide variety of physical environments, many of
which are well-suited to outdoor recreation. Many Californians
pride themselves on being rugged outdoor types; the modern life
styles have surely found expression here.

City parks in California began comparatively early, by national
as well as by state historical standards. Golden Gate Park was
famous relatively early in city park history in the United States,
as were also the magnificent grounds of the state capital. Many
cities in California have developed outstanding park systems over
the years, especially since the war. Most California cities, like most
cities everywhere, lack park and recreation areas in their lowest
income parts, where they are needed most. California city parks are
actively in use, and use and activities are increasing steadily in
them. In California, counties have played a larger role in providing
parks than in many parts of the nation. In many states, especially
in New England, counties are weak and relatively ineffective, or,
as in the South, small and poorly financed. Most California counties
are large, have relatively great governmental powers, and have
large financial resources. Large urban counties in California have
established outstanding park and recreation programs.

The California state park system is one of the best in the nation.
Historic areas have had special attention, and in few parts of the
country have the important historic areas been better preserved

and maintained than those in California. However, outstanding natural areas have also been included in the state park system, from the redwoods to the desert, and popular park areas nearer the large cities are also included in the system.

California has many federally owned, developed, or managed outdoor recreation areas, some of outstanding character. Yosemite is the oldest of the national parks in California, which now include Sequoia, Kings Canyon, Lassen, and the new Redwoods national park. Point Reyes is a national seashore; Joshua Tree is a desert national monument; and there are several other units in the national park system. Substantial parts of the coastal mountain ranges and of the Sierra Nevada are included in national forests. Wilderness and primitive areas include outstanding areas which are to be preserved against intruding uses; but their availability to recreation use will subject them to severe pressures. The national forests contain scores of campgrounds, fishing streams and lakes, and other popular recreation areas. The major reservoirs built by federal agencies, such as Shasta Lake, Millerton Lake, Isabella Reservoir, and others have become immensely popular for water sports. The state, in its water development plan, is giving special attention to outdoor recreation. On top of all these are wildlife refuges, grazing districts, and other types of federal areas, where outdoor recreation is both provided for and encouraged.

In thus describing the wealth of city, county, state, and federal park and recreation areas in California, all, of course, is not perfect. There is need to expand the acreage and to increase the facilities of outdoor recreation areas at all levels. The system is deficient now, particularly for lower income city dwellers, and continuously increasing population and rising real incomes will result in greater and greater demands for parks and other outdoor recreation areas. The struggle to provide enough outdoor recreation capacity in California will be a never-ending one—the various governments and private organizations will have to work very hard simply to avoid falling further behind.

Californians have many kinds of outdoor recreation areas and many specific sites to choose among. There are the high mountains, especially the Sierras, but others also, which have their charms in summer, winter and at other seasons. The desert is more attractive in winter and early spring than at other seasons. There are numerous water bodies, many man-made rather than natural, extending from the lower Colorado River and the Salton Sea, through the many foothill reservoirs up the Central Valley to Shasta Lake. There is the sea and the seashore.

Californians, at least the more affluent lovers of the outdoors can, and do, visit any or all of these areas. One has only to note that a long summer weekend will find hundreds of motorboats towed from the Los Angeles metropolis to Shasta Lake to gain some understanding of the passion for the outdoors of some persons. Californians are in some ways fortunate in their accessibility to resource-based outdoor recreation areas. National parks such as Yosemite, Sequoia, and Kings Canyon lie so remote to much of the population that visits are possible only on vacations. Glacier, Yellowstone, Mesa Verde, and Grand Canyon—to name but some of the best known—are so remote from all but a handful of local people that a visit to one of them is possible only as part of a vacation. However, the major California parks are, to a large extent, weekend areas for Californians. A long weekend permits Californians by the scores of thousands to visit their major national parks. To a large extent, the ready availability of what would elsewhere be considered resource-based areas of kinds other than national parks, leads to similar use patterns for them.

This ready accessibility to resource-based areas has its disadvantages also. A prime problem is the great influx of visitors on weekends, especially long ones. Everyone (or at least it seems like everyone!) seeks to visit them at the same time, and road congestion (and accidents) are one result. It may be argued that the relative abundance of resource-based areas was, and perhaps still is, an inhibiting factor in development of enough more closely located intermediate areas. Legislators and taxpayers may, perhaps subconsciously, conclude that developed parks nearer the population were not necessary as long as mountains, deserts, reservoirs, lakes, and ocean were so accessible. If this viewpoint ever had any validity, it has none now—the demand for easily accessible outdoor recreation, especially for the lower income population, is simply too great.

Every serious effort to look at California's future has concluded that the total population of the state would continue to rise, real incomes per capita would continue to increase, and emphasis upon an outdoor style of life would continue and perhaps intensify. The total demand for outdoor recreation can only rise steeply—there may be differences of opinion as to just how fast this rise will be, which forms of outdoor recreation will be in the greatest demand, the role of various public and private organizations in providing the needed recreation places, and other issues. There may come a time when the average person has all the outdoor recreation he wants or can afford—or, at least, is willing to buck the traffic for—and then per capita consumption of outdoor recreation will no longer rise. However, that day does not seem in sight now. Even if it should come, a rising population would still mean greater demand for outdoor recreation. Resource planners and managers in California must count on a rising total demand for outdoor recreation.

6. SIGNIFICANCE FOR URBAN-MARINE ENVIRONMENT

All of the foregoing is significant for the urban-marine environment, and I conclude by briefly making some of these consequences explicit.

A substantial part of the total population of California lives relatively near the sea—within 50 miles. This has always been so, is true today, is likely to be true for the indefinite future ahead. There has been some shift in emphasis on a location near the sea; the great postwar growth of population in California has, in general, meant some modest moving away from the sea, in part because the best locations near the sea were already occupied. In the Los Angeles metropolitan area, intensive residential use of land has moved inland to some degree; in the San Francisco metropolitan area, a great deal of the postwar expansion has been down the Peninsula, away from the deeper parts of the Bay and from the sea; and much of the East Bay expansion has been over and behind the hills, also to a degree away from the sea. However, areas near the sea have also expanded, and even this movement away from the sea has been within a zone of relative proximity to it. In spite of population growth in the Central Valley and other basically inland locations, California is closely oriented to the sea.

Californians have always turned to the sea and to the beach for an important part of their outdoor recreation, and probably always will. The ocean off California has severe limitations for swimming and some other water sports, yet it has great usefulness as a recreation area also. The beaches have been alienated from public ownership, or public access to them has been cut off, in all too many instances. Yet some beach areas are open, and heavily used. Use pressures will almost certainly rise.

The beaches have been an important scenic asset, an important part of the natural environment of California; and, in spite of much diversion of beach area to other uses and much disfigurement of the beach areas, they still are. There are a number of superb ocean drives in California, as well as others of lesser but still high quality. The opportunity to view such areas at intervals is one of the advantages of living in California. I think the use and the value of such areas will increase in the future.

On a strictly economic calculation, it is highly probable that ocean and beach areas will have a rising value for recreation and for scenic purposes—rising probably faster than for most other uses. It is difficult to place a defensible value on natural resources used for these purposes, but not impossible to do so. However, no detailed and careful calculation will be needed to demonstrate the increased value of these natural resources for these purposes. It will find expression in the words and the actions of the ordinary people, as they talk about the resources and as they seek to use them.

Regardless of the strict economics of the situation, I think there will be a rising tide of popular interest and concern about the ocean and beach resources and their use, for instance the popular outcry in the winter of 1969 over the beach despoliation from the leaking offshore oil well.

This event provoked an outcry in California; but the incident was front page news all over the United States for several days. I think this but symbolic of the growing popular concern; should any such incident occur again, I venture to assert that the resulting outcry will be vastly greater than it was in 1969. People will demand different use of marine and beach resources in the future. As I have suggested, their demands may not be wholly logical or consistent, but that will not reduce their insistence.

It seems to me that every present and potential user of the marine and beach resources must take this changing popular attitude into account in their private calculations. Business and other enterprises have obtained control over beach properties to the exclusion of the public in the past, and others may well do so in the future; it is true that the general public is often more capable of indignation than of action. However it is also true that the public can be capable of action, when the issues are, or seem, simple enough and are readily dramatized. The user of California beaches whom the public disapproves of, should begin now to study how activities elsewhere can be shifted or accommodate the public's needs to at least some degree; the public interest can not be indefinitely thwarted to an unlimited degree. Popular interest in marine and beach use will not be limited to private uses but will extend to public agencies as well.

REFERENCES

1. Conrad Taeuber and Irene B. Taeuber, *The Changing Population of the United States,* Wiley, New York, 1958; Irene B. Taeuber, *Population Trends in the United States: 1900 to 1960,* U.S. Bureau of the Census, Technical Paper No. 10. Washington, U.S. Government Printing Office, 1964.

2. Calvin L. Beale, "Natural Decrease of Population: The Current and Prospective Status of an Emergent Phenomenon," *Demography,* Vol. 6, No. 2 (May 1969).

3. Advisory Commission on Intergovernmental Relations, *Urban and Rural America: Policies for Future Growth,* Government Printing Office, Washington, D.C., April 1968.

4. Hans H. Landsberg, Leonard L. Fischman, and Joseph L. Fisher, *Resources in America's Future,* Johns Hopkins Press, Baltimore, 1963.

5. Marion Clawson, "Statistical Data Available for Economic Research on Certain Types of Recreation," *Journal of American Statistical Association,* March 1959.

6. James C. Charlesworth (Ed.), *Leisure in America: Blessing or Curse,* monograph 4 in a series sponsored by the American Academy of Political and Social Science, Philadelphia, April 1964.

7. Marion Clawson, "The Emerging American Life Style," *American Forests,* Vol. 74, No. 2 and 3, February 1968, pp. 14–16, 59–62; March 1968, pp. 32–35.

8. President's National Advisory Commission on Rural Poverty, *The People Left Behind,* Government Printing Office, Washington, D.C., September 1967.

9. Henry Jarrett (Ed.), *Environmental Quality in a Growing Economy,* Johns Hopkins Press, Baltimore, 1966.

10. Outdoor Recreation Resources Review Commission, *Outdoor Recreation for America,* Government Printing Office, Washington, D.C., January 1962.

11. Marion Clawson and Jack L. Knetsch, *Economics of Outdoor Recreation,* Johns Hopkins Press, Baltimore, 1966.

CHAPTER 5

Traffic and Transport Needs at the Land-Sea Interface

EDWARD M. MAC CUTCHEON

Ever since man first floated down a river on a log, the coastal zone has been important. The coast and the fall line have always been the interface between one form of transportation and another, and the coastal zone continues to be the major transfer point in our transportation systems. Even airlines use coastal airports as terminals or transfer points. Industry has congregated at the coast to benefit from all types of transportation; the military has had to focus on the coast because here a potential enemy must transfer vehicles. For the same reason it is usually the borderline of the sovereign state.

The result of this trend over the ages is that 45% of the population of the United States now lives at or near the coast. Now centuries after the first water-borne explorer boarded his log, commercial transportation is the biggest user of the coastal zone from an economic standpoint.

The impact of the water-borne trade affects greatly the coastal communities. The direct charges levied on cargo flowing through the port are less than one half of its total economic impact. In addition to direct charges, the cargo-generated port activities include a heavy cash flow from port-dependent industry, foreign consulates, trade and labor associations, and commerce-related branches of Federal and Local Government. The total cash flow from all of these activities has been estimated for the port of Seattle, Washington. It proved to be about $50 per short ton of cargo flowing through the port.

Port-dependent industries include the direct shipping support such as stevedoring and logistics, but that is not all. Many non-shipping industries seek port locations. These include both water-borne and shoreside industries. The water-borne industries include fishing, and the shoreside industries include all those which seek locations where shipping costs of raw materials and finished products are at a minimum.

In the twentieth century we find new types of demands for use of the waterfront properties. We find that recreation and esthetic pleasures are generating a purchasing leverage which permits them to compete for space, even along the crowded waterfronts of our major ports. This keen competition for the shoreline in way of deepwater piers has driven the price higher and higher. Costs of more than $4000 per linear foot per year are common for major United States waterfronts.

The water-borne traffic and related industries do not constitute the entire traffic and transport of the ports by themselves. These primary activities generate hundreds of collateral activities, including automobile, rail, and air traffic; signals and sounds of all types; cables; pipelines; and a host of other supporting systems.

All of these systems are squeezed into the narrow strip called the coastal zone. There they compete with one another for the limited resources of the area. These limited resources include the adjacent sea, shoreside real estate, air space, a share of the chemical and ecological processes offered by the sea and local use of the crowded electromagnetic communication channels.

The competition for these resources is already very keen. This is evident from the price that must be paid to compete. Now, however, another factor is being recognized. This is the social and ecological value of the coastal zone. It is not a new factor but it is extremely important to our future well-being. The profit-motivated ocean commerce and industrial uses of the coastal zone generate systems which compete with the people who seek to use this zone for recreation and other private purposes. The economic motivation of the past has run headlong into the present-day necessity of satisfying more intangible social needs and the necessity for the future survival of the human race. The economic values of the market place no longer suffice to measure the new needs of our society, and we are at a loss to reconcile the important intangibles of ecological balance or human satisfaction with the more entrenched and quantitative values of commerce and industry, backed as they are by the power of tradition, habitual views and practices.

Commercial values are now head to head with social values in a manner which complicates greatly any appraisal of the conflicts at the coastline or their resolution. The situation is bad now but is bound to get worse as the population grows, leisure time increases, commerce flourishes, and new technology places added demands on old systems.

Ships are getting larger, and they will require deeper channels or offshore terminals. Containerization is becoming more prevalent, and it is shifting the itineraries of the ships and the ports of delivery. Also it is requiring much more shoreside real estate to marshall the greater cargoes. Burgeoning pleasure craft fleets, underwater tourism, and possible 100-knot surface-effect ships will demand new forms of coastal traffic control. Offshore petroleum exploitation, mining operations, and aquaculture will vie for space with major freshwater, petroleum, or power pipelines and signal cables. All of these will compete with the more traditional merchant marine, fishery, and naval activities which will still be present.

The conflicts involving traffic and transport at the coastal zone affect every one of us in the sense that we are beneficiaries of the national economy. They involve all of us as custodians of our natural heritage, and more than half of us because our livelihood is directly dependent on them, and most of us because we want to enjoy the recreation and the beauty of the coastal zone or at least to relish the seafood. Figure 1 illustrates the many interactions between uses of the coastal zone and the potential for conflicts involving traffic and transport systems.

Who must solve the problems of the coastal zone? The list is almost as long as the list of the beneficiaries. It involves practically every profession and trade in the nation: conservationists, engineers, attorneys, economists, naval architects, civil engineers, fishermen, oceanographers, biologists, physicists, and such. Everyone is involved; there are no laymen.

The purpose of this chapter is to review the traffic and transport facets of the situation, looking specifically at the goals and conflicts involved. It examines the conflicts which arise when systems are developed and utilized in the achievement of independent uncoordinated goals, and when a primary consideration has been the impact of the environment on the system rather than vice versa. This chapter covers the nature of the traffic and transport systems, their goals, the nature of the conflicts which exist or may arise, some examples of major conflicts, and some thoughts on the implications of the situation.

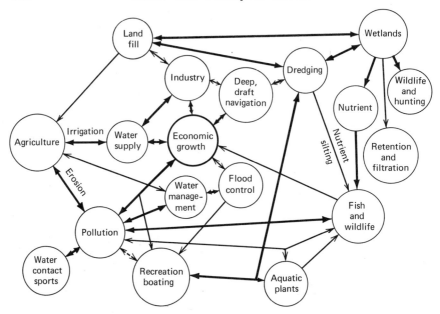

Figure 1. Interacting uses of the coastal zone. Traffic and transport is involved in every activity and circumstance shown in this coastal zone maze. Probably the core labelled "economic growth" should be supplanted by or teamed with a core labeled "public welfare." *Source:* National Council on Marine Resources and Engineering Development.

1. THE NATURE OF TRAFFIC AND TRANSPORT AND SUPPORTING SYSTEMS

National concern for the coastal zone commences with attention to water-borne commerce and defense. In the United States the first investments by the Federal Government to improve shipping facilities were made in 1787 when the Union was very young. Commerce continues to dominate coastal activities and to be the recipient of major Federal resources. Between 1824 and 1966 more than $2 billion of Federal funds were invested in facilities for water-borne commerce. This investment was more than matched by private funds.

Mention of oceans, coasts, and ports conjures thoughts of great ocean liners, cargo ships, battleships, and occasionally fishing boats or tugs. This follows from the romance of our heritage of literature, radio, and television, but this is only a small part of the picture. Looking more widely and searching the future, we find that the ships include not only the traditional displacement ships, which have carried the world's trade for centuries but also they now include submersibles, surface-effect ships, and amphibious vehicles. The traffic at the land-sea interface is not limited to ships. It includes also the aircraft and the land vehicle; the automobile, truck, bus, and train traveling over and under the interface via bridges and tunnels. Not all of the traffic is transport; it includes people crossing bridges and enjoying swimming. The communication channels are filled with signal traffic; acoustical, optical, and radio, and the floor of the ocean is lined with cables, pipelines, and tunnels carrying signals, bulk commodities, or vehicular traffic.

Classes of systems and supporting subsystems

The following list is not a complete inventory of all of the important traffic and transport systems but it will illustrate the wide variety of systems involved and the difficulty of visualizing a total problem. Later in the chapter some of the classes are expanded to amplify the complexity of the interactions.

    Classes of traffic and transport
        Vessels—ships
            Surface ships
            Submersibles—submarines
            Surface-effect ships
            Amphibious vehicles
        Aircraft
        Land vehicles
            Automobiles
            Trucks
            Buses
            Railroad trains
        People
            Pedestrians
            Swimmers
        Animals
        Signals
            Acoustic
            Optical
            Electromagnetic—radio
        Commodities
    Classes of conveyor-type supporting and related systems
        Cables

Pipelines
Conveyors
Bridges
Tunnels
Waterside supporting systems
  Platforms
  Moorings
  Piers
  Quays
  Buoys
  Fish nets and traps
  Tunnel vent towers
  Land substitute systems (floating or pile mounted)
    Offshore airports
    Offshore city modules
Shoreside supporting systems
  Shipyards
  Bases
  Marinas
  Canals and locks
  Marshalling areas
  Tank farms
  Navigational ranges

Certainly the ships or vessels are an important class of systems. A closer examination of their anatomy should help to elaborate the backdrop of coastal zone conflicts.

Functions of vessels

In examining conflicts it is necessary to look at the functions within the vessel as well as those nominal functions by which the vessel is usually characterized. The internal systems such as propulsion and communication may participate in a conflict as well as the external or characterizing system, for example, dredging.

The basic systems of a ship include the platform (i.e., the supporting or buoying system) and the transporting system. If it is self-propelled it will usually have propelling, positioning, maneuvering, navigating, surveillance, and communicating systems as well. Usually it will include some degree of life support and shelter for cargo and crew. If it is an ocean passenger liner it will include all of the so-called hotel systems such as heat, light, food, recreation, and such, right down to the manicurist.

Except for transport ships, it is not these basic systems which usually characterize the ship; instead the ship is characterized by a system which it customarily transports, for example, the guns make the warship, or net handling equipment makes the fishing boat. Thus ships can be considered in two broad groups; those which are intended to engage primarily in the carriage of people and goods, which are loaded and unloaded, and those which are carrying a system whose function is other than transportation. The difference is important to the types of conflicts because the transport ships shuttle through the coastal zone in going to or from a berth for loading. Other types may spend a great deal more time moored or meandering through the waters in or near the coastal zone.

There are many characterizing ship functions other than transportation. Here are fourteen examples: lift, look, listen, sense, manufacture, signal, educate, accommodate, dig, survey, store, amuse, fight, and police. These nontransport ships and craft constitute the water-borne traffic of the port and coastal zone.

Types of traffic vessels

The aforementioned functional titles have an unfamiliar ring when related to ships. This is because ships have been with us so long that we have tagged typical types with descriptive names. Usually the characterizing functional systems are apparent from the names even though we seldom think of them in these functional terms.

There is a very wide range of vessel traffic. Here are 27 examples to illustrate the variety:

Seaweed harvester	Oceanographic research ship
Oil drilling ship	Schoolship
Salvage vessel	Houseboat
Police patrol boat	Sailing yacht
Fireboat	Sport fisher
Surfboat	Naval cruiser
Buoy tender	Warehouse ship
Coast Guard cutter	Fuel barge
Cable layer	Dredge
Fishing boat	Derrick barge
Garbage scow	Destroyer
Survey ship	Bum boat
Pilot boat	Motor yacht
Industrial ship	

There are some exotic vessels operating and generating some unique conflicts, for instance, the prospecting or geological survey ships using explosives to generate acoustic echoes so as to examine the subbottom. These ships seek petroleum, but one result is usually dead fish and cries of righteous indignation from the naturalists.

Federal government involvement in ocean exploration and exploitation has been slow, but the private investment is heavy in the oil industry. Through 1968 almost $13 billion have gone into offshore petroleum activities. The need for major amounts of prospecting and other offshore work is apparent if an industry of this size is to remain healthy. Thus petroleum has received preference over fish.

Meanwhile the objecting naturalists may be amusing themselves on special boats which hire out at certain ports to convey the people who want to watch migrating whales. These boats too are traffic.

The growth in ocean science and engineering is not limited to increasing the use of the more prosaic survey ships, it also is generating some strange craft of its own. These include the small submersibles, but they also include some more unusual types. For instance, the FLIP (Floating Instrument Platform) looks like a well-stretched cigar. When it is at sea it upends and drifts about with its long spar-shaped body penetrating quiet subsurface layers of the ocean and three or four stories of superstructure extending upward for meteorological measurements. Another different craft is the CURV (Controlled Underwater Recovery Vehicle), which is a highly effective unmanned submersible operating on the end of an umbilical control cable.

Traffic of practically all these types join shoreside and other systems in impinging on the biota of the coastal zone. The result is that we now are witnessing a new kind of vessel. The function of this new vessel is to measure the intensity and other features of aquatic pollution. These vessels also add to the traffic.

Types of transport vessels

The total water-borne trade of the United States is more than 800 million short tons per year, one half of which is foreign. This trade generates a very large income for the port communities and enhances the standard of living of all of us.

There is a passenger-carrying trade, but the advent of the jet aircraft has done much to weaken this portion of our foreign commerce. The oceangoing passenger traffic is on the wane throughout the world and is almost extinct in the United States.

There are some 19,000 merchant ships plying the oceans of the world. These are the major ships of over 1000 gross tons. They collectively provide a carrying capacity of 260 million deadweight tons. Of these less than 1000 are American flagships with an aggregate tonnage of some 11 million. However the theme of this chapter is conflicts. The United States foreign commerce, which is not carried in American flagships, is carried by foreign bottoms. These foreign ships enter and occupy American ports, and in so doing they generate all of the conflict potentialities which could be expected of our own ships. The net result of the situation is that there are about 1000 major ships in United States ports at any one time and their goings and comings create conflicts without regard to the fact that only one half of them are United States flag.

There is no tidy way of classifying the transport vessels. Each author has his own pet scheme. For purposes of this discussion on coastal area conflicts we can use eleven classes or types; passenger liner, combo (combination passenger and cargo liner), troopship, hospital ship, ferryboat, trampship, dry bulk carrier, general cargo liner, lighter or barge, and tug or towboat.

All of these ships float in the water displacing an amount of water equal to their weight, that is, they are displacement ships. Looking to the future there are two new types which may become important. One is the hydrofoil ship. When operating at cruising speed this vehicle is supported by hydrofoils, that is, underwater wings. The use of this principle is likely to be limited to relatively small craft, but they can be quite fast (can be expected to be used at speeds up to about 60 knots) so they may create a traffic control problem. The other type is the surface-effect ship. These craft glide over the surface of the water riding on a cushion of air or enjoying the extra efficiency of an aircraft operating so close to the surface as to be in the "ground effect" domain of aerodynamic lift as illustrated in Figures 2 and 3. The surface-effect ship is a potentially critical vehicle in creating conflicts. Its speed is high. Serious consideration has been given to 4000-ton 100-knot vehicles. However, for some configurations the maneuverability is poor, and some very effective traffic control will be required.

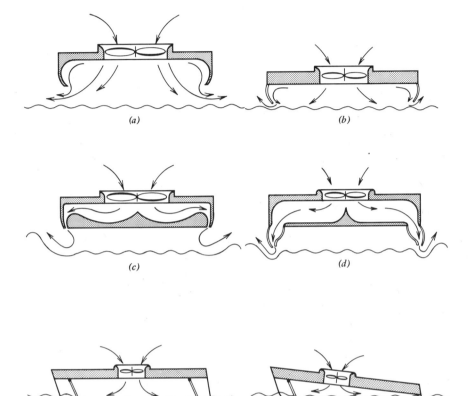

Figure 2. Various concepts illustrating the aerostatic lift principle. (*a*) The plenum chamber. (*b*) The plenum chamber with "skirt." (*c*) The annular jet. (*d*) The hydroskimmer (annular jet with "trunks"). (*e*) The captured air bubble. (*f*) The hydrokeel. *Source:* U. S. Department of Commerce.

Other types of systems

Pipelines, tunnels, and cableways are a major source of conflict. It has always been difficult to keep nautical charts up-to-date so that these navigational hazards are correctly depicted. The problem has become increasingly acute. Pipelines crisscross the Gulf of Mexico in all directions, and every harbor is bordered with signs saying "cable crossing, do not anchor." Now there is serious consideration of a major freshwater aqueduct running from northern to southern California. This would be a very large diameter pipe.

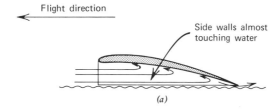

(a)

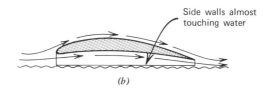

(b)

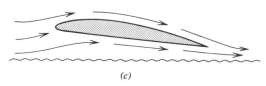

(c)

Figure 3. Various concepts illustrating the aerodynamic lift principle. (*a*) The ram wing. (*b*) The channel-flow wing. (*c*) The wing-in-ground effect. *Source:* U. S. Department of Commerce.

One concept calls for running the pipe at about 40 fathoms below the surface. We cannot even imagine the conflicts this pipeline may generate.

The diminution of shoreside available real estate is illustrated by two serious studies which have been conducted during the past year. In one of these studies the Federal Aviation Agency has contracted to examine the economic and operational aspects of offshore airports. In the other study the Department of Housing and Urban Development has contracted to examine the feasibility of floating city modules which can be constructed at a shipyard and floated to a suitable site.

Pollution is also a form of traffic at the coastal zone. Great care must be taken that all waterfront arrangements acknowledge the location of sewer outfalls and that navigation locks do not interfere with the necessary circulation. Someday we must minimize this traffic or escort it promptly to sea so that our beaches will be more available for recreation.

Swimming and other body-contact activities demand a high quality of water. Normally we do not think of the swimmer as a form of traffic. However, an inventory of the traffic would not be complete without the swimmer. To begin with swimming is a major part of the coastal zone utilization. By one estimate there were 33 million participants in 1964, and the projection is 40 million by 1975. The annual expenditure ranges from $1.5 to 2.0 billion. This large group of people interact with the environment in several ways. They use boats, they get in the way of boats, and they demand a special quality for the environment which conflicts with the operation of boats. Above all, however, the swimmer demands the most pollution control of any of the traffic or transport.

Interacting uses

This chapter deals with traffic and transport. The first thought which comes to mind is the interaction between two ships—a collision. There are too many collisions, but they are only a small part of what the chapter is about. The interaction between two ships is a part of the picture as is the interaction between a ship and a pier. There is, however, a much broader picture. We must include the entire coastal zone environment if the total interaction picture is to be complete. Some of the most important interactions are between a ship and the environment.

The environment of the coastal zone includes:

- Dry land adjacent to the shore.
- Wetlands over which the water ebbs and flows due to tidal action and other natural forces.
- Water adjacent to the shore, including its chemical characteristics, predominant wave and current action, depth, and other parameters.
- Submerged land adjacent to the shore.
- Microscopic plant and animal life which exists because of particular physical and chemical conditions in the coastal zone.
- Visible species of plant life which exist in the water, wetlands, or dry land of the coastal zone.

An obvious addition to this list is the airspace and the electromagnetic spectrum of the coastal zone.

The air traffic in the coastal zone exemplifies the broader picture of interactions as it contributes materially to the variety. The real estate for the air fields competes with marinas or marshaling yards. The exhaust of the jets pollutes the same air as the stacks of the ships, and the signals from both compete for room in a crowded frequency spectrum.

Looking toward the future we can see another interesting interaction muddle in the institutional area. The dynamic-lift surface-effect ships do not touch the water when they are in operation. In this regard they are like aircraft. On the other hand, they fly so low that they are in the ship traffic pattern.

The foregoing catalogue of the dimensions of the interaction situation makes it clear that it is not a simple one. Man did not manufacture this whole situation; part of it was the business of nature. Nevertheless, if man is to examine the complete inventory of possibilities in a port study he will be pleased that he has invented the computer to help him.

2. GOALS OF TRAFFIC AND TRANSPORT AT THE LAND-SEA INTERFACE

The goals of traffic and transport at the land-sea interface are as numerous and as varied as are the systems involved. The goals are also as numerous as the persons identifying them. Probably the only goals that have been really quantified to date are the profit-related goals of private industry and commerce. We could class these under the broader class of private satisfaction. This class would include many other economic and noneconomic goals such as recreational joys or esthetic satisfaction.

The private satisfaction group of rather mercenary goals certainly does not cover the whole gamut of goals. There are goals related to curbing the satisfaction of one person at the expense of another. Also there are resource conservation goals. This group of more altruistic goals could be identified as public welfare. Private satisfaction and public welfare seem to cover the goal possibilities, but they are not very useful groupings for the purpose of examining the conflicts at the land-sea interface. Perhaps a look from another direction would be more helpful.

Let us consider the purposes rather than the goals, and perhaps this will yield more useful groupings for analytical application. For traffic and transport at the land-sea interface one can name ten types of purposes which seem to cover most cases. They are commerce, industry, defense, surveillance, science, safety, health, recreation, education, and esthetics. The list lacks pedantic purity but it appears more useful for studying the conflict problem.

Each type of goal or purpose appears to be in an individual dimension of its own. The purposes are not in apparent conflict as vice with virtue or positive with negative. Goals and purposes exist in the multidimensional and boundless realm of thought and inspiration. A conflict among goals per se is possible, but the real conflicts occur when we develop, build, and operate systems to achieve the goals and carry out the purposes. The systems exist and operate in a physical world of finite space and resources, and they perform at the direction of purposeful humans. Here the conflicts start.

Each system has a purpose or private goal which is of one or more of the types listed. Seldom are these purposes coordinated with one another, with the few exceptions where some form of regulation is already invoked. The consequence is a great independence and divergence of purpose. Two systems devoted to goals falling in different type groups will be developed without mutual consideration except where regulations apply. Today regulation is largely limited to taxation, rate control, or immigration. Public welfare considerations are largely limited to safety and import control. It is little wonder that there are conflicts. These conflicts are very real and not limited to physical collisions. Sometimes little wars result; as in the case of the oystermen of the Potomac or the stevedores in almost every port.

3. NATURE OF CONFLICTS

It has been pointed out that goals or purposes are seldom in real conflict with one another, and that the real conflicts occur when we install and operate the systems intended to achieve the goals or purposes. The conflicts are not just between systems, however; many of the most important conflicts are between the system and the environment.

Many examples of each type of conflict exist in the interactions among our present systems and with the environment. Forecasts of future growth make it clear that the frequency and intensity of conflicts will increase. Probably all of our remedial efforts will fail to prevent an increase in conflicts. However, lacking remedial measures, the conflicts will achieve such enormous proportions that the public welfare will be threatened. The conflicts with the environment will become especially more important because we are approaching the exhaustion of our natural resources of the coastal zone; the useful elements of the land, the sea, and the atmosphere.

Aspects of conflicts

Every interaction, between one system and another system or between the system and the environment, which serves to frustrate or degrade the purpose of the system, constitutes a conflict. It would make this discussion much easier and it would help the resolution of the conflicts if it were possible to provide a discrete categorization which would serve as a check-off inventory and permit analysis of the conflicts by applying a neat formula for each type. However, there appears to be no such simple procedure.

The interactions are complex and multiple, and the conflicting aspects occur in various intensities and combinations in each interaction. Some of the conflicting aspects involve the materiel of the system; examples of these physical aspects would be collision and pollution. There may be management aspects in conflict in institutional or economic domains, or social aspects involving the people of the system or of the environment. Finally an aspect may involve the ecology of the environment which is depicted in Figure 4 along with the other factors that affect interactions of traffic and transport systems.

Conflict theory

In order to compare alternatives for multiple use of the coastal zone it would be most desirable to quantify the importance of the multiple conflicts which accompany each interaction. If this could be done, the cost of the conflicts might be balanced against the benefits expected of the proposed system or combination of systems.

Certainly collisions are an important aspect of conflict. Application of some operations-research theory might permit us to quantify the collision aspect.

During World War II, Lancaster, one of the fathers of operations research developed some very useful theories involving striking power and hit-or-miss probabilities. These became known as Lancaster's equations of warfare and continue to serve as a basis of some of the operations research applied to modern warfare. The theories include equations for the probability of hitting a target given certain information about the missile and the target.

Let us consider the missile as a vehicle or vessel. It would have characteristic navigating, surveillance, tracking, and maneuvering systems as does the missile. The target might be a navigational buoy, which is effectively a point; it might be a piling or a bridge

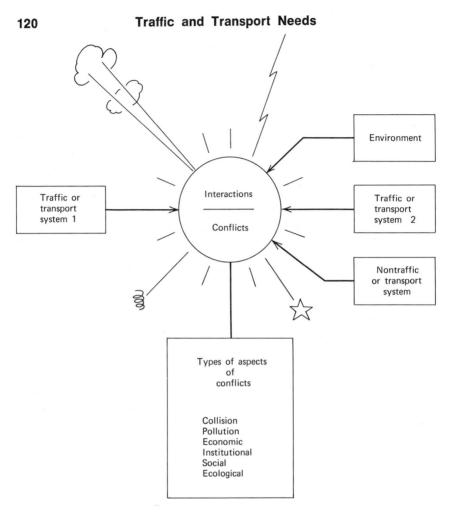

Figure 4.   Interactions of traffic and transport systems.

deck, which is essentially one-dimensional; it might be a pierside or a quayside, which is essentially two-dimensional; or it might be the topography of the bottom, which is three-dimensional. The target would have a definable signature; optical in good weather, radar in poor weather, or sonar for the underwater portions. Its speed and course could be fed in—zero for bridges and tunnels. Its itinerary also could be included.

Now we have postulated a complex though manageable problem. We next apply the equations in reverse because we are interested in misses rather than hits. Now we get some numbers.

This aspect was taken for the example because it is one of the few which may be amenable to mathematical treatment. The other aspects of the conflicts are probably much more difficult to treat analytically. However, what do these numbers mean unless all aspects can be reduced to a unified solution?

Imponderables and intangibles

There are several reasons why other aspects of the conflicts are more difficult to handle. One is that there are generally no Lancaster's equations available to handle the analysis. This part of the problem might be solved by resolute application of our more powerful modern mathematical and computer capabilities. A much more difficult part, however, is that of identifying the beneficiaries, measuring the magnitude of the benefits, and in quantifying the impact of these other aspects of the conflicts.

What number, for instance, shall we assign to the pollution aspect; garbage, sewage, smoke, noise, radioactive fallout, odor, or the waves generated by passing vessels? These are examples of the imponderables, and there are dozens of other examples in the economic, institutional, social, and ecological aspects of the conflicts.

Some of the imponderables lie close to economic quantification. For instance, the finger piers in the downtown areas of most large cities are becoming obsolete for ship use. They are used increasingly for eating, drinking, shopping, fish-processing, or parking. Economic values can be placed on most of these activities, but it is harder to measure the value of an afternoon stroll.

Rafts, trellises, or cages are increasing in aquacultural applications. Any sport sailer or fisherman who has run into a fish trap in the middle of the night appreciates the hazard of such obstacles. It is true that zones for such installations are charted, but the small-craft operational areas are being encroached upon more and more by such structures. The values in this conflict are imponderable. Although the benefit to fisheries can be quantified, the value to recreational boating cannot. At this point the imponderables begin to become intangibles.

How much would a major oil spill from a ship in the arctic change the ecology? Would it change the climate? What premium is reasonable to ensure against the chance of an unpredictable change with an immeasurable impact?

The waterfronts of many major cities are blocked by piers and pollution for miles from the downtown area. The trip is too long and too expensive for many of the downtown residents. Low-income groups cannot afford the long trip so they are denied recreational opportunities at the beaches. What is the cost of this denial of opportunity?

What is the value of the ecology of the wetlands? A marina can use much wetland acreage while at the same time block the migration of the sand along the beaches so that they are not restored by natural processes. Here the intangible value of certain wildlife and of natural swimming beaches is in conflict with the intangible value of the yachtsman's recreation and the measurable marina promoter's profit.

We are squandering and polluting the global natural resources of our space ship—earth. We must soon find national and international bases for value judgements weighing ecological depletion against so-called economic growth. What will be our standard of total conservation? Shall we use the continuous replenishment standard or some other?

Until there are means for quantifying the values which are now imponderable and until there are some forms of measures for the intangibles it will not be possible to produce fully effective analytical models for optimizing the conflicts involving traffic and transport at the land-sea interface.

A multidimensional problem

It will be very difficult to isolate any of the systems or interactions for study. Most plans call for studies on a regional basis. The U.S. Army Corps of Engineers has been making port studies for many years. Their regional studies deal directly with comprehensive surveys of regional port-transportation requirements. The relationship of recreation and conservation of estuarine resources is given continuous consideration but is not a direct element of the study. The National Council on Marine Resources and Engineering Development takes a broader view. They would provide the best use or combination of uses of water and related land facilities to meet contemporary and long range needs for safe, efficient, and convenient water transportation at the lowest practicable cost in a manner consistent with other national goals and objectives. Or is this really different? Neither approach embodies all of the national goals, and both approaches minimize the more imponderable and intangible factors. Are these factors relegated to a peripheral position because of the policy, or because they are difficult to analyze?

One thing appears clearly from the plans for these studies. This is the great cost of performing them. Planning for any of the ports would involve inputs from numerous Federal activities in addition to state and municipal inputs. The total cost of a study of a major port is estimated to run $2½ to $6 million and to take 6 years. The reader can appreciate the scope and complexity of such studies with attendant costs by considering the Port of New York as an example shown in Figure 5.

The new study of Chesapeake Bay would be even more expensive because it involves some of the pollution and conservation factors.

Figure 5. Traffic and transport in the port of New York. Note entrance (bottom center) and vent tower (left of center) for Battery vehicular tunnel. Note famous old Brooklyn Bridge which carries vehicles and trains over the East River (right center). The North-Hudson River (center top) is spanned by train and vehicular tunnels and the George Washington Bridge. The bottoms of rivers and harbor are carpeted with telephone cables, power cables, and pneumatic tubes. *Source:* The Port of New York Authority.

It would start with the construction of a major hydraulic facility, similar to those which are in use for the Mississippi River and for San Francisco Bay. Extensive laboratory, field, and analytical studies of Chesapeake Bay will also be conducted.

A discussion of the conflicts would not be complete without mention of the fact that many of the apparent solutions are two-edged swords. We have already mentioned the compromise which must be made between the yachting recreational value of the marinas and the threat to swimmer recreation which they pose. A less evident compromise will be made in cleaning up our harbors. Just about the time that we have purified the water of the harbors to our satisfaction we shall find that we have generated a new problem for ourselves. The marine life will enjoy the clean water just as much as we do, and this will be a mixed blessing. We can expect the improvement to be accompanied by much destruction of our piers by marine borers and accelerated fouling of ship bottoms.

4. EXAMPLES OF MAJOR CONFLICTS

The foregoing discussion has indicated the complexity and the numerous conflicts which may be involved in a single interaction. It has also covered the lack of comprehensive analytical methods for most of the conflicts. A total analysis intrigues the imagination and might be academically attractive, but probably would collapse of its own weight and fail to resolve any traffic conflicts.

Since principles and practices are not available to the student or potential problem solver, the next best thing is some illustrations of some of the more important interactions. For these it will be possible to identify important conflicts, examine the aspects, and note where compromises will be necessary.

We now explore six examples of interactions involving traffic and transport at the land-sea interface. For each example, apparently important trends will also be mentioned.

The weather versus traffic and transport

Weather information has been provided in the United States by the Weather Bureau of the Environmental Science Services Administration* (ESSA). Special services are provided for ships and

---

* With the establishment of the National Oceanic and Atmospheric Administration (NOAA) as a part of the Federal Administration, ESSA is indicated at the time of this printing to undergo significant organizational restructuring.

craft. These services include the prediction of seas and swells in the North Atlantic and Pacific. The ships and craft also enjoy the benefits of the Hurricane Warning Service of ESSA. This latter service is operated to save lives and property, and it provides information on the position, intensity, direction, and rate of movement of important storms. The warning also includes a prediction of the wind-driven tides (storm tide), strength of winds expected along the coast, and the amount of rainfall. All of these services are very important to major commerce and to small-craft operations. An example of this importance is the use of these services during hurricane Camille in August 1969.

Camille was perhaps the most vicious storm that ever struck the United States. At the time that she crossed the coast near New Orleans the winds had reached a speed of 190 miles per hour and she brought storm tides ranging from 15 to 30 feet above normal near the eye. This storm surge carried ships and small craft inland, and then within 20 to 30 minutes receded carrying much of the burden back into the Gulf of Mexico. More than 6000 homes were destroyed, and 32 boats were destroyed or severely damaged. The Port of Gulfport, Mississippi, was almost completely destroyed and at least 94 vessels were sunk or grounded in the Mississippi River. Figure 6 shows three of the damaged vessels at Gulfport. Out in the gulf, oil rigs foundered and pipelines were destroyed.

The toll from Camille was 140 dead and 76 missing. The total bill will probably exceed $1 billion, but there is a very bright side to the picture. The nature and point of arrival of Camille were predicted about 15 hours before the storm struck and this warning had been preceded by a series of prior advisories over a period of two days. Everyone was fully warned and 99% of the populace living at altitudes less than 20 feet above sea level was evacuated. This was a total of 81,000 persons, and through effective warning an estimated 50,000 persons were saved.

Large enterprises like the shipping companies prudently prepared for the onslaught of Camille and greatly reduced their losses through their preparedness. The general public, however, could not relate the power of the storm to anything in their experience. The winds of 190 miles per hour and 20-foot tides were incredible to them. As a result many refused to leave their homes. Some were arrested and carried to safety. In one case 34 others were known to have been warned but refused to leave and lost their lives.

In spite of the great loss to shipping it is clear that the active response by the owners and operators went far to ameliorate the

Figure 6. Three large freighters; *Hulda, Alamo Victory,* and *Silver Hawk* ashore at Gulfport, Mississippi, after hurricane Camille. *Source:* Coast and Geodetic Survey, ESSA, U. S. Department of Commerce.

effects of the storm. If the general public had heeded the warnings as well as major industry the loss of life would have been trivial. ESSA is conducting an intensified public awareness campaign so that the warnings will receive more effective attention in the future.

Pollution from traffic and transport versus the public

This example covers the pollution aspect of a large group of conflicts and includes several types of pollution which are commonly generated by ships and small craft.

Sewage. One hundred ships generate an amount of sewage equal to that of a city of 5000 people. However, this is not the whole picture; much ship sewage is raw. If it were all raw sewage, the strength would be equal to that of a city of 50,000 equipped with adequate treatment facilities. About 1000 major ships are in our harbors at any one time; thus the dispersal of the sewage is a sizeable problem.

The sewage problem does not involve only that from the large ships however. There are some 8½ million small craft in United States coastal waters and the Interior Department estimates that 1.3 million have toilets. Almost all of these toilets pump raw sewage directly overboard. Also one cannot help but note that there must be 7.2 million small craft with people and no toilets. The latter statistic is an imponderable.

There are already many ports and marinas which are having difficulties. The projected growth of the number of small craft in the United States is almost unbelievable and there is no question but that the sewage problem will be getting more notoriety because of the increasing pollution consciousness of our present-day society.

Waves. Large ships and high-speed power craft can generate sizeable waves. The uninitiated may not see this as a problem, but watermen, shore-side dwellers, and yachtsmen find the waves from other craft a considerable problem. They would cheer to find this discussion under the heading of pollution.

Most marinas and restricted channels have speed limits posted. These are frequently ignored and are somewhat unrealistic in any event. A slow moving tug and tow will generate much more havoc than a small power boat going at the same speed. This inequality may be one of the reasons that speed rules are often ignored; the quiet of the mooring is disturbed; and your lunch lands in your lap.

The problem is much more serious, however, when a large ship ignores speed postings. In restricted waters this can result in costly damage to floats, piers, or retaining walls. Along man-made channels erosion is accelerated and maintenance made more costly. Waves from passing ships and craft are not a crucial problem but the rapid growth of the small craft fleet is bound to build this into a sizeable and expensive nuisance.

Smoke. Smoke in major ports has always been a problem, and ships have been important contributors. Probably the ships alone could be tolerated, but the ports where they exchange cargoes are in the environs of large cities where automobiles, jet aircraft, power plants, and thousands of home and building heating plants join the ships in asphyxiating the public.

The contribution of ships to this problem will probably diminish. Automated combustion control is reducing the frequency of imbalance in the burning so the smoky emissions are almost eliminated. The ships are tending to get larger with the result that more elaborate controls are justified to ensure economical operation, and finally the terminals are moving more and more from the center of the city so the ships' smoke is not being fed in at the worst point of the pollution pattern.

Radioactive fallout. There has been much talk of the possibility of radioactive fallout, but the subject is easily over emphasized because of the novelty. We have grown up in a dirty yellowish black haze and tend to accept it even though we know that it is contributing to a degree of selective extermination. However, radioactivity is different because it introduces the unknown.

Fallout is different in other ways. For one thing it is not continuous like smoke from a funnel. There is a very low probability that it will occur at all. On the other hand, we know and must respect the fact that heavy fallout would be lethal. The danger is hard to ignore when the third party liability of shore-based power plants and that of the nuclear ship *Savannah* is covered by $500 million under the Price-Anderson Act.

The Atomic Energy Commission has developed such effective safeguards that the jeopardy from radioactive fallout is practically nonexistent. The threat of accidental radioactive fallout is small compared with that of potentially lethal collisions of large jet aircraft. The real problem is one of familiarity and a feel for the probabilities. Nevertheless the subject must be mentioned because the trend for the future is for an increase in the number of nuclear-powered ships. This growth will not be as precipitous as one would expect. The reason is that we incorrectly view the *N.S. Savannah* as the base for the growth. The *Savannah* alone is not the base for the growth. The U.S. Navy has been operating a large number of nuclear ships in and out of United States ports for many years, so a large growth has already quietly occurred.

The excellent "no pollution" record of the nuclear ships could lead one to believe that the risk of fallout may be more than offset by the elimination of the smoke and the oily black soot that decorates most fossil fueled steamships.

Signals. Less needs to be said about the interference of signals in a busy port. Optical and acoustical signals have been with us for centuries. Who can forget the mournful sound of the fog horn, the bleat of the whistle, or the flashing light from the bridge of a naval ship. Even the radio signal has been with us long enough to be familiar.

All of us know about the limited range of horns, bells, and whistles. Some of us are familiar with the interferences with underwater sound signals, and some are also aware of the crowding of the radio spectrum with frequency assignments so close that there is continuous threat of interference. There is no interference-free form of signaling.

All that can be said is that the situation will continue to get worse as the demands increase. So far the technological advances have increased the traffic but the operational compromise continues to permit considerable noise. The system designer must not fail to consider noise and interference which are increasing in importance as system design factors.

Oil spills. The man who recommended pouring oil on troubled waters certainly said it backward. In the last few years we have had more than enough trouble pouring from our oily waters. Not only have we had the usual oil slicks from ships pumping overboard their oily ballast but we have had a number of groundings and collisions and finally a breakout from a well.

There are about 100 oil handling terminals, 100 commercial and naval shipyards, and over 60 oil tank-cleaning firms in the United States. Oil is released to the sea during the normal operation of these facilities. In spite of regulations to the contrary oil slicks continue to arrive at our beaches from ships which have pumped oily ballast at sea. This problem will probably decrease as technology provides better solutions and as regulations are strengthened.

A larger threat to the future purity of our coastal zones is the leakage from underwater pipelines. The number of these pipelines is increasing, and as the large deeper draft ships come increasingly into operation the need for offshore terminals with connecting pipelines will increase. Public officials are becoming sensitive to the rising public apprehension toward offshore pipelines. In the summer of 1969 the beaches of New Jersey from Barnegat to Ocean City were soiled by oil presumably pumped from the bilges of an unidentified tanker. Shortly afterward the Governor of New Jersey found himself in the awkward position of reviewing a project to run a 7½ mile pipeline offshore to a proposed new tanker unloading terminal. His initial public reaction to the offshore pipeline was very negative.

Not only will there be an increasing need for piping to offshore ship terminals but also there will be an increasing mileage of underwater piping carrying oil in the vicinity of the oil-producing fields. There are 12,000 wells off the United States coasts at this time and the number is increasing at the rate of 1400 wells per year. Soon we shall have to provide moorings for our ships so that they do not drop anchor inadvertently on an underwater pipeline.

By far the largest pollution threat involving ships or craft, is the threat of an oil spill from a damaged oil tanker. Oil is not the only culprit however; in the group we must include also the increasing quantities of all sorts of chemicals and other liquid cargoes being carried in ships. During the past decade there have been an increasing number of disastrous spills from tank vessels of all types.

This type of casualty is definitely on the upswing for two reasons. First there are an increasing number of vessels carrying liquid, and gaseous cargoes of all types. Second the vessels are getting larger and larger. It is not necessarily a question of the lethality of the cargo. In one case for instance the oils involved were soybean oil and salad oil. Both of these are acceptable dining table products, but when 2,500,000 gallons of soybean oil was let loose with 500,000 gallons of salad oil, 2000 ducks died and 130 miles of recreational and wildlife areas were fouled by the oils.

In March 1967 when the *Torrey Canyon* grounded and released 800,000 barrels of crude petroleum she spread a film of oil over miles and miles of the coasts of England and France. Extensive damage was done to aquatic birds and marine life. It is not known whether the damage will be relatively permanent. An accident involving the tanker, *Golden Eagle,* resulted in damages similar to those of the *Torrey Canyon.* The disabled *Golden Eagle* and the shore damage are shown in Figures 7 and 8. Now contemplate the consequences of releasing, not 800,000 but 2,250,000 barrels of oil. This is the size of the cargo of the new 312,000 ton tankers such as the *Universe Ireland.* Certainly we must avoid the full consequences of such a disaster.

The U.S. Coast Guard is tackling the problem from all angles. They are devising ways to avoid such casualties through ship design and through operational safety measures intended to reduce the probability of grounding and collision. They are developing evasion techniques and ways of minimizing the leakage from damaged tankers, and they are engaged in studies of how to handle the oil if it escapes. Moreover, similarly constructive efforts to solve this worldwide problem are in process in other countries.

The latter area has been the source of some of the greater disappointments. The emulsifiers employed to help disperse the oil slicks have turned out to be more lethal than the oil itself and some are not readily degraded or dissolved in the ocean.

Figure 7. The bow of the tanker *Golden Eagle* after she ran aground and broke in two. The ship was entering the harbor of San Juan, Puerto Rico, with a cargo of 5.7 million gallons of crude oil. March 1968. *Source:* U. S. Coast Guard.

Is shipborne pollution a serious problem? The answer to the question, as far as the welfare of our coastal zone is concerned, is that the problem is definitely serious. However the problem can be handled in terms of technology and ability to regulate in all but two areas. The two areas that will give increasing difficulty are sewage and oil spills. Both problems can be helped by more advanced technology, but both will demand some soul-searching compromises along the way.

Ships versus the bottom

There are some 1000 ships in the U.S. Merchant Marine and several hundred United States owned major ships under foreign flags of convenience. These along with about 1000 foreign ships are the frequenters of our ports. During a 1-year period the U.S. Coast Guard reports about 4000 marine accidents involving these ships. The total loss is about $81 million and the casualties involve about 650 groundings.

Figure 8. View on the 11 miles of Puerto Rico resort beach which were contaminated by 2 million gallons of crude oil leaking from the stranded tanker *Ocean Eagle. Source:* U. S. Coast Guard.

United States territorial waters are well marked. Each year the National Oceanic and Atmospheric Administration (NOAA) issues almost 3 million copies of 822 different charts covering these waters. About 500 of these charts are reissued each year to embody the natural and man-made changes in zones covered by the charts. Lack of good charts cannot explain the large number of groundings in United States waters.

Other remedies have been applied. In 1854 the U.S. Naval officer who came to be known as the father of oceanography, Matthew Fontaine Maury, suggested the idea of providing traffic lanes for ships. It took until 1967 for the idea to achieve general international acceptance. Now in 1970 these lanes are a fact. The traffic routing system is known internationally as the "direct traffic scheme." The Coast and Geodetic Survey charts now show these lanes for San Francisco and New York harbors and for the channels of the Delaware River and the Santa Barbara Islands.

Another improvement resulted from necessity. The numerous oil rigs in the Gulf of Mexico presented an increasing hazard. Finally it was agreed that the above-water structures would be so located that paths would be left between them, so that ship traffic could enter and leave major ports on fairly straight routes. These paths are known as fairways.

The good charts and the other remedial measures have improved the casualty situation but there is no reason to rest easy. In the year 1970 it is expected that our ports will handle 440 million short tons of cargo; but by the year 2000 the prediction is for 1400 million short tons of cargo through United States ports.

Trends in ship development will intensify the grounding problem. The international standard for obstacle location on charts is 11 fathoms or 66 feet. The new tankers draw more than that; for instance, the *Universe Ireland* shown in Figure 9, draws 76 feet. However, that is not the only problem generated by technological advances. Another problem relates to the surface-effect ships. If they grow in number and size as some people predict, we can expect 100-knot 4000-ton ships to be plying the oceans. When this occurs the directed traffic scheme will have to be extended far to sea; safety zones will be required for fishermen; and new traffic controls will have to be instituted. The situation is bound to get more serious in spite of the remedies contemplated.

Small craft versus other craft or the bottom

The U.S. Coast Guard estimates that there were 8½ million small craft in United States waters in 1968. The Coast and Geodetic Survey in an effort to satisfy the special needs of the small-craft operators has issued 65 special small-craft charts. In areas not covered by the special charts the small-craft operator may use the appropriate folio of the 822 standard charts which are available to him. In spite of the availability of this information the Coast Guard reported 239 groundings of small craft in 1968. Every small-craft operator knows that only a small fraction of the groundings reach the attention of the Coast Guard, so we know there were numerous additional groundings not reported.

In 1969 the population of the United States was in the 200+ million zone; by the year 2000 it is expected to reach 350 million. Another factor in the picture is the growth of leisure time as a proportion of our 24-hour day as illustrated in Figure 10. The combined effect of these two factors is that there will be many more

Figure 9. The *Universe Ireland* is one of six 312,000-ton-deadweight capacity tankers used by Gulf Oil Corporation. The ships ply between deep-water terminals in Kuwait and Bantry Bay, Ireland. Later terminals will be built at Okinawa and Nova Scotia. The great size of the ship can be judged by comparison with the tugs. The upper deck area is sufficient to construct two football fields. *Source:* Gulf Oil Corporation.

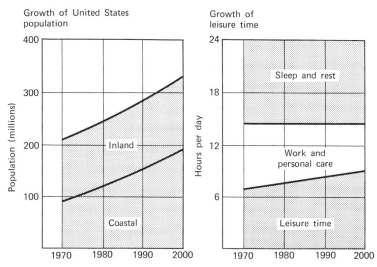

Figure 10. Growth of United States population. Growth of leisure time.
Source: National Council on Marine Resources and Engineering Development.

man-hours for recreation. One of the fastest growing forms of recreation is small boating. According to Coast Guard data there were 3½ million small boats in the United States in 1950. By 1968 this figure had grown to 8½ million, and by the year 2000 it is predicted that there will be 26 million small craft about our coastline. The problem is already such that in August 1969 a Coast Guard officer reported, "It's really bad around Annapolis. You look around the (Chesapeake) Bay and you can hardly see any water. It's all boats."

The growth of conventional small craft will not be the whole problem. There are new types of craft in the making. Many high-speed hydrofoil supported craft are already in use. A type of surface-effect craft is coming into use in smaller sizes. These speedy craft have been tested for ferrying airline passengers around San Francisco harbor and are being widely used by the military in Vietnam. A third class of problem maker will be the small submersible. Probably we shall see a new sport of underwater tourism, and when we do we shall see some new safety problems.

All of the trends point to increases in the problems of small craft in the coastal zone. It is going to be extremely difficult to provide services and controls which will effectively minimize the accidents accruing from rapid growth in the use of the many novel types, coupled with the prodigious increase in the numbers of the more conventional types.

Wetlands versus commerce

Estuaries and their surrounding wetlands are the spawning grounds of two-thirds of the world's entire fisheries harvest. Seven of the most valuable of American commercial fish species spend all or an important portion of their lives in estuarine waters, and at least 80 other commercially important species depend on the estuaries. The estuaries and the wetlands are also the home of water fowl and other wildlife. This is what is known as an "exacting" use because this wildlife cannot exist elsewhere. Further destruction of the wetlands will cause the extinction of many species.

The United States had about 27 million acres of estuaries of which 8 million acres constitute important habitat. Of these 8 million acres of important habitat 570,000 acres have already been preempted by dredging and filling. This is only 7% and it might seem little, but the statistics include Alaska and other areas where little destruction has taken place. The state of California has filled 67% of its habitat area and the 300 square miles of tidal wetland in the San Francisco Bay area have been 80% filled in.

Essential spawning grounds and sanctuary areas have been damaged beyond restoration. In this case the loss is partly measureable, partly imponderable, and partly intangible. Only recently have the people and the governments awakened to the desperate situation which is occurring around almost all of our major port cities. Some stiff compromises will be required.

Technological trends are going to make the choices even more difficult. The merchant marine trend is toward larger and larger ships. Tankers are becoming huge; large dry bulk carriers are planned; and the new container ships and barge carriers are many times larger than their predecessors. Cargoes must be marshaled for these large ships. Figure 11 depicts how this requirement for marshaling containers is met at Port Elizabeth, N.Y. The larger the ships the larger the marshaling area required. The container ships now require about 20 acres of land per ship berth, and they require an enlarged quayside to accommodate the special container cranes such as illustrated in Figure 12. It is no wonder that the downtown piers are falling into disuse. The Port of Seattle has recently renovated five berths and provided 40 acres of holding space. Three more berths and 54 acres of holding space are under

Figure 11. Acres of containers marshaled at Port Elizabeth, New Jersey. Ships load and unload in the foreground. Warehouses in the background provide shelter for cargo being loaded into or removed from containers. Containers arrive and leave by truck, rail, or barge. *Source:* The Port of New York Authority.

construction. The Port of New York Authority is planning to complete development of a 25 berth container facility by 1975, and 919 acres will be required to support it.

Of course the oil storage tanks and the container holding fields are not the only demands on the wetlands near the great ports. The port activities include many transport related activities which find it economical to be near the transhipping points. A good example of space demand is the space demand of the oil refineries which like to congregate between the crude oil terminals and the major customers.

In 1970 the U.S. Army Corps of Engineers working with the Interior Department commenced studies of port areas with special attention to the conservation factors including wetland preemption. These studies, now under review, are expected to support the de-

Figure 12. A container ship being loaded by specially designed cranes. *Source:* Sea-Land Service Inc.

velopment of workable solutions. Some states such as California have taken steps to provide legal protection to the wetlands so that they will not be further destroyed before sensible and balanced planning can be invoked.

This situation is so desperate that it has prompted serious consideration of offshore airports and floating city modules. It will be very difficult to reach a well-balanced compromise with the intangibles of conservation needs in the face of shoreside real estate values in which such expensive alternatives appear to be becoming competitive.

Large ships versus ports

There is an irrevocable motivation toward the construction of larger and larger ships. It is the lust for money. The arithmetic is quite simple. About the greatest cost of ship operation is the crew cost. The crew cost does not increase in proportion to the size of the ship. In fact, the crew of a very large oceangoing ship is not much larger than that of a ship of average size. Once the billets are iden-

tified for around-the-clock watch stations, the bulk of the crew size
is determined. A man can watch a large piece of machinery as
easily as a small one, and he can scan the same horizon even more
easily from a large ship. There are other savings in going to the
relatively large ships and these include the fuel cost per ton of
cargo carried; however, crew savings dominate.

As a modest example consider the savings from doubling the
size of a Maritime Administration C-4 class cargo ship. The savings
in operating cost would be 15 to 17% on each ton of cargo carried.
Of course some of the initial savings might have to be plowed back
into terminal modifications, but the trend is clear. It is practical
to build very large tankers. Ships of as much as 1,000,000 tons
deadweight have been projected. For purpose of comparison,
Figure 13 depicts operating cost against tanker size for the T-2

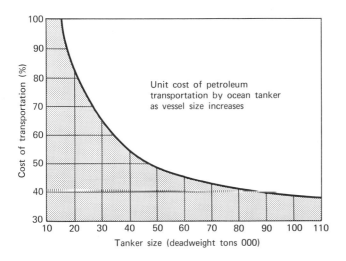

Figure 13. Relationship of transport operating cost to tanker size. Total unit
operating costs of a T-2 Tanker, including capital costs, were taken as equivalent to 100%. Costs for larger vessels are related to this as a percentage of the
T-2 costs. *Source:* Department of Army, Corps of Engineers.

tanker, which was the 16,000 ton deadweight workhorse of World
War II, a one million ton ship could deliver cargo at a 63% cost
saving.

No one million ton deadweight ships are under construction but
the new Gulf Oil Corp. super tankers such as the *Universe Ireland*

are a giant step toward one million tons. The *Universe Ireland* is a 312,000-ton deadweight ship. She makes 14.6 knots and draws 76 feet. The Department of Transportation has made a projection of ship sizes for use in planning as shown in Table 1. It can be seen from what has been happening in the last ten years that ocean shipping has not been in a state of evolution, it has been in a state of revolution.

Another important trend in shipping, especially for the general cargo carriers, is the trend toward modularization. Containers, barges, and detachable hulls all have been introduced or planned. There are two reasons for this trend. The first reason is that 60% of the total door-to-door cost of delivering cargo by break-bulk methods is the cost of packaging and small claims. If containers, barges, or other means are used to better protect the cargo and eliminate transhipping much of this cost is saved. As an example, to send a 75,000 pound baking machine from Indianapolis to Trinidad by breakbulk would cost $8617, but if the shipment is containerized the cost is only $4505.

The second reason for going to modularized cargo carriage is that faster ship turnaround can occur. This in itself brings about economies because the highly capitalized portion of the system is kept in fuller use and the ship crew does not sit idle during a lengthy loading period.

An example of the new types of ships evolving is the Lykes Lines' *Seabee* illustrated in Figure 14. These are fast 19-knot 875-feet ships and exemplify a good degree of courage on the part of private industry. The three ships and the complete set of 266 barges (98 foot length) will run about $150 million to build.

One important consequence of this new trend will be a change in the itinerary of the ships. The large master vessels will have a very limited itinerary, perhaps between two ports which will serve as distribution centers. The *Universe Ireland* runs from Kuwait to Bantry Bay in Ireland. From Bantry Bay the cargo is distributed throughout Europe by smaller ships. In the case of the *Seabee* the barges will be offloaded at master terminals and then they will fan out toward their ultimate destinations.

Another fascinating new development is the possibility of opening the Northwest Passage. After centuries of attempts, the level of technology and the economic motivation have joined hands to produce a system which may permanently open the passage. In the summer of 1969 the 144,400-ton tanker *Manhattan* illustrated in Figures 15 and 16 successfully made an experimental voyage. The

TABLE 1
Projected Vessel Characteristics, 1970 to 2000

	1970	1980	1990	2000
General Cargo or Container Ships				
Maximum deadweight tons				
in world fleet	25,500	33,500	43,500	50,000
Length (feet)	850	930	1,010	1,050
Beam (feet)	108	117	127	132
Depth (feet)	74	80	85	88
Draft (feet)	36	39	40	40
Average deadweight tons				
in world fleet	8,168	8,583	9,043	9,350
Dry Bulk Carriers				
Maximum deadweight tons				
in world fleet	105,000	185,000	317,000	400,000
Length (feet)	870	1,040	1,230	1,325
Beam (feet)	125	152	183	198
Depth (feet)	71	84	99	106
Draft (feet)	48	57	66	71
Average deadweight tons				
in world fleet	14,750	18,750	23,575	27,350
Tankers				
Maximum deadweight tons				
in world fleet	300,000	760,000	1,000,000	1,000,000
Length (feet)	1,135	1,460	1,570	1,570
Beam (feet)	186	252	276	276
Depth (feet)	94	129	142	142
Draft (feet)	72	98	104	104
Average deadweight tons				
in world fleet	39,825	76,225	90,000	94,325

Source. Department of Transportation, Assistant Secretary for Policy Development.

Note. There have been several recent projections of vessel characteristics which have reflected somewhat different estimates of maximum vessel size. One such projection forecast dry bulk vessels as large as 800,000 deadweight tons by the year 2000 while another recognized the technological feasibility of 1,000,000 deadweight tons tankers but assumed that, because of the limited uses for such extremely large vessels, tankers would probably not exceed 500,000 deadweight tons. It is clear that such projections involve judgments which may vary and it is important to recognize the existence of these differences.

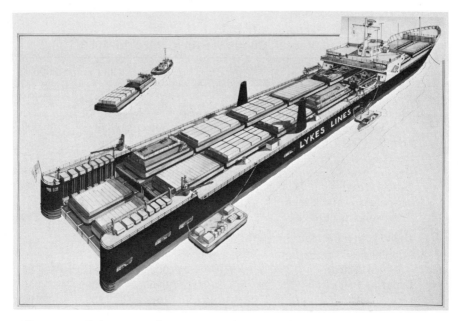

Figure 14. Lykes Lines *Seabee* carries barges and containers. These 875-foot-long, 50,000-ton ships can carry 38 loaded barges or 1800 containers each. They may also handle roll-on roll-off cargo. The 98-foot-long 1000-ton barges are lifted on board by a special powerful stern elevator. *Source:* Lykes Brothers Steamship Co. Inc.

experiment was focused on the technical problems, notably the ability of the ship to break ice. The voyage provided the information necessary to determine the economic feasibility of using this route in comparison with pipeline to bring oil from the North slopes of Alaska to the refineries on the East Coast of the United States and to Europe.

It has been estimated that bringing the oil by this route will save between $500 million and $1 billion per year in shipping costs, and this will accrue to the benefit of domestic consumers. This is not the end of the potential benefit however; there are other ores in the northern Alaska wilderness. With the aid of new slurrying processes it may be possible to carry such ores out of the area in tankers. Finally there is the possibility that opening the arctic may provide new shipping routes through the Arctic Ocean providing all the technical problems can be managed and such operations made economically feasible. The introduction of a shorter route from En-

Figure 15. The 144,000-ton tanker *S. S. Manhattan* was fitted with a special ice breaking bow for her experimental voyage through the Northwest Passage. The sloped prow causes the bow to ride up on the ice and break it downward. The crosses painted on the ship's side are targets for photographic recording of speed through the ice. *Source:* Humble Oil and Refining Company.

gland to Japan over the North Pole is also interesting to contemplate. Certainly it will affect the nature of transport in our coastal zone. One wonders whether the changes will include an increase or a decrease.

The cost of building and operating the special ships to handle the Alaskan oil will be great indeed but the cost of alternatives is not low. As a clue we can use the cost of the 48-inch pipeline from Prudhoe Bay to Valdiz Alaska. It will be the initial leg of the oil supply from the North slope to the U.S. West Coast, and it is expected to cost between $800 million and 1.2 billion.

What major conflicts will be generated by the large ships? We have already discussed some of them. The obsolescence of the finger piers in the downtown area of our major port cities is one of the conflict areas. Another conflict is the intensification of the threat

Figure 16. The *S. S. Manhattan* in Arctic ice. Ice crews obtain samples of tough old ice for analysis in the shipboard laboratory. *Source:* Humble Oil and Refining Company.

of oil spills. The special new feature here is that some of this threat may be in the arctic where the bacteria will not be so vigorous in cleaning up the mess and special provisions may be necessary. Another conflict which we have already mentioned is the preemption of wetlands.

There are two other conflicts generated by the larger ships and these have not been discussed in this chapter. These are the shift of the work force of the waterfront and the problems stemming from the deeper drafts of the new ships.

Over the centuries the oceangoing ships have unloaded their cargo at the traditional interface, the ocean port. The current trend will change this for all types of significant cargoes. (Passengers will continue to be handled in the cities but this traffic is dwindling). In the planned operation of the large tankers and the barge carriers the loading and the unloading of cargo will not occur at the large ports.

It is too early to predict the entire impact of this change. Will the ship fueling, ship chandlery, and other ship support move from the ports? It is clear that for the general cargo it will be necessary for the stevedores to be located where the cargo is ultimately destined. One can forecast some interesting discussions between stevedoring and trucking unions. In the end economics will dictate the trend and those ports which view port levies as a tribute to their vested rights are going to find it increasingly difficult to sustain their position.

The conflict due to the increasing draft of the large ships is of another kind. The *Manhattan* draws 50 feet and the *Universe Ireland* draws 76 feet. Most channels to harbors of the United States are from 35 to 45 feet deep. What is perhaps worse is that the slope of the continental shelf off northern Alaska, of the bottom of the Gulf of Mexico near Texas, and even of the continental shelf off the major ports of the East coast is quite gentle. As an example the 50-foot contour is 28 miles offshore from Sabine Pass in East Texas. This means that channels must be dredged deeper or the ships must stand far offshore.

The cost of further dredging in many of our ports would be very great because of the natural and man-made obstructions. The soft clays have been penetrated in several harbors such as New York and further dredging would have to be be through bed rock at ten times the cost of the earlier dredging. There are other problems; at some places the bedrock contains natural aquafers which must not be contaminated with salt water. In still other cases there are vehicular tunnels under the channels which could be moved only at very great cost. Compounding all of these problems is the increasing pressure to avoid further disturbance of the ecology through the dredging and the disposal of the spoils from the cuts.

In one harbor study the estimated cost of partial deepening coupled with a pipeline and an offshore terminal was $132 million less than the cost of a traditional harbor deepening project. This potential saving coupled with the other motivations which have been mentioned would make it easy to decide on an offshore terminal. Not all of the decisions may be that simple but they are likely to end up with the same answer even if preceded by a bitter struggle, so we can conclude that we shall see more and more offshore terminals.

5. CONCLUSION

The traffic and transport systems important to the study of conflicts at the coastal zone include not only the ships but also other
waterborne craft, land vehicles, aircraft, and the bridges, tunnels,
and supporting systems necessary for the effective locomotion of
all people, vehicles, and commodities through the port area. The
conflicts are seldom found among the goals or purposes of these
systems, instead the conflicts occur when the systems are installed
and operated to achieve the designated purposes or goals. The
systems compete with one another and conflict with the environment in response to their needs for sea space, land space, air space,
or a share of the electromagnetic spectrum.

The interactions among the systems at the coastal zone are multiple, and each interaction may generate several conflicts. It would
help if there existed some theory to determine the value or cost of
the conflicts, but none seems to exist. It is not even easy to classify
the systems much less the conflicts. It appears that one useful way
of handling problems is to group them by geographical regions and
handle the problems of each region collectively. This at least offers
a chance of a comprehensive view of the problems even if it does
not offer a means for their solution.

Probably the most frustrating part of tackling the coastal zone
interactions involving traffic and transport is the presence of so
many imponderables and intangibles among the quantities which
should be measured if an analytical study is to be attempted. These
imponderables and intangibles are most prevalent among the public
welfare aspects of the interactions but they exist in the other
aspects as well. How much is a swimmer's satisfaction worth? And
what is the value of the stroll along the waterfront?

There are important trends which impact on the status of traffic
and transport at the land-sea interface. These trends include population growth, the increasing proportion of leisure time, and
increasing public awareness of conservation and the threat of
pollution. A revolution is occurring in ocean shipping with the
introduction of supertankers and large container and barge carriers. The new types of large and small craft such as the surface-
effect ship and the hydrofoil may change the pattern of operations
and the advent of major efforts to explore and exploit the oceans is
introducing a host of new types of ships and craft. Finally, despite
operational and technical problems there is the possibility of sea

routes through the Arctic Ocean. Collectively all of the trends portend changes in maritime traffic and transport which stagger the imagination.

Important conflicts involving the traffic and transport at the land-sea interface already exist. These conflicts include sewage, signals, and oil spills. All of these problems are likely to be more severe in the future, and the threat from oil spills is perhaps the most acute. The ever-increasing drafts, as the oceangoing ships become larger and larger, is a difficult problem which promises to get worse. The number of small craft is becoming a threat in itself, but the more serious problems will involve adequate safety provisions for the exotic new types which are beginning to come into vogue.

The human factors in shifting work forces to new sites and the coveting of precious wetlands by marina promoters and container-holding operations are a part of what is perhaps the most difficult general problem of all. This problem is the lack of a system of quantitative values for many of the ecological and social factors which are now in direct competition with private enterprise in the coastal zone. New measures and associated quantities must be devised to manage the public welfare in important planning decisions. The solution of this problem is long overdue. Evidently we have already created irreversible reactions. The fact that we initiated these reactions unintentionally and sometimes unknowingly is certainly alarming. We must learn to plan these things and not let them occur by default.

There are many other systems operational at the coastal zone, and each will have its conflicts and problems. It is clear, however, that the traffic and transport by themselves offer a plethora of conflicts. Not only that but also the methods of solution of the problems are largely lacking. It looks as though there will be plenty of challenging work for the scientists, statesmen, engineers, and economists of future generations.

BIBLIOGRAPHY

Battelle Memorial Institute, Research Report to the U.S. Department of Commerce, Coast and Geodetic Survey, *A Study of the Coast and Geodetic Survey's Products and Services as Related to Economic Activity in the U.S. Continental Shelf Regions*, January 1966.

Commission on Marine Science, Engineering and Resources, *Industry and Technology, Keys to Oceanic Development*, Panel Reports, Vol. 2, Superintendent of Documents, U.S. Government Printing Office, Washington, D.C.

Commission on Marine Science, Engineering and Resources, *Our Nation and the Sea*, Superintendent of Documents, U.S. Government Printing Office, Washington, D.C., January 1969.

Committee on Oceanography, *Oceanography 1966, Achievements and Opportunities*, National Academy of Sciences—National Research Council, Publ. 1492, 1967.

Committee on Oceanography and Committee on Ocean Engineering, *An Oceanic Quest*, National Academy of Sciences, Publ. 1709, 1969.

Federal Interagency Committee on Multiple Use of the Coastal Zone, *A Report on the Seminar on Multiple Use of the Coastal Zone*, National Council on Marine Resources and Engineering Development, November 1968.

House, Donald C., A Report to the Administrator of ESSA, *Hurricane Camille*, Department of Commerce, ESSA/PI 690034, September 1969.

Interdepartmental Ad Hoc Task Group of Committee on Multiple Use of the Coastal Zone, *Conceptual Plan for Harbor and Port Development Studies*, National Council for Marine Resources and Engineering Development, November 1968.

Management and Economic Research Incorporate, *Shoreline Utilization in the Greater Seattle Area*, PB 183026, January 1968.

National Council on Marine Resources and Engineering Development, *Marine Science Affairs—A Year of Transition*, Superintendent of Documents, U.S. Government Printing Office, Washington, D.C., February 1967.

National Council on Marine Resources and Engineering Development, *Marine Science Affairs—A Year of Plans and Progress*, Superintendent of Documents, U.S. Government Printing Office, Washington, D.C., March 1968.

National Council on Marine Resources and Engineering Development, *Marine Science Affairs—A Year of Broadened Participation*, Superintendent of Documents, U.S. Government Printing Office, Washington, D.C., January 1969.

Panel on Oceanography of the President's Science Advisory Committee, *Effective Use of the Sea*, Superintendent of Documents, U.S. Government Printing Office, Washington, D.C., 1966.

SESOC Advisory Committee of Commerce Technical Advisory Board, *Surface Effect Ships for Ocean Commerce*, Superintendent of Documents, U.S. Government Printing Office, Washington, D.C., February 1966.

Taylor, Lorne G., Presentation to Institute of Navigation, *Modern Charting Requirements for Marine Navigation and the National Economy*, ESSA, Coast and Geodetic Survey, June 1965.

Taylor, Lorne G., Presentation to Institute of Navigation, *Safety Lanes for Marine Navigation*, ESSA, Coast and Geodetic Survey, October 1966.

Trident Engineering Associates, Inc., *Chesapeake Bay Case Study*, PB 179844, September 1968.

U.S. Army Corps of Engineers, *Harbor and Port Development: A Problem and an Opportunity*, July 1968.

CHAPTER 6

Conservation of Mineral Resources of the Coastal Zone

FRANCIS J. HORTIG

For this chapter to serve as the basis for a rational discourse on conservation of mineral resources of the coastal zone, we must start with the application of a time-honored cliché, "Let's define our terms."

Neither the term *conservation* nor *coastal zone* have a standard universally applicable definition. *Conservation* definitions range between the extremes of that of the arch-preservationist that the natural conditions of the total environment may not be disturbed or altered by man to that of the self-serving single-purpose statement that conservation is achieved in a resource development program if the operation can be conducted in a manner to maximize economic profit. This chapter is presented within the constraints of the definition:

> Conservation of all natural resources is the result of achieving the best feasible ecological balance while developing the necessary resources for the benefit of man.

We next consider the *coastal zone*. A report by the Commission on Marine Science, Engineering and Resources, "Our Nation and the Sea," suggests that the coastal zone contains the nearshore area together with the entire continental shelf and the resources of the overlying waters as delimited by existing international agreements. A study conducted for the California Advisory Commission on Marine and Coastal Resources on California's coastal zone recommended planning evaluation of a coastal zone identified as a strip of land and water running from the northern to the southern boundary of the state, with an arm extending 80 miles up the delta to

include the Sacramento and Stockton areas. The seaward limit is
the fisheries limit which lies 12 miles out to sea, with the exception
that the line has been drawn outside all the channel islands off
southern California along a 100 fathom (600 feet) *average depth*
contour and in that section is approximately 65 miles from the
mainland. The landward limit has been established on the basis
that economic, climatic, topographic, or recreational influences tied
closely to the coast or ocean were encompassed by the coastal zone
boundary. The landward line runs about 20 miles back from the
coast and generally parallels the shore, although it swings far
inland up the delta to include Stockton and Sacramento and the
areas bordering San Francisco Bay. It also bulges inland to include
the San Bernardino-Riverside portion of the Southern California
metropolitan area. The California Interagency Committee on Ocean
Resources established by Executive Order of the Governor is
charged with the development of a comprehensive ocean area development plan for the state. This committee is focusing primary
planning considerations on a coastal zone area identified as that
which includes publicly and privately owned lands inland to a
variable distance from beaches and the margins of bays and estuaries, but normally does not extend further than the highest elevation in the nearest coastal mountain range. It further includes tide
and submerged lands lying seaward to variable distance from the
beaches but normally does not extend further seaward than the
outermost limit of the state's boundaries.

NEEDS FOR DEVELOPING MINERAL RESOURCES

Now we know what we wish to accomplish by conservation and
in general where—but why? Does the mountain climber's challenge,
"because it's there," justify confronting the technological problems
of mineral extraction from a hostile marine environment? Obviously not. However, there is as yet little general awareness of the
absolute necessity for full mineral development of the offshore to
offset otherwise adverse impacts on the economy and security of
the nation and particularly the economy of the individual state.

To support optimum development of offshore mineral resources,
the National Commission on Marine Science, Engineering and Resources in January 1969 recommended:

1. "The Nation should establish as a major goal the advancement of an
understanding of the planetary oceans as a principal focus for its basic
marine science effort.

2. "The basic science effort required to achieve the understanding of the planet . . . should be supported as a necessary National effort to provide the basic geological and geophysical knowledge of the oceans required for the National program of marine mineral resource development.

3. "Extensive field experiments should be conducted to describe physical processes associated with ocean fluctuations. Parallel efforts in geophysical fluid dynamics should be mounted which can provide the theoretical and practical framework for the establishment of physical techniques for ocean prediction."

The United States is an importer of aluminum, bromine used primarily as a gasoline additive, cobalt used in high-strength alloys, copper, industrial diamonds, gold, ilmenite and rutile used for their high-strength titanium metal content, thorium used principally for high-strength alloys, and crude petroleum and petroleum products. The supply of all these essentials is always tenuous depending upon the international situation as to whether the resources can be produced or transported to the United States. Technological developments have increased the requirements for nonenergy resources such as tungsten, titanium, and platinum to the point where the availability of these resources is generally critical.

The need for expansion of energy resource production has been projected at an even greater rate of acceleration than the requirements for nonfuel minerals. Oil and gas provided approximately three-fourths of the total energy consumed in the United States during 1968 (approximately 62×10^{15} Btu), an increase of more than 80% in 20 years. Neither the definition of a Btu (the heat energy to raise 1 pound of water $1° F$ in temperature) nor the electrical energy measurement equivalent of a kilowatt-hour permit a simple relative concept of the amount of energy represented. However, a barrel of oil (containing 42 gallons) can be visualized readily and therefore the following energy requirement projections will be stated in barrels of oil-equivalent. From approximately 30 million barrels daily oil-equivalent total energy use in 1968 (which should be more easily visualized than 62×10^{15} Btu), projections indicate 45 million barrels daily oil-equivalent demand for total energy use by 1980—a one and one-half fold increase only 10 years hence. In the event of continuing difficulty with visualization of the magnitude of this demand, the numbers can be made smaller by considering the number of supertankers which would be required to transport the total equivalent mineral fuel requirement. The largest supertanker which can be handled currently at Los Angeles Harbor has a capacity of 870,000 barrels. Therefore the 1968 oil-equivalent total energy requirement can be translated into the arrival into United States ports of 35 supertankers every day of the year. Concurrently, during the period 1960 to 1968 fewer new oil and gas reserves were discovered in the United States than the amounts consumed domestically during the same period.

As with all projections there is a range from which to choose. The values reported here are approximately at the median. However, even the most conservative projections spotlight the severity of the future resource problems, particularly as to energy sources. Figure 1 (translated into barrels) shows an overwhelming cumula-

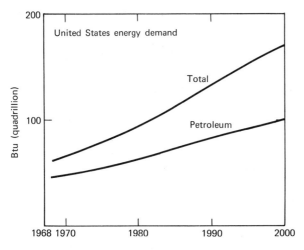

Figure 1. Projected cumulative energy demand for United States (to year 2000).

tive demand for over 200 billion barrels of petroleum product requirements in the United States within the next 30 years—more than five times the currently proved United States reserves available for production. This demand projection includes the factor that petroleum will contribute a decreasing proportion of the total future energy supply—estimated at 60% of the year 2000 total energy demand of 169 quadrillion Btu or 9.6 billion barrels.

California is an outstanding example of the petroleum supply-demand imbalance on the West Coast. California, Alaska, Arizona, Hawaii, Nevada, Oregon, and Washington comprise the U.S. Department of the Interior Petroleum District V. For July 1969

District V production was 1,311,000 barrels daily, of which 1,043,801 barrels daily was produced in California. During July 1969 the total District V petroleum product demand was 2,074,000 barrels daily necessitating the importation into the District of the major segment of the supply deficiency for operation of the refineries and petrochemical plants. The minor segment was supplied from inventories of stocks on hand. The entire subject of Federal policy with respect to required controls on importation of crude oil and product supplies is under study by a presidential commission.

An area of upland adjoining the ocean is inseparably related to the activities of, in, and under the adjoining ocean. Generally, mineral resource extraction operations on the upland, particularly in urban areas, are subject to additional institutional controls such as local zoning ordinances. Ocean extraction operations include all of the dry-land technological problems and a host of greater problems unique to the marine environment. With such a concentration of interrelated problems, this chapter is directed primarily to the underwater segment of the coastal zone.

CONTROLS ON MINERAL RESOURCES DEVELOPMENT

The majority of statutory controls over offshore mining operations in California have been assigned to the State Lands Commission. This commission is composed of the Lieutenant Governor, the State Controller, and the Director of Finance. It must be stressed that all extraction operations must be conducted *on balance* with all of the user groups with requirements for the same environment. Such user groups have been catalogued by the Environmental Science Services Administration (ESSA) of the U.S. Department of Commerce prior to establishing the National Oceanic and Atmospheric Administration (NOAA) as follows:

1. Mining and petroleum
2. Marine engineering
3. Recreation
4. Health and welfare
5. Transportation
6. Food and agriculture
7. Defense and space
8. Research (both academic and industrial) and development
9. Other industries
10. State and local agencies

Offshore California is divided into two zones of jurisdiction—the *territorial sea* and underlying lands which are owned by the state, generally out to 3 geographic miles from the mainland and including a 3-geographic mile belt around offshore islands, and the *outer continental shelf* lying outside of the state's ownership and in which the United States exercises jurisdiction only over the resources in the lands of the *shelf*. The International Convention of the Continental Shelf in 1958 provided for mineral development on such lands by the adjoining sovereign state to a distance offshore where the water depth is 200 meters or where the depth of the superjacent waters permits exploitation. Under this definition the seaward limit appears to be determined by the limit of technological capability for mineral recovery. The general terms of the International Convention of 1958 reflect the average conditions of the continental shelves —reasonably flat and sloping slowly to a line of precipitate drop off the edge of the continents at an average water depth of 200 meters. In contrast, the *shelf* adjoining the Pacific Coast of California as a continuation of the continental mass has a very rugged topography including extremely deep water areas before the change from continental to oceanic basin geology is reached. Because of this distinctive submarine topography the area is referred to as a *continental borderland.*

Inasmuch as the *continental borderland* adjoining California is a currently submerged area of the same geology and mineralogy as the adjoining upland, the majority of the minerals existent in the upland can be expected to be found in the submerged lands. Thirty-two of these minerals, including petroleum and natural gas, were produced commercially in California from the upland during 1966 and 1967. Offshore exploration and development have been limited to areas of concentrated mineralization such as oil and gas reservoirs, phosphorite deposits, sand and gravel placers, and to the less-concentrated higher-value minerals such as gold and titanium. Minerals are also being produced from sea water, principally bromine, magnesium compounds for industrial purposes, and sodium chloride for domestic and industrial uses. Worldwide, subsea deposits have been investigated and developed in varying degrees also containing aragonite (calcium carbonate crystals), coal, diamonds, ferromanganese nodules having significant concentrations of nickel, copper and cobalt, glauconite (*green sand*) with a high potash content, iron, platinum, and tin.

The development and conservation of the mineral resources are inextricably intertwined with the conservation of other nonliving extractive resources such as geothermal energy and with the dynamics of the ocean environment. All development should be capable of being conducted in such manner as to assure minimization of detrimental effects on the living resources of the sea. Graphical presentation of these interrelationships as a guide to optimum resource management requires a multidimensional matrix for which there are as yet only imprecise criteria, which will permit reasonably objective evaluation and assignment of priorities.

Having hinted at the complexity of the problem of mineral resource conservation, we can consider herein only the status of some of the principal resource management developments and the inevitability of interrelationships, because no extractive operations can be conducted in the ocean environment without varying degrees of impact on the balance of the entire environmental system.

Extraction of low unit-value sand from the coastal zone should be an uncomplicated process for an initial review. Mechanically, this is relatively correct, whether the removal is undertaken from the beach and surf zone with a bulldozer and scoop, or from deeper water areas with a clamshell or hydraulic dredge. However, particularly in southern California, the construction of debris dams and channelization of virtually all of the water courses which flow into the ocean have eliminated the normal transport of sand to the coastal zone. Therefore, the natural mass balance of spring flood replenishment of the coastal sand eroded by winter storms has already been effected adversely to a serious degree. Artificial removal of such deposits (i.e., by the interposition of the structures and activities of man) can and has upset the existent imbalance even further, accelerating coastal erosion to the degree that extensive protective works have had to be installed with facilities for artificial and costly replenishment of the sand.

For construction purposes, as a generalization, sand removed directly from a beach is of lower quality than river or quarry sand. However, higher quality sand removal from a river mouth or upstream has a necessary adverse impact on beach erosion although the effects of delayed open beach erosion are not as dramatically apparent as when the sand is removed artificially directly from a beach. All California urban areas have either prohibited or severely restricted most upland sand quarrying operations, thereby focusing the increasing market demand on the stream systems and further depleting the natural beach replenishment sources. As the economic value of sand increases in California, as it must, it may become economically feasible to return to the coastal beaches the tremendous volumes of sand carried by the littoral drift along shore into such deep water areas as Monterey Canyon in Monterey County, Redondo Canyon in Los Angeles County, Newport Canyon in Orange County, and Scripps Canyon in San Diego County, as well as from other offshore areas. On the Atlantic Coast offshore sand extraction for construction purposes is under evaluation as a competing use to beach replenishment, which has been a comparatively extensive material utilization in that area.

Specialty sands with physical and chemical properties uniquely suitable for glass manufacture and other specialized industrial processes are in comparatively short supply and are produced almost entirely from beach deposits in Monterey County. Nevertheless, despite the economic asset to the County represented by these resources, as recently as September 1969 the Association of Monterey Bay Area Governments and the Board of Supervisors of Santa Cruz County by formal resolutions requested a moratorium on coastal zone sand extraction pending a determination of the source of the sands, their movement along the coast and their rate of replenishment.

The aforementioned elements are all inputs to the solution of the resource allocation equation in the best public interest. Inasmuch as this last element ordinarily cannot be quantified with precision, completely satisfactory objective solutions are seldom achieved. In addition, the best public interest includes considering the impact of sand removal on living resources of the ocean through disturbance of the subsurface, and the creation of turbidity by the removal operation, as well as restrictions to recreational access and again the adverse effects of turbidity on recreational activities such as skin diving.

A current operating example of effective resource allocation is the authorization for sand removal from the mouth and a portion of the state-owned bed of the Russian River in Sonoma County. This coastal operation 70 miles north of the San Francisco Bay complex is under development as a source of construction aggregate because of the virtual embargo on sand production in the San Francisco metropolitan area. The distinctive resource allocation feature of the operation requires that the royalty payments to the state for sand removal must be invested in land for expansion of the existent adjoining state beach park. An additional spin-off benefit will be the improvement of navigability for recreational boating and fishing.

All other nonhydrocarbon minerals under current or recent evaluation offshore California (e.g., gold, ilmenite, and magnetite) have extraction problems and institutional control problems similar to those for the extraction of sand. The higher unit-value for these minerals should assist measurably in making such operations economically feasible.

Gold, ilmenite, and other heavy minerals have been the subject of recent Pacific Coast reconnaissance surveys by both the U.S. Geological Survey and the U.S. Bureau of Mines. Currently these programs are virtually inactive because of budgetary limitations. Offshore prospecting and evaluation is continuing under permit authorizations from the California State Lands Commission but, as yet, no bases have been developed to support a viable, large-scale offshore mineral extraction industry.

Phosphorite nodules are known to exist offshore southern California on *outer continental shelf* lands. One uncompleted attempt at commercial exploitation of these deposits has been made. This year the possibility of a question of jurisdiction over at least a portion of the deposit has been raised by an announcement of the Mexican Government of the intent to assert ownership over a 12-mile territorial sea. Such extended limit could overlap an extensive segment of area previously considered *outer continental shelf* lands of the United States.

Now, let us consider some of the problems of conservation of the principal energy minerals, oil and gas, which are of general interest and are most essential to the economy and our mode of living.

On the basis of national policy it has been decided that as much of available petroleum and petroleum products shall be imported into the United States as will not affect the viability of the domestic petroleum industry adversely to the extent that effective domestic productive capability would be hampered in the event of an international crisis. Petroleum conservation in California, however, cannot be discussed in the terms of national norms, averages, or parameters. One of the many unique features of California is that it is the only major petroleum production area, ranking third nationally, where the market demand exceeds the local production capability. As stated previously in introducing the mineral conservation problems, the total petroleum production in California during July 1969 was 1,043,801 barrels per day of the District V total production of 1,311,000 barrels per day. During this period 2,074,000 barrels per day were required for input to the District V refineries and petrochemical plants. This current inability to meet the local market demand coupled with the projections for increased energy requirements constitute the primary motivations for increased exploration effort for petroleum reserves in offshore areas.

California offshore fields discovered as early as 1927 are still in production. Such areas particularly require the application of more recently developed reservoir engineering technology to assure optimum utilization of reservoir energy and the maximum ultimate recovery of oil and gas. Prominent among these applications are vastly improved well completion practices and primary recovery methods, secondary recovery operations for enhancement of the natural processes of recovery from reservoirs through application of pressure, and tertiary recovery stimulation through the application of heat and solvents. Original expectations of recovery efficiencies of only 10% of the oil in place have in many instances been increased to 50% by the application of developing technology. Similarly, in the instances of reservoirs especially susceptible to the application of miscible flooding (i.e., by the introduction of pressure and improvement of fluid flow through a material which is miscible in crude oil) anticipated recovery efficiencies may be in the order of 90%.

A unique experimental project for direct oil recovery, representing conservation in the absolute sense, is in operation offshore Santa Barbara County. The technique of covering an ocean-floor oil leak with a fabric enclosure and recovery system has been utilized in efforts to control the aftermath of a blow-out on a drilling well. The unique application is in an area of known natural ocean-floor oil seeps offshore Coal Oil Point identified as early as the 18th Century by Padre Pedro Font. Recovery by this one unit has been complete, and its ultimate effectiveness is being given a maximum performance test by the winter storms. A most intriguing prospect of a successful project is, of course, that the water quality and beach conditions could be enhanced above the preexisting natural conditions to the benefit of all types of recreational activity.

While not considered a *mineral* resource by popular classification, the development of geothermal resources offshore presents a challenging and potentially highly prolific source of energy. To date, the production of geothermal steam has been restricted to upland areas throughout the world. In California exploration and development of geothermal steam for electrical power generation has been conducted fairly continuously since 1955 with the demonstrated capability of generating in excess of 250,000 kilowatts of electrical energy. However, exploration for subsea locations for possible development of geothermal energy has been extremely limited as to the area reviewed and even more so as to the percentage of the total area with a general potential for geothermal resources available for exploration. Initial subsea production will probably be from locations selected as they have been on the upland, where there is natural steam emission, or steam flow can be secured by drilling into subsurface areas of high temperature with a natural supply of subterranean water to be flashed into steam. In view of the known volcanic activity along the West Coast of the United States, a segment of the *Pacific Ring of Fire*, there must be many areas with a high potential for subsea production of geothermal resources. Under the oceans wherever a high temperature anomaly can be localized by geothermal exploration, almost unlimited supplies of water are available from the overlying ocean. Under these conditions it should be technologically feasible to drill two boreholes into the subsurface; the first for controlled injection of seawater and the second for production of the resultant steam.

For the benefit of those who might be concerned over the inclusion of geothermal resources in the broad domain of mineral resources it should be explained that the first California authorizations for geothermal resource development were issued under mineral leasing statutes. These statutes provided for effective control and development of the normal extractive resources ranging literally from A to Z, for instance, asbestos to zinc. With the advent of a better understanding of the nature and energy characteristics of geothermal resources, specific geothermal resource development statutes were adopted to provide the flexibility and control conditions required by the unique physical nature and geologic occurrence of the resource. Chapter 1398 Statutes of 1967 for California (Appendix 1) defines "geothermal resources" as "the natural heat of the earth, the energy in whatever form below the surface of the earth present in, resulting from, or created by, or which may be extracted from, such natural heat, and all minerals in solution or other products obtained from naturally heated fluids, brines, associated gases, and steam, in whatever form, found below the surface of the earth, but excluding oil, hydrocarbon gas or other hydrocarbon substances." Prospecting permits and leases for the extraction and removal specifically of geothermal resources from lands belonging to the state may be issued by the State Lands Commission under rules and regulations to encourage the greatest ultimate recovery of geothermal resources.

Between 1920 and 1969, 133 wells were drilled in California for exploration and development of geothermal resources in 19 areas with geothermal potential.

An interesting classification of geothermal energy is found in a July 31, 1969 Federal Tax Court decision in *Arthur E. Reich and Carolyn G. Reich et al.* v. *Commissioner* (*of Internal Revenue*). The Tax Court determined that the commercial product of geothermal wells is steam. This steam is a gas taken from a natural subterranean reservoir of fixed capacity and is an exhaustible natural resource, the taking of which causes depletion.

Bromine and magnesium compounds are being extracted from sea water in three California plants while the principal production of sodium chloride for domestic and industrial uses results from the operation of large area solar evaporation vats. Inclusive of the costs of refining, this latter process is becoming economically tenuous in areas of high land values as exemplified in California. Because of the low unit-value of the product, transportation costs are probably one of the principal determinants as to the ability of the product to compete in a specific market area. Anomalously, in view of the comparatively high concentration of sodium chloride in seawater and the probability that formation and accumulation are continuing processes, sodium chloride is probably one of the minerals requiring the least concern as to conservation under any definition.

Some beach areas on the southeastern seaboard of the United States have been a source of radioactive thorium sands. These sands, in theory, upon refining could provide fuel for nuclear energy facilities. Transportable nuclear energy generators have been utilized in isolated offshore operations particularly because of the long fuel life and thus have supplanted less operationally efficient ordinary fuel minerals. However, the principal current utilization of thorium continues to be in the production of high strength alloys.

While not susceptible of classification as a mineral resource, certain physical resources must also be considered in any overview of conservation, particularly to the degree that these physical resources have a potential for supplementing and, currently in limited instances, replacing fuel minerals. Most prominent of these resources under evaluation are the conversion or utilization of tidal energy, ocean currents, and the conversion of the thermal energy in the ocean potentially available from the significant temperature differentials existent at various depths.

A tidal energy utilization project to generate electricity is in operation in a tidal estuary system in France. This system is actuated by the potential energy of the differential in the extreme stages of the tides. A different, unique, prototype system has been announced recently in California for conversion of the tidal energy to provide a high pressure compressed air reservoir for equipment operation. While designed initially as the integral power source for a seawater desalination system, the Aqualectra power system should be universally applicable as an energy source derived from the ocean. The power system operation of the prototype model is described as follows:

The initial power input to the system would be supplied from the energy contained in the ocean waves. A wave is an energy pulse which uses the ocean as a conductor. The waves are allowed to raise and crest into a specially designed trough. The stored water then flows from the elevated trough through a vena contracta which entrains quantities of air into the water. The flowing water delivers the air to the underwater storage chamber. Large quantities of power would be generated under carefully controlled conditions in a very useable form, compressed.

Optimum resource allocation requires the most effective application of the principles of *multiple use* to a specific area to the maximum degree feasible, if for no other reason than that the essential mineral deposits are as located in nature and must be developed at such location without any other feasible alternatives. Required governmental institutional arrangements and protective constraints add yet another dimension of complication to the efficiency of conservation of nonliving resources offshore, primarily because these have been extrapolated from an upland base of experience to an operating domain where experience is comparatively limited. The unique dynamics and environmental factors of the offshore further limit the effectiveness of transferring onshore program designs to offshore developments. Not the least of the complications from institutional arrangements results from artificial, arbitrary offshore political boundaries with each involved jurisdiction specifying varying exploration and development requirements. Obviously, neither living nor nonliving resources give any recognition to such artificial constraints.

As reported in Chapter 3, ocean mining, including petroleum, can include four categories of effects that can have important impact on the living resources of the sea: effects of geophysical prospecting; direct damage to benthic (ocean floor) organisms by mining operations; effects of deposition of mining spoil and other waste materials arising from the mining process; and pollution from beneficiation and processing at sea. All authorizations by the State Lands Commission for offshore operations control any adverse effects of geophysical prospecting through operating constraints specified by the State Lands Commission and the Fish and Game Commission in concurrent permits and through continuous field monitoring during operations by the State Lands Division and the Department of Fish and Game (Appendices 2, 3, 4, and 5). Similarly, direct damage to benthic organisms is minimized by operating permit controls specified by the State Lands Commission and the Fish and Game Commission, while waste discharge and pollution controls prescribed by the Fish and Game Commission and the State Water Resources Control Board are again included in State Lands Commission operating authorizations. All of these control conditions are based upon extensive research and operating experience to assure the elimination of any previously existing defects in the optimization of area multiple use and the conservation of all natural resources.

The effectiveness of directed technological improvements is illustrated by the advances in offshore oil production installations as an example. Figure 2 shows the Summerland Oil Field in Santa

Figure 2. Summerland oil field—1906.

Barbara County on and adjacent to the beach in 1906. At the peak of development over 400 wells were scattered over miles of beach, surf, and the nearshore waters. Figure 3 shows current operating facilities 2 miles offshore the earlier Summerland beach operation which has been eliminated completely. This single compact facility provides the total support for the operation of 22 oil and gas wells. Figure 4 shows an artificially constructed island which provided the complete base for development and production of 42 oil and gas wells. Finally, the unbroken expanse of ocean surface (Figure 5) is typical of the actual location of ocean-floor production operations in California in up to 235 feet of water depth. This type of development is generally most appealing because of the complete elimination of any *visual pollution.* Forty-two such installations have been completed in the Ventura and Santa Barbara County off-

Figure 3.   Platform "Hazel"—Summerland offshore.

Figure 4.   Artificial island operations Rincon oil field.

Figure 5.   Site of ocean-floor oil wells.

shore, twenty-nine for oil and thirteen for gas (Appendix 6, 7). Unfortunately such installations are not yet universally adaptable to all reservoir production conditions, even without consideration of possible economic limitations. The specific gravity and viscosity of the oil to be produced in the low ocean-floor temperatures and the frequency of required repairs, replacements, and cleaning necessitated by sand scouring and wax and other solid depositions, all determine the mechanical feasibility of a specific installation. Here again, technological advances are continuing with the development of superior equipment, ocean-floor containers, and servicing capability through manned submersibles, many types of which are beyond the drawing board stage. Some equipment is already operational, and the balance is undergoing fabrication and prototype testing.

Other primary inputs for balancing the multiple use equation are the compatibility of development operations with other structures, both civilian and military, such as pipelines, cables, protective works, transportation facilities, and offshore loading terminals as reviewed in Chapter 5. Multiple use inputs include also the elimination or minimization of pollution, whether toxic, thermal, or visual, the minimization of detrimental effects on the recreational utilization of the offshore, and the effective preservation of specific areas as marine reserves. Establishment of specific areas has been authorized by statute and are under study for classification as underwater parks, ecological preserves, and for educational marine laboratory purposes and industrial research facilities.

Mathematical economists have approached the resource allocation complex from the standpoints of quantitative measurement of conservation and the establishment of conservation policies. Publications outlining the methodology for the mathematical determination of the degree of conservation by calculation of resource use rates and the determination of the optimum state of conservation appear to be reasonably practicable primarily for analyses of individual resource development.

A technique for an initial one-dimensional graphical analysis of the interrelationships and conflicts of area multiple uses is illustrated by a compatibility matrix (Figure 6). This illustration was provided by Dr. Gordon Lill, Vice-Chairman of the California Advisory Commission on Marine and Coastal Resources. The scope of uses presented is not exhaustive but does list typical uses of priority concern. Specifically, reading both from left to right across the top and top to bottom along the left side of the list, these are as follows.

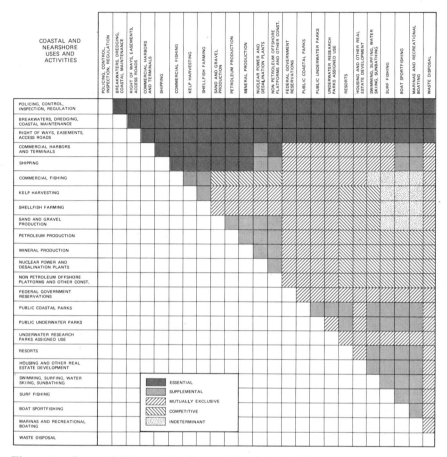

Figure 6. Compatibility matrix. *Source:* Dr. Gordon Lill.

1. Policing, control, inspection, regulation
2. Breakwaters, dredging, coastal maintenance
3. Rights of way easements, access roads
4. Commercial harbors and terminals
5. Shipping
6. Commercial fishing
7. Kelp harvesting
8. Shellfish farming
9. Sand and gravel production
10. Petroleum production
11. Other mineral production

12. Nuclear power and desalination plants
13. Nonpetroleum offshore platforms and other construction
14. Federal government reservations
15. Public coastal parks
16. Public underwater parks
17. Underwater research parks
18. Resorts
19. Housing and other real estate development
20. Swimming, surfing, water skiing, sunbathing
21. Surf fishing
22. Boat sportfishing
23. Marinas and recreational boating
24. Waste disposal

The compatibility terms for uses depicted on this chart are defined as follows.

1. *Essential.* Coastal uses or activities that are essential to orderly coastal and offshore development.

2. *Supplemental.* Coastal uses that eventually tend to supplement one another economically without conflict.

3. *Mutually exclusive.* Only one such coastal use can be accomplished to the exclusion of all others.

4. *Competitive.* Activities that can go on simultaneously, but between which there will always be argument for priority, political favor or position, legal precedence, and such.

5. *Indeterminant.* No discernible relationship; at least none of any consequence.

It must be noted that in this list by grouping uses with the most potential for conflict, the visual impact of the unbroken central area, identified as requiring an exclusive use, may not be precisely related in all instances to the degree of difficulty in effective resource allocation.

In view of the complications for arriving at a preferred discrete solution for optimum resource development, the techniques of operations research, linear programming, and mathematical and analog simulation immediately suggest themselves for application. Here, examples of the state of the art have been reported during the past year in the descriptions of a mathematical model for simulating three-dimensional, three-phase fluid flow in reservoirs, and a petroleum reservoir mathematical model and computer program for prediction of reservoir flow for three immiscible phases (i.e., oil, gas, and water) in two-dimensional geometry. Such analytic tools will be invaluable for optimizing petroleum reservoir development and operation to the best attainable conservation level. This is only a segment of the total conservation complex. However, this does afford a clue to what may be the only currently practical approach to a solution. This approach would require segmenting the problem, analyzing within boundary limits, and combining the segment solutions into entire project solutions, again, within boundary limits.

The petroleum reservoir mathematical models cited were developed for digital computer simulation. In many instances, involving solutions for continuous dynamic systems that can be described by differential equations with time as an independent variable, simulation may be accomplished more efficiently (i.e., in terms of cost and solution time required) by using an analog computer. Obviously the sophisticated analyses available from a hybrid analog-digital computer system are particularly applicable to solutions of a segmented problem.

Then, finally, the selection of a specific conservation solution, or range of solutions, for implementation is currently still primarily dependent upon technical and administrative management decision.

APPENDIX 1. PUBLIC RESOURCES CODE (Excerpts)

DIVISION 6. PUBLIC LANDS

PART 2. LEASING OF PUBLIC LANDS

Chapter 3. Oil and Gas and Mineral Leases
Article 5.5. Geothermal Resources

6903. For the purposes of this chapter, "geothermal resources" shall mean the natural heat of the earth, the energy, in whatever form, below the surface of the earth present in, resulting from, or created by, or which may be extracted from, such natural heat, and all minerals in solution or other products obtained from naturally heated fluids, brines, associated gases, and steam, in whatever form, found below the surface of the earth, but excluding oil, hydrocarbon gas or other hydrocarbon substances.
(Added by Ch. 1398, Stats. 1967 (SB 169))

6904. Prospecting permits and leases for the extraction and removal of geothermal resources from lands belonging to the state may be issued by the commission as provided in this article. For purposes of this article, state lands shall be defined as all lands owned by the state, including school lands, proprietary lands, tidelands, submerged lands, swamp and over-flowed lands, and beds of navigable rivers and lakes, and lands in which geothermal resources have been reserved to the state.

(Added by Ch. 1398, Stats. 1967 (SB 169))

6906. Administration of this article shall be under the principle of multiple use of public lands and resources, and shall allow coexistence of other permits or leases of the same lands for deposits of other minerals under applicable laws, and the existence of permits or leases issued pursuant to the provisions of this article shall not preclude other uses of the areas covered thereby. However, operations under such other permits or leases or such other uses shall not unreasonably interfere with or endanger operations under any permit or lease issued pursuant to this article, nor shall operations under permits or leases issued pursuant to the provisions of this article unreasonably interfere with or endanger operations under any permit or lease issued pursuant to the provisions of any other act. Nor shall this article be construed as superseding the authority which the head of any state department or agency has with respect to the management, protection, and utilization of the state lands and resources under his jurisdiction. The commission may prescribe in its rules and regulations those conditions it deems to be necessary for the protection of other resources.

(Added by Ch. 1398, Stats. 1967 (SB 169))

6907. Where it is determined by the commission independently or on advice of the Geothermal Resources Board that the production or use of geothermal resources is also susceptible of economically producing other of the geothermal resources in commercially valuable quantities, and a market therefor exists, production of such other geothermal resources may be required by the commission.

(Added by Ch. 1398, Stats. 1967 (SB 169))

6908. An application for a prospecting permit or lease shall not be made for less than 640 acres nor more than 2,560 acres and shall embrace a reasonably compact area; provided, however, that a permit or lease may be issued for a parcel less than 640 acres if such parcel is isolated from or not contiguous with other parcels of land available for permit or lease hereunder. The commission may provide for compensatory agreements on those parcels of state land which it feels should be subjected to such agreements rather than to leasing thereof. No person, association, or corporation shall take, hold, own, or control at one time, whether acquired directly from the commission under this act or otherwise, any direct or indirect interests in state geothermal leases exceeding 25,600 acres. Prospecting permits or leases for lands beneath lakes and rivers, and below the mean high tide level of tide and submerged lands, may be issued for not less than 640 acres nor more than 5,760 acres and shall embrace a reasonably compact area, except that a permit or lease may be issued for a parcel less than 640 acres if such parcel is isolated from or not contiguous with other parcels of land available for permit or lease hereunder. No limitation shall apply to the number of permits or leases granted under this act.

(Added by Ch. 1398, Stats. 1967 (SB 169))

6909. Subject to the provisions of Section 6906, for the commission shall issue a permit to the first qualified applicant therefor under such rules and regulations as it may prescribe for lands which have not been classified as known geothermal resources lands, upon the payment to the commission of one dollar ($1) per acre for each acre of lands included in the permit, in accordance with subdivision (c) of Section 6913 of this code. An application for a permit shall be denied if, prior to the issuance of the permit, the lands are classified or reclassified as known geothermal resources lands pursuant to subdivision (b) of Section 6912.

(Added by Ch. 1398, Stats. 1967 (SB 169))

6910. A permit shall give to the permittee the exclusive right for a period of three years to prospect for geothermal resources upon lands included within said permit. The commission may, in its discretion, extend the primary term of any permit for a period not exceeding two years; provided that the combination of the primary term and extension of any permit shall not exceed a total of five years. The commission may amend or terminate any permit issued by it within the primary term period or within the extension, if any, with the consent of the permittee.

(Added by Ch. 1398, Stats. 1967 (SB 169))

6911. Upon the classification of any of the lands included within a permit issued under this article as being known geothermal resources lands, the permittee shall be entitled to a lease for such lands in accordance with Section 6918 of this code. The classification of any such lands shall be made in accordance with subdivision (b) of Section 6912 of this code. The terms of such lease shall include the royalties and other terms contained in Section 6913 on the effective date of the lease.

(Added by Ch. 1398, Stats. 1967 (SB 169))

6912. (a) If the lands to be leased under this article are within a known geothermal resources area and no permit thereon has been issued, such lands shall be leased to the highest responsible qualified bidder under such rules and regulations as the commission may prescribe for notice to the public of terms and conditions of the sale, conduct of the sale, receipt of bid, and awarding of the lease, and bidding shall be by competitive bid and on the basis of a cash bonus, net profit, or other single biddable factor.

(b) The classification of a known geothermal resources area, which shall contain at least one well capable of producing geothermal resources in commercial quantities, shall be made by the commission independently or upon recommendations of the Geothermal Resources Board.

(c) The commission shall have the power in leasing lands hereunder to prescribe a development program. In prescribing such program, the commission shall consider all applicable economic factors, including market conditions and the cost of drilling for, producing, processing and utilizing of geothermal resources.

(Added by Ch. 1398, Stats. 1967 (SB 169))

6913. Each permit and lease issued under this article shall provide for the following rentals and royalties with respect to geothermal resources produced, saved and sold from the lands included within said permit or lease:

(a) A royalty of 10 percent of the gross revenue, exclusive of charges, approved by the commission, made or incurred with respect to transmission or other services or processes, received from the sale of steam, brines, from which no minerals have been extracted, and associated gases at the point of delivery to the purchaser thereof.

(b) A royalty of not less than 2 percent nor more than 10 percent of the gross revenue received from the sale of mineral products or chemical compounds recovered from geothermal fluids in the first marketable form as to each such mineral product or chemical compound for the primary term of the lease.

(c) An annual rental payable in advance of one dollar ($1) per acre or fraction thereof for each year of a permit or lease.

(d) If, after the discovery of geothermal resources in commercial quantities, the total royalties due to the state during any calendar year do not equal or exceed a sum equal to two dollars ($2) per acre for each acre or fraction thereof then included in the permit or lease, the permittee or the lessee shall, within 60 days after the end of the year, pay such sum as is necessary to equal a minimum royalty of two dollars ($2) per acre.

(e) The royalties specified herein shall be subject to renegotiation after 20 years from the effective date of the lease and at 10-year intervals thereafter based upon recommendations of the Geothermal Resources Board, and such renegotiations shall not be limited by the maximum royalties specified in subdivisions (a) and (b).

Royalty payments shall be made pursuant to the provisions of subdivisions (a) and (b) for all geothermal resources used by the permittee or lessee and not sold, with the gross revenue therefrom to be determined as though said geothermal resources had been sold to a third person at the then prevailing market price in the same market area and under the same marketing conditions; provided, however, that no royalties shall be payable for steam used by the permittee or lessee in the production of any geothermal mineral products or chemical compounds recovered from geothermal fluids in first marketable form subject to the payment of royalties under subdivisions (a) or (b).

(Added by Ch. 1398, Stats. 1967 (SB 169))

6914. The holder of any geothermal resources permit or lease may quitclaim or relinquish his rights under such permit or lease pursuant to the provisions of Section 6804.1 of this code.

(Added by Ch. 1398, Stats. 1967 (SB 169))

6915.　Subject to the other provisions of this article, the permittee or lessee shall be entitled to use so much of the surface as is reasonably necessary as determined by the commission for the production and conservation of geothermal resources.

(Added by Ch. 1398, Stats. 1967 (SB 169))

6916.　The commission independently or upon the advice of the Geothermal Resources Board, may waive, suspend, or reduce the rental or minimum royalty for the lands included in any permit or lease, or any portion thereof, and waive, suspend, alter or amend the operating requirements contained in the lease or regulations promulgated hereunder affecting operations of the lease or permit, in the interests of conservation, and to encourage the greatest ultimate recovery of geothermal resources if it determines that such action is necessary or beneficial to promote development or finds that the permit or lease cannot be successfully operated under the permit or lease terms or under the regulations. The commission shall file a report with the Legislature annually on all waivers, suspensions, reductions, alterations or amendments made by the commission pursuant to the provisions of this section together with the reasons therefor.

(Added by Ch. 1398, Stats. 1967 (SB 169))

6918.　Leases under this article shall be for a primary term of 20 years and so long thereafter as geothermal resources are being produced or utilized or are capable of being produced or utilized in commercial quantities from such lands or from lands unitized therewith; provided, that such leases shall not exceed a term of 99 years.

(Added by Ch. 1398, Stats. 1967 (SB 169))

6920.　Any person engaged in the production of geothermal resources under a lease issued by the commission may commingle geothermal resources from any two or more wells without regard to whether such wells are located on the lands for which such lease was issued or elsewhere, provided, however, that said lessee shall install and maintain meters or other measuring devices satisfactory to the commission to measure the amount of geothermal resources produced from lands for which leases were issued by the commission.

(Added by Ch. 1398, Stats. 1967 (SB 169))

6921.　A permittee or lessee may upon the approval of the commission drill special wells, convert producing wells or reactivate and convert abandoned wells for the sole purpose of reinjecting geothermal resources or the residue thereof.

(Added by Ch. 1398, Stats. 1967 (SB 169))

6923.　For the purpose of more properly conserving the natural resources of any geothermal resources areas, or any part thereof, the lessees thereof may unite with each other or with others in collectively adopting and operating under a cooperative or unit plan of development or operation of such geothermal resources lands, consistent with the provisions of Section 3756 of this code. The commission may, with the consent of the holders of leases involved, establish, alter, change, and revoke any drilling and production requirements of such leases, permit apportionment of production, and may make such regulations with reference to such leases, with like consent on the part of such lessees, in connection with the institution and operation of any such cooperative or unit plan, as the commission deems necessary or proper to secure the proper protection of the interests of the state.

(Added by Ch. 1398, Stats. 1967 (SB 169))

APPENDIX 2.   PUBLIC RESOURCES CODE (Excerpts)

DIVISION 6.   PUBLIC LANDS

PART 2.   LEASING OF PUBLIC LANDS

Chapter 3.   Oil and Gas and Mineral Leases
Article 2.   Provisions Relating to Oil and Gas Leases Generally

6826. The commission may permit geological or geophysical surveys on state lands and may grant permits therefor upon such terms and conditions as the commission shall specify by regulation, but any such permit shall not give the permittee any preferential right to an oil and gas lease. The taking of cores and other sample may be conducted on and under state lands; provided, that the commission shall require that a permit first be obtained covering such types of drilling operations for the purpose of obtaining geological samples as the commission may determine by regulation, such permit to be issued upon such terms and conditions as the commission may specify by regulation, but any such permit shall not give the permittee any preferential right to an oil and gas lease.

The commission shall require, as a condition to the issuance of any permit for the conduct of geological or geophysical surveys on tide and submerged lands under this section, that the permittee make available to the commission, upon request, all factual and physical exploration results, logs, and records resulting from the operations under the permit. Any such factual or physical exploration results, logs, or records which the permittee is required to make available to the commission shall be for the confidential use of the commission and shall not be open to inspection by any other person or agency without the written consent of the permittee.

It is a misdemeanor for any member of the commission, any officer or employee of the commission, or any person performing any function or work assigned to him by the commission, to disclose to any person who is not a member, officer, employee of the commission or to any person who is not performing any function or work assigned to him by the commission, any information obtained from the inspection of such factual or physical exploration results, logs, or records, or to use such information for purposes other than the administration of the functions, responsibilities, and duties vested in the commission by law, except upon the written consent of the permittee making available such information to the commission.

(Amended by Ch. 1945, Stats. 1963.)

APPENDIX 3. PERMIT FOR THE CONDUCT OF GEOPHYSICAL SURVEYS ON TIDE AND SUBMERGED LANDS OF THE STATE OF CALIFORNIA

W.O. _____

P.R.C. _____

Date _____

Permission is granted hereby to _____ for the conduct of submarine seismic exploration work during the period _____ through _____, on those tide and submerged lands under the jurisdiction of the State Lands Commission in the area lying between the seaward extension of the northern boundary of Mendocino County and the southern boundary of the State of California, excepting the following-described areas:

A. San Francisco Bay and other inland waters draining therein;

B. Lands included in Section 6871.2(b) of the Public Resources Code;

C. Lands lying adjacent to the mainland between a line forming the Northwesterly Boundary of the City of Newport Beach, Orange County, and the seaward extension thereof, and a line forming the Southeasterly Boundary of Orange County and the seaward extension thereof.

D. All tide and submerged lands in Monterey County including Monterey Bay.

The conduct of any operations under this permit is subject to the following specific conditions:

1. No explosives shall be discharged under any circumstances unless an inspector of the State Lands Division is aboard the recording boat of each seismic crew in operation, or permission to proceed with the discharge of explosives has been given by such inspector of the State Lands Division. In the event that the inspector determines that the proposed discharge of explosives at any location within the area covered by this permit may affect the safety of any vessel, structure or person, said inspector shall prohibit the proposed discharge of explosives.

2. Operations shall be suspended on order of the State Lands Division inspector whenever and for such time as may be required to establish that the conditions of this permit are being complied with.

3. A copy of the schedule of operations to be conducted during the following 24-hour period shall be furnished to the State Lands Division inspector on or before the close of the preceding day's shooting schedule. Such schedule shall be complete in detail as to location, number size, and type of placement of shots to be fired. Divergence from such schedule may be permitted only upon specific authorization of the State Lands Division inspector prior to firing.

4. A copy of a daily log of operations, showing date, location, number, size and type of placement of detonation shall be furnished to the State Lands Division inspector within 24 hours of the completion of the day's shooting schedule.

5. Specific compliance must be had with any and all requirements of any permit issued by the State Department of Fish and Game operations in the permitted area.

6. Only explosives of a size or type as authorized under concurrent permit by the Fish and Game Commission shall be used in submarine seismic exploration operations whether shots are "jetted" or are "open". No shots shall be permitted at a distance closer than one-quarter statute mile from the ordinary high water mark or one-half statute mile from any structure.

7. Explosive charges may be placed only in areas of water sufficiently clear of kelp to minimize physical damage from the detonation of any submarine seismic exploration shots.

8. No shots shall be permitted:

    (a) At distances closer than one statute mile from the ordinary high water mark in the offshore Santa Barbara County area between a line drawn due South from Gaviota and the projection seaward of the Santa Barbara-Ventura County Line.

    (b) At distances closer than one-quarter statute mile from the ordinary high water mark in the balance of the Santa Barbara County offshore area.

    (c)   At distances closer than one statute mile from the ordinary high water mark in the adjoining residential areas of the cities of Ventura and Port Hueneme, Ventura County.

9.   Violation of any of the provisions of this permit, or of any permit issued by the State Department of Fish and Game for the same area, shall result in immediate suspension of all operations on orders given by the State Lands Division inspector assigned to the project, and may result in termination of the permit by order of the Executive Officer, State Lands Commission. Such terminated permit may be reinstated only by action of the State Lands Commission.

10.   For each seismic crew in operation, the permittee shall make an advance deposit of $800 before the commencement of operations under this permit, and $800 every calendar month thereafter, as a minimum deposit to defray the costs of the State Lands Division that are involved in inspection under this permit. Actual costs to the State Lands Division of such inspection which are in excess of the aforesaid minimum deposit shall be remitted by the permittee upon receipt of a statement of such additional costs.

11.   The permittee agrees to indemnify the State against any and all losses, damages, claims, demands, or actions caused by, arising out of, or connected with the operations of the permittee hereunder.

12.   This permit shall be effective only when a concurrent permit for the same operating area specified herein is authorized by the State Fish and Game Commission.

13.   The State Lands Commission reserves the right to inspect and, upon request by the Commission, the permittee shall make available for such inspection all factual and physical exploration results, logs, and records resulting from the operations under this permit for the confidential use of the Commission.

This permit is revocable at any time by the State Lands Commission.

STATE LANDS COMMISSION

_____

MAILED IN TRIPLICATE

All terms, conditions and provisions
of the foregoing permit are accepted
by the applicant:

By   _____

Title   _____

Date   _____

APPENDIX 4

Excerpt from Title 14, California Administrative Code (Revised June 1962)

225. Seismic Explorations. The following are the regulations under which permits are granted to use explosives in the waters of this State inhabited by fish, insofar as such explosives may be used for seismic explorations.

(a) Applications to the Commission for seismic permits shall be made to the Commission at least thirty (30) days prior to the date of the Commission meeting at which the application will be considered, and shall be made according to a standard form supplied by the Commission. Applications for renewal, supplemental action, or amendments shall be made at least fifteen (15) days prior to such meeting.

(b) Permits shall be issued in such a manner as will result in a minimum destruction to marine life and fisheries.

(c) No explosives shall be used except the following:

(1) Deflagrating explosives, such as black powder, or any other "low" explosive which in the opinion of the department is equivalent to it. For exploding black powder, no more than one (1) electric blasting cap and one (1) length of detonating fuse not to exceed six (6) feet in length or of greater strength than fifty (50) grains of explosive per foot, shall be used for each container. Means for exploding deflagrating explosives other than black powder are subject to approval of the department. The amount of deflagrating explosives to be used at each shot point shall not exceed ninety (90) pounds.

(2) Detonating explosives, such as nitro-carbo-nitrate, or any other "high" explosive which in the opinion of the department is equivalent to it. For exploding detonating explosives of the nitro-carbo-nitrate type, no more than one (1) electric blasting cap and one (1) commercial booster shall be used for each container. Means for exploding detonating explosives other than nitro-carbo-nitrate are subject to approval of the department. The amount of detonating explosives to be used at each shot point in waters of less than two hundred (200) feet in depth shall not exceed five (5) pounds. The amount of detonating explosives to be used at each shot point in waters of greater depth than two hundred (200) feet shall not exceed twenty (20) pounds.

No unjetted explosive charges shall be detonated within one-half (½) mile of any breakwater, jetty, pier, or anchored fishing boat or barge. No explosive charges shall be detonated in a kelp bed as designated by the department observer or within three hundred (300) feet of the fringe thereof, or within one-half (½) mile of the mouth of any stream when the department observer finds that a concentration of fish may be endangered.

(d) An employee of the Department of Fish and Game shall accompany the boat or crew which is conducting the exploratory work. This observer shall have the authority to stop operations in any given area if, in his opinion, undue damage to marine life occurs, or to stop temporarily or slow up operations until the observer can clearly determine the amount of animals killed. Operations also may be temporarily suspended when in opinion of observer, after consultation with party chief, it is determined that weather conditions make further operations unsafe for personnel and equipment or when equipment breakdowns result in unsatisfactory observations of marine life.

A boat and crew, satisfactory to the department, shall be provided for the observer at all times and during operations shall not be used for any other purpose. One of the crew members must be competent in the operation of the communication and fish-detecting devices described below. Radio-telephone communications between the observer boat and the operating boat shall be maintained at all times when explosives are being detonated. A recording depth-indicator and a modern-type of sonar or fish-detecting device satisfactory to the department shall be provided for the observer boat. The observer boat shall carry, and the crew shall help operate such gear and equipment for determining damage to marine life as the observer shall furnish, and permittee shall meet any expense of gear rental or operation that may be incurred. The observer boat and all equipment, including communication and fish-detecting devices, must be kept in good working condition at all times.

(e) The applicant shall defray the cost of such observer's services and all administrative and incidental costs by payment to the Department of Fish and Game, Sacramento, California, for the benefit of the Fish and Game Preservation Fund the minimum deposit of seven hundred fifty dollars ($750) per survey crew for each month for which a permit is requested, said month commencing the date on which said permit becomes effective, whether operations are commenced on that date or not. A similar minimum deposit of seven hundred fifty dollars ($750) per month shall be made fifteen (15) days prior to the addition of every crew not specified in original application for permit.

This sum shall be paid as follows:

(1) The minimum payment due prior to issuance or a renewal of a permit shall be seven hundred fifty dollars ($750) for each month or

fraction of a month covered by the permit, and shall accompany the application.

(2) Expenses as they accrue to the department shall be charged against this minimum deposit.

(3) At the expiration of the permit, the cancellation of operations, or the denial of the application, any sum remaining over and above those expenses incurred by the department shall be refunded within thirty (30) days.

(4) Any expenses incurred by the department in connection with the permit over and above the minimum deposits shall be due and payable upon billing by the department.

(5) Any temporary cessation of seismic operations of thirty (30) days or less shall be considered as an expense to the department in the amount of the observer's monthly salary and associated administrative costs.

(f) Before beginning any day's operations, permission to detonate must be obtained from the observer and such permission must also be obtained during the day if the observer has temporarily stopped work due to excessive damage to marine life.

(g) All fish of edible size which may be killed shall be picked up by the operating crew, and arrangements made by the permittee for their disposal subject to approval of the department. If sold any money received from such sale shall be paid into the Fish and Game Preservation Fund. When in the judgment of the observer an excessive amount of fish has been killed and washed onto any shore in such quantities as to endanger public health or create a nuisance, the permittee shall immediately gather up and dispose of such fish in a manner satisfactory to the observer.

(h) Anyone applying for or holding a permit shall notify the Sacramento Headquarters Office of the Department of Fish and Game, or the office designated in the permit, in writing not less than fifteen (15) days before beginning operations or before adding a survey crew, and not less than five (5) days before transferring a crew between permits held by the same permittee. Notification of intention to terminate operations or to suspend operations more than thirty (30) days shall also be given in writing not less than fifteen (15) days in advance of such termination. Copies of all notices and reports shall be sent to the Sacramento Headquarters Office. At least twenty-four (24) hours before commencing operations within three (3) miles of shore, or in any new area whose boundaries shall be defined in the permit, where he has not operated during the preceding one (1) month, the permittee shall discuss the forthcoming operations with the department at Sacramento Headquarters or other office as designated in the permit.

(i) On the fifteenth and last days of each month of operation, the permittee shall submit a report of dates, location, and number of detonations made in the preceding period. A report shall be submitted for each permit for each half-month period whether operations were actually conducted or not. The report shall include the species and weight of edible fish disposed of, as provided in paragraph (g), and the name of the recipient. Reports shall be submitted in duplicate in the manner provided for above in (h).

(j) All permits shall be issued for a period of not to exceed six (6) months, but may be renewed from time to time thereafter, for such periods not to exceed six (6) months at a time, as the Fish and Game Commission may approve. Separate permits are required for: (1) The ocean waters; (2) Each inland water operation regardless of location.

(k) Every permittee shall post a copy of said permit in a conspicuous place aboard the main survey vessel where it can be inspected by the observer and survey crew at any time.

(l) No permit granted pursuant to these regulations shall be valid or exercised unless at the same time the permittee has a permit in full force and effect issued by the State Lands Commission of California and authorizing such seismic operations.

(m) All permits shall be subject to revocation at any time.

APPENDIX 5

Seismic Permit

To Whom It May Concern:

In accordance with authorization granted by the Commission at its regular meeting on   and insofar as the Department of Fish and Game is concerned, permission is hereby granted to

to use explosives in the waters of the Pacific Ocean for seismic exploration purposes in offshore waters between the seaward extension of the boundary between Oregon and California and the seaward extension of the boundary between Mexico and California.

The permittee shall not be required to supply a separate boat and crew for the Department observer provided an observer is aboard each shooting boat when explosives are being used on two such boats. Each shooting boat shall be equipped with a fish detecting device in good operating condition with a competent operator in attendance. The Department observer shall be accorded any desired use of the fish detecting device. A separate observer boat and crew shall be provided by the permittee when only one shooting boat is being used in the exploration work.

The permittee is authorized to use a total of   charges of explosives weighing   pounds each, and   charges weighing   pounds each. The permittee shall confine the use of these special explosive charges to the area within the Santa Barbara Channel as outlined on charts previously presented to the Department, and in the area offshore from the general vicinity of Santa Cruz County and San Mateo County. Such explosives shall not be used within three (3) nautical miles of the low tide line of the mainland shore or the shore of any island.

The following additional restrictions, limitations and requirements shall apply to this permit:

1. Permittee shall, if requested by the observer, immediately suspend shooting activity and shall allow the observer full use of the shooting boat to survey and assess damage or suspected damage to fish life, and shall assist the observer in recovering any specimens of fish killed at a shot point.

2. North of Point Ano Nuevo, operations may be conducted inside the 40 fathom curve only as specifically approved by Terminal Island personnel. Detailed plans showing the proposed shot lines within the 40 fathom curve and the approximate dates when shooting will be done shall be submitted to the Terminal Island office of the Department for review.

3. At least 15 days prior to commencing any seismic work under this permit, permittee shall submit copies of proposed plans of operation to the Wildlife Protection Branch, Department of Fish and Game, 511 Tuna Street, San Pedro, for additional evaluation of the effects such operations may have on aquatic life. Such plans shall be explicit in regard to area and proposed dates of operation. Seismic work shall not be conducted contrary to recommendations issued by Wildlife Protection personnel.

4. The permittee, prior to using explosive charges of 100 or 300 pounds weight offshore from Santa Cruz and San Mateo Counties, shall discuss the proposed use with appropriate Department personnel at the Marine Resources Operations Office in Menlo Park, and shall use the explosives only in accordance with their recommendations and upon their approval.

5. All other standard provisions of the seismic regulations shall apply to this permit. A copy of the seismic regulations, Section 225, Title 14, California Administrative Code, is attached to this permit and is a part of this permit.

This permit shall be valid from   through

DEPARTMENT OF FISH AND GAME

Director

APPENDIX 6. PUBLIC RESOURCES CODE (Excerpts)

DIVISION 6. PUBLIC LANDS

PART 2. LEASING OF PUBLIC LANDS

Chapter 3. Oil and Gas and Mineral Leases
Article 2. Provisions Relating to Oil and Gas Leases Generally

6829. Every oil and gas lease executed under this chapter shall include the following:

(a) Such terms, conditions, and provisions as will protect the interests of the State with reference to securing the payment to the State of the proper amount or value of production.

(b) Such terms, conditions and provisions as will protect the interests of the State with reference to the spacing of wells for the purpose of properly offsetting the drainage of oil and gas from state lands by wells drilled and operated on and within privately owned lands; diligence on the part of the lessee in drilling wells to the oil sands and requirements as to depth of such wells for the purpose of reaching the oil sands and producing oil and gas therefrom in commercial quantities.

(c) Provisions specifying methods of operation and standard requirements for carrying on operations in proper and workmanlike manner; the prevention of waste; the protection of the safety and health of workmen; and the liability of the lessee for personal injuries and property damage.

(d) Security for faithful performance by the lessee, including provisions for the forfeiture of the lease, as set forth in Section 6805, and the requirement that the lessee shall, at the time of execution of the lease, furnish and thereafter maintain a good and sufficient bond in such sum as may be specified by the commission, in favor of the State, guaranteeing faithful performance by the lessee of the terms, covenants, and conditions of the lease and of the provisions of this chapter.

(e) Such other covenants, conditions, requirements, and reservations as may be deemed advisable by the commission in effecting the purpose of this chapter and not inconsistent with any of its provisions; provided, that any provision of an oil and gas lease executed under this chapter which purports to deprive the State or a lessee of any right or benefit secured by law, or is otherwise inconsistent with the provisions of this chapter, shall be void, and shall be deemed separable from and without effect upon the valid provisions of such lease.

6830. All oil and gas leases issued by the commission for lands under its jurisdiction as set forth in Chapters 3 and 4 of Part 1 and in Chapter 3 of Part 2 of Division 6 of this code shall contain a reservation to the commission of the right to determine the spacing of wells and the rate of drilling and rate of production of such wells so as to prevent the waste of oil and gas and promote the maximum economic recovery of oil and gas from, and the conservation of reservoir energy in, each zone or separate underground source of supply of oil or gas covered in whole or in part by leases issued under this chapter.

6830.1 It is hereby found and determined by the Legislature of the State of California as follows:

(a) That the people of the State of California have a direct and primary interest in assuring the production of the optimum quantities of oil and gas from lands owned by the State, and that a minimum of oil and gas be left wasted and unrecovered in such lands.

(b) That the state owns tide and submerged lands, which lands have been developed under oil and gas leases issued by the state to such extent that it is desirable that secondary operations be undertaken within such lands in an effort to obtain the maximum economic ultimate recovery of oil and gas from said lands; and that it is desirable that the carrying on of secondary recovery operations in such lands be encouraged, which operations the holders of such leases may otherwise not undertake because certain of the leases covering such lands provide for the payment of graduated royalties dependent upon daily per well rates of oil production (which, in the case of multiple completions, means the separately measured average daily production from each zone produced through a separate string of tubing or through casing which is not in communication with any other zone), which graduated royalties were established without contemplation of secondary recovery operations and the economics respecting such operations.

The definition relating to multiple completions set forth herein shall apply to leases executed on or after the effective date of the amendments made to this section at the 1966 Second Extraordinary Session of the Legislature and may, with the approval of the commission, apply to oil produced from leased lands with respect to which the commission and the holder of the lease shall, on or after the effective date of such amendments, enter into an amendatory agreement pursuant to Section 6830.2. It is not the intention of the Legislature in enacting this paragraph to declare the law relating to the computation of daily per well rates of oil production from multiple completions before the effective date of such amendments or in the absence of such an amendatory agreement. (Amended by Ch. 7, Stats. 1966, 2d E.S., effective October 7, 1966.)

6830.2 Whenever the holder of an oil and gas lease of state-owned lands proposes to engage in secondary recovery operations within such lease, the commission and the holder of the lease may mutually agree to modifications of the lease in furtherance of such proposal and with the object of obtaining the maximum economic ultimate recovery of oil and gas from the lands included within such lease, so far as such is reasonably practicable.

Any such amendatory agreement shall contain provisions to assure, so far as reasonably practicable:

(a) That the total royalty production to which the state shall thereafter be entitled shall be no less than the total royalty production to which the state would thereafter have been entitled if such lease had continued to be operated under primary recovery methods, absent any secondary recovery operations, and (b) that the royalty production accruing to the state from the additional oil produced, if any, as a result of the conduct of secondary recovery operations shall be calculated and determined in such manner as to be at least as great in proportion to such additional oil as the royalty production agreed upon in conformance with subdivision (a) of this section is in proportion to the total remaining primary production agreed upon in conformance with subdivision (a).

As a basis for making a determination that it is in the best interests of the state that it enter into such an agreement, and before authorizing the execution thereof, and to determine the appropriate royalty rates on primary and on additional production, the commission shall, using all information available to it, make a calculated projection of the volume of primary royalty to which the state would be entitled under the existing royalty provisions of the lease for the zone or zones involved in the proposal, absent secondary recovery operations, and shall compare its determinations with those of the holder of the lease in an effort to arrive at a mutual agreement.

(Amended by Ch. 7, Stats. 1966, 2d E.S., effective October 7, 1966.)

6830.3 In satisfaction of the requirements of subdivisions (a) and (b) of Section 6830.2, the commission may consider, use, apply or adopt any means, methods, formulas or data available to it in order to arrive, in accordance with generally recognized good engineering practice, at any provisions to be included in any agreement amendatory to the lease, mutually acceptable to the holder of the lease, including the rate or rates of royalty to be applied, and otherwise in conformity with the provisions of this section and Section 6830.2.

The royalty rate or rates to be applied during secondary recovery operations shall in no event be less than the minimum royalty provided by the lease prior to any amendment thereof entered into pursuant to this section and Section 6830.2, but nothing in this section and Section 6830.2 is intended to require that the holder of the lease shall account to the State for a guaranteed quantity of royalty production, but neither shall it prohibit the holder of the lease from guaranteeing to the State any given quantity of royalty production.

Amendatory agreements entered into pursuant to and in conformity with this section and Section 6830.2 may be made in conjunction with agreements entered into for the purpose of effecting a co-operative or unit plan of development pursuant to the provisions of this code, including Section 6832 thereof.

6832. For the purpose of more properly conserving the natural resources of any oil or gas pool or field, or any part thereof, lessees hereunder and their representatives may unite with each other jointly or separately, or jointly or separately with others owning or operating lands not belonging to the State, including lands belonging to the United States, in collectively adopting and operating under a cooperative or unit plan of development or operation of the pool or field, or any part thereof, whenever it is determined by the commission to be necessary or advisable in the public interest. The commission may, with the consent of the holders of leases involved, establish, alter, change, and revoke any drilling and production requirements of such leases, permit apportionment of production, and may make such regulations with reference to such leases, with like consent on the part of such lessees, in connection with the institution and operation of any such cooperative or unit plan, as the commission deems necessary or proper to secure the proper protection of the interests of the State.

6833. The commission, upon such conditions as the commission shall prescribe, may approve operating, drilling or development contracts made by one or more lessees holding oil or gas leases on State lands with one or more persons, associations, or corporations, whenever in the discretion of the commission the conservation of natural products or the public convenience and necessity require it, or the interests of the State may be best subserved thereby.

6873. When leasing tide or submerged lands or beds of navigable rivers or lakes, the commission shall prepare a form of lease which shall contain, in addition to other provisions deemed desirable and necessary by the commission, appropriate provisions contained in this chapter and the following:

(b) Pollution and contamination of the ocean, and tidelands, or navigable rivers or lakes, and all impairment of and interference with bathing, fishing or navigation in the waters of the ocean or any bay or inlet thereof, or any navigable river or lake, is prohibited, and no oil, tar, residuary product of oil or any refuse of any kind from any well or works shall be permitted to be deposited on or pass into the waters of the ocean or any bay or inlet thereof or any navigable river or lake; provided, however, that this subsection (b) shall not be deemed to apply to deposit on or passage into said waters of water not containing any hydrocarbons or vegetable or animal matter.

6873.2 Before offering any tide or submerged land area or beds of navigable rivers or lakes in any area for an oil and gas lease, the commission shall publish notice thereof, and any affected city or county may, within thirty (30) days after the publication of such notice, request in writing to the commission that a hearing be held with respect thereto.

Upon receipt of such request, the commission shall hold such a hearing and give not less than ten (10) days' written notice thereof to the city or county, or both such city and county, making such request, and to the Department of Parks and Recreation, and shall publish such notice. The commission in its discretion and irrespective of any such requests may hold such hearings as it shall determine. Published notices shall be given in the manner prescribed in Section 6834 of this chapter.

In not less than thirty (30) days after such hearing the commission shall determine whether or not to offer the lands for lease, as provided under Sections 6871.3, 6872 and 6872.1. In such determination the commission shall consider whether the issuance of a lease as to all or a part of such lands would result in an impairment or interference with the developed riverbank or shoreline recreational or residential areas adjacent to the proposed leased acreage, or whether to offer such land for lease as to all or a part thereof and include in the offer for lease such reasonable rules and regulations which, in the opinion of the commission, are necessary for the exploration, development, and operation of said lease in a manner which will not impair or interfere with said developed riverbank or shoreline recreational or residential areas; provided, however, that no tide or submerged lands or beds of navigable rivers or lakes shall be offered for lease under any conditions, rules, or regulations which will result in a discrimination between bidders as prohibited by Section 6874.

The commission in determining whether the issuance of such lease or leases would result in such impairment or interference with the developed riverbank or shoreline, recreational or residential areas adjacent to the proposed leased acreage or in determining such rules and regulations as shall be necessary in connection therewith shall at said hearing receive evidence upon and consider whether such proposed lease or leases would

(a) Be detrimental to the health, safety, comfort, convenience, or welfare of persons residing in, owning real property, or working in the neighborhood of such areas;

(b) Interfere with the developed riverbank or shoreline, residential or recreational areas to an extent that would render such areas unfit for recreational or residential uses or unfit for park purposes;

(c) Destroy, impair, or interfere with the esthetic and scenic value of such recreational, residential or park areas;

(d) Create any fire hazard or hazards, or smoke, smog, or dust nuisance, or pollution of waters surrounding or adjoining said areas.

Authority to hold the hearings provided in this section may be delegated by the commission to its officers or employees.

APPENDIX 7.   CALIFORNIA ADMINISTRATIVE CODE

TITLE 2.   ADMINISTRATION

DIVISION 3.   STATE PROPERTY OPERATIONS

Inclusive of Register 64, No. 17—8/15/64 (Excerpts)

ARTICLE 3.   Oil and Gas Leases, Exploration Permits, and Operating Requirements

2122.   Lease Operation Offshore.

For all wells drilled from filled land or other drillsites or structure or structures located seaward of the ordinary high water mark, operations that may be conducted shall conform with the following:

(a) The lessee shall remove the derrick from each well within sixty (60) days after lessee has ceased making use of such derrick in its operations on and with respect to such well.

(b) In the discretion of the commission, all permanent operating sites shall be landscaped with shrubbery, or fenced, so as to screen from public view as far as possible the tanks, pumps or other permanent equipment. Such landscaping and shrubbery, or fencing, are to be kept in good condition.

(c) Oil, tar, or other residuary products of oil, or any refuse of any kind from any well or works, shall be disposed of on shore in a dumping area in conformance with local regulatory requirements.

(d) Suitable and adequate sanitary toilet and washing facilities shall be installed and maintained in a clean and sanitary condition at all times for the use of lessee's personnel.

(e) All drilling and production operations shall be conducted in such manner as to eliminate as far as practicable dust, noise, vibration, or noxious odors.

(f) Pollution and contamination of the ocean and tide lands and all impairment of and interference with bathing, fishing, or navigation in the waters of the ocean or any bay or inlet thereof is prohibited, and no oil, tar, residuary product of oil or any refuse of any kind from any well or works shall be permitted to be deposited on or pass into the waters of the ocean or any bay or inlet thereof.

(g) No permanent filled lands, piers, platforms, or other fixed or floating structures in, on, or over the tide and submerged lands covered by the lease or otherwise available to the lessee shall be permitted to be constructed, used, maintained, or operated where service of less than 20 wells is provided for, without specific authority by the commission. Operating wells not meeting the foregoing requirement shall be completed below such elevation as may be required in each case by the United States, the State, or other competent authority, with the production piped along or below the floor of the ocean to such receiving points as the commission may determine or approve. For nonoperative wells the structures or facilities used for their drilling shall be removed to the satisfaction of the commission within ninety (90) days' time after such wells have been determined to be nonoperative unless a longer period is approved by the commission.

2123.   Lease Operations on Uplands.

For all wells drilled from an upland or littoral drillsite landward of the ordinary high water mark, operations that may be conducted shall conform with the following:

(a) The lessee shall remove the derrick from each well within sixty (60) days after lessee has ceased making use of such derrick in its operations on and with respect to such well.

(b) In the discretion of the commission, all permanent operating sites shall be landscaped with shrubbery, or fenced, so as to screen from public view as far as possible the tanks, pumps, or other permanent equipment. Such landscaping and shrubbery, or fencing, are to be kept in good condition.

(c) All drilling and production operations shall be conducted in such manner as to eliminate, as far as practicable, dust, noise, vibration or noxious odors.

(d) Suitable and adequate sanitary toilet and washing facilities shall be installed and maintained in a clean and sanitary condition at all times for the use of lessee's personnel.

(e) No sign shall be constructed or erected, maintained or placed on the premises except those required by law or ordinance to be displayed in connection with the drilling or maintenance of the well.

(f) Pollution and contamination of the ocean and tide lands and all impairment of and interference with bathing, fishing, or navigation in the waters of the ocean or any bay or inlet thereof is prohibited; and no oil, tar, residuary product of oil or any refuse of any kind from any well or works shall be permitted to be deposited on or pass into the waters of the ocean or any bay or inlet thereof.

(g) Oil, tar, or other residuary products of oil, or any refuse of any kind from any well or works, shall be disposed of onshore in a dumping area in conformance with local regulatory requirements.

BIBLIOGRAPHY

Bendix, Bradberry Associates and Copley International Corporation, *California's Coastal Zone* (report prepared for the California Advisory Commission on Marine and Coastal Resources and The Interagency Council on Ocean Resources), September 1968.

California State Division of Mines and Geology, Bulletin 191, *Mineral Resources of California, 1966.*

Commission on Marine Science, Engineering and Resources, *Our Nation and the Sea,* House Document 91–42, Report January 1969.

State of California, *Marine Resources Conservation and Development Act of 1967.*

State of California, Statute, Public Resources Code, Division 6.

U.S. Naval Ordnance Test Station, T.P. 4122, *Undersea Geothermal Deposits,* July 1966.

PART 2
SYSTEMS PLANNING AND ENGINEERING

CHAPTER 7

Systems Planning and Control:
Coastal Regions

DAVID STERNLIGHT

The purpose of this chapter is to describe the planning of physical and organizational systems for the use of the coastal zone. Planning includes systems structuring, analysis and design, programming, and subsequent feedback and evaluation. Each use of the coastal zone requires an "internal" subsystem of its own. The entire zone is composed of a series of such subsystems, each for its special purpose, interacting in a network of local, regional, state, and national subsystems, public and private, in pursuit of goals which are sometimes independent, complementary, and conflicting. Previous chapters show many examples of such systems and their conflicts; repeated examples of the increasing seriousness of these conflicts are well known to all of us.

Following this introduction, the chapter discusses some methods for conflict resolution. An examination of the key questions about such systems (activities) is followed by a description of the systems planning and design process, and the analytic process embedded in it. Policy techniques for achieving objectives are considered next. The conclusion to the chapter is a discussion of some examples.

1. CONFLICTS AND THEIR RESOLUTION

Most of the coastal-zone conflicts that concern us are man-made, not natural. Our increasing command of analytic, planning, and management techniques can be used to deal with these conflicts through new technology, better planning, more careful and responsible management, and by removing basic causes where in the overall social interest. In many cases a complex chain must be

193

isolated, described, and analyzed. A direct analysis of the subsystem causing the conflict is often adequate, provided full consideration is given to interaction effects and external economies and diseconomies. Such an analytical subsystem approach requires examination of alternatives. However, with structured planning, it is not necessary to know "all about everything."

The key to rational choice is to add up the benefits arising from a decision (action), policy or system, and compare them with the costs. Care must be taken to ensure that all relevant benefits and costs are considered, not just those of the proposer or proprietor of the system. Externalities, joint costs, and benefits, and non-monetary costs and benefits must all be considered. Often, simple engineering solutions serve initially or permanently. For instance if ships collide, establish sea lanes. Two central objectives, free economic choice and economic efficiency, guide our approach. Often they are complementary; sometimes compromises are required. Free economic choice requires that wherever possible, without significant social loss, the free action of the marketplace is the mechanism of choice. Oil leases should be offered on the public's lands in competitive bidding. Economic efficiency requires these leases to be offered in a way that will permit economies of scale in extraction. The number, rate, size, and location of tracts to be offered can be used to encourage such economies. A social loss results if firms submit inappropriately low bids for such public property. Thus the government must gather enough information to assess a probable value for such lands and establish a minimum bid. In a following part of this discussion, policy techniques for achieving objectives are treated.

Pool (see Bibliography) includes in his classification of modes of influence: providing information, modifying certainty, providing a behavioral model to the influencee, changing the objective environment, and changing the influencee's resources (Figure 1). All of these techniques are now being used for conflict resolution in international affairs and are appropriate for our purposes as well. Providing information as a result of research, development, or exploration can increase the productive intensity of use of the coastal zone. Modifying certainty is being used now in court actions to reduce further the belief that the public will do nothing when private users of the coastal zone transfer some of their costs (for pollution abatement, for example) to the public. "Raising certainty may help if the objective is to teach a conclusion; lowering it may help if the objective is to compel caution and indecision" (Pool,

MODES OF INFLUENCE:

● providing information

● modifying certainty

● providing a behavioral model

● changing the objective environment

● changing the influencee's resources

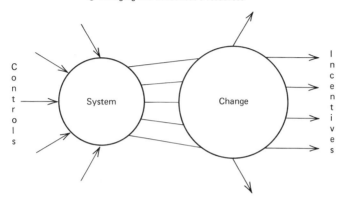

Figure 1. Modes of influence.

see Bibliography). Seed money and pilot programs provide behavioral models for others. Through the use of grants, loans, tax shelters, contracting power, regulatory power, and market aggregation, the objective environment is being changed in ways that can aid in coastal zone conflict resolution and more productive and efficient usage. The successful participant in these programs has his resources changed. Imposition of more stringent regulations or economic penalties are another way to change the resources of program participants.

2. THE KEY QUESTIONS

Our approach is to analyze a particular use (subsystem) of the coastal zone, considering interactions with other systems when such interactions have a significant effect on the target subsystem being examined or on an external system. In such an examination, some decision or action is being contemplated. It may be the structuring of a new system, the modification or elimination of an existing system, or the well-known "do nothing" decision.

The first set of questions to be asked is: what should be done? Why? Should, for example, the California commercial fishery system be improved? Should it produce more fish? Should it preserve the jobs of fishermen (income redistribution)? Should it increase profitability?

The second set of questions is: who should do it? Why? Are there any large fishing firms? Should they do it? Will they get benefits from such action comparable with their costs? Who else will obtain these benefits? Should the government do it?

The third set of questions is: what are the relevant factors in allocating resources? Is there free entry into commercial fishing? Will any increase in attractiveness of the industry attract more firms, until profitability is back where it was? Is the problem one of restricting entry? What about those present operators who are inefficient? Is there an economic need for more, or cheaper, fish? Will an equal expenditure on some other industry, such as mineral extraction, produce greater benefits?

The fourth set is: how should it be done? What should the activity level be? What should the schedule be? What is the plan? How have conflicts been treated? The final set is: how should the plan be monitored, controlled, evaluated and modified through feedback? Who will perform this function?

3. THE SYSTEMS PLANNING AND DESIGN PROCESS

The questions raised in Section 3 represent a few of the principal and subsidiary questions that must be treated during systems planning. A sequential, evolutionary planning process permits orderly treatment of these and other issues. The process is an iterative one; information developed during later stages is used to check, modify or repeat earlier stages when a significant improvement can be expected and planning time permits. The process is a continuous, dynamic one, even after the system has been installed. The main steps in the process are problem definition, structuring, and analysis; systems synthesis; implementation planning and programming; and installation, monitoring, and evaluation.

Problem definition, structuring, and analysis

The basic elements of a problem of economic choice are objectives, alternatives, costs and benefits, criteria, and models. If one or more of these five elements are absent, there is no problem, choice, or solution. Analysis of these elements is not always extensive, complex or formal; it is performed in the detail necessary to solve the problem at hand.

Objectives. Objectives are our aims or goals in a particular problem of choice. Consider the problem mentioned in Chapter 10. How should wastes from a city sewage collection system be treated for subsequent disposal? The objective is disposal of the waste. The protection of the receiving body and the conservation of the city budget also enter the decision process. For the purposes of this discussion, we assume that the question, "Who should do it?" has already been answered—"the city."

Alternatives. Alternatives are different ways or systems for achieving objectives. Alternatives in the example were using an intensive-treatment, costly plant at the end of a short pipeline near the city to dispose of the effluent in a river; using a medium intensity plant of intermediate cost at the end of a longer pipeline to dispose of the effluent in an estuary fed by the river; using a low intensity plant of least cost at the end of the longest pipeline to dispose of the effluent to the open coast (Figure 2). Note that these alternatives reflect some preanalysis. Each plant meets the dilution requirements of the receiving body to maintain its water quality, which is one of the elements of the criterion function. Such pre-analysis is quite common in systems planning. Often, before complex cost-benefit structuring, modeling, and data collection take place, alternatives meeting nonmonetary criteria are preselected from all possible alternatives to save considerable time and effort. Such a process must be conducted with great care to avoid ignoring an apparently unacceptable alternative which, in terms of the criteria, with some redesign could become an acceptable alternative. Note also that in the list of alternatives above, there is only one plant of each type. In reality, many combinations of components may be used in a plant of a given type to produce the same final dilution.

Costs. Costs are the resources used up by each alternative. Costs in this simplified example include those of the pipeline and plant of each alternative. In complex systems, a detailed cost structure is often used (Figure 3). Costs are subdivided using a *top-down breakdown* of the system similar to the system work breakdown structure. This "life-cycle cost structure" is often divided into the phases of development (the advanced planning and

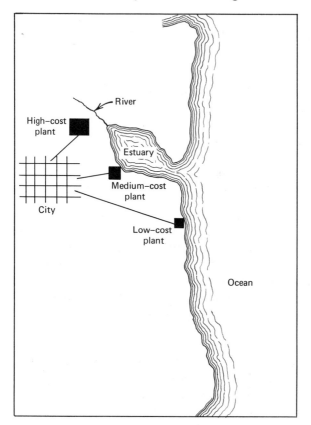

Figure 2. Waste disposal alternatives.

prototype stage), investment (the system construction and installation phase), and operations and support (the system's useful life
phase). Cost categories and subcategories are used to predict and
accumulate costs in sufficient detail for planning, monitoring, and
control by homogenous cost category. In the present case, the
"benefit consequences" are the same for each alternative: disposal
of the waste at an acceptable rate of dilution.

   In calculating costs, much depends on who calculates and for
what purpose. If the effect of a program is being examined, the
cost and benefit structure used must include costs to others for the
different alternatives. These external diseconomies and economies
are often critical to the selection of policies by governing bodies
to regulate or control third parties. For example, if manufacturers

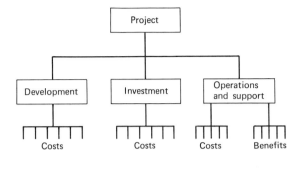

Figure 3. Cost/benefit structuring and analysis.

of soft drinks had to pay the extra waste disposal costs incurred when deposit bottles were replaced by throwaway cans (perhaps, by a tax on each can sold), such waste might not have been generated so quickly. The true cost of throwaway cans is hidden from the purchaser, who does not see the higher tax bills that result from this use. In general, if an action by one party causes a second party to incur additional costs, the social calculation must take this external diseconomy into consideration. The same thing is true of external economies. Transfer mechanisms are necessary for such externalities if we are to preserve a market economy. This subject is explored further in a later section. When systems being compared have different time patterns of costs or different useful lives, discounting and salvage value calculations are often made to permit equal comparison. The process of cost estimation and prediction is necessary for choice; when the selected system is operational, measurement of actual costs and validation of estimates (with some incentives or penalties associated with validation) is necessary to ensure diligence in the original estimates, to spot divergencies between predicted and actual costs due to system degradation (in order to control such degradation), and to accumulate experience for future systems design. The RAND Cost Analysis reference contains much useful material on structuring and calculating systems costs.

Criteria. Criteria are rules for choice. They are explicit. The weighted share of gross state product is a number. This number can be a criterion only if there is a specified manner in which it is used for choosing among alternatives. A criterion is a test of preferability. Criteria need not always be numeric; they can be comparative rankings if appropriate. There may be two sets of criteria, as in the present case, one describing a cost universe, and the other describing a performance or benefit universe. One general formulation of the criterion function is minimum cost for a specified level of performance. That is the criterion in the present example: minimum total cost (pipeline plus plant) for specified dilution levels of pollutants in the receiving body. Criteria must be derived from objectives. In this case each alternative meets the objective of disposing of the waste. Conservation of the receiving body is ensured with the performance criterion of dilution level. Efficient use of city funds is secured by the decision rule of selecting the minimum total cost alternative, meeting the other criteria. In the formal analysis, we would compute the sum of pipeline and plant construction costs, land and equipment costs, and operating and support costs (perhaps discounted if the alternatives have different expenditure patterns over time) for each alternative, and then compare the resultant sums.

There are other forms of criterion functions (Figure 4). In some cases we may use maximum performance or benefit for a fixed cost

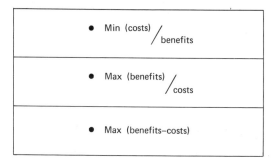

Figure 4. Alternative criterion functions.

as the decision rule. Many organizations operate under fixed budget constraints, and one would expect such a decision rule to be used frequently. Because of the ease of comparing costs of alternatives and the institutional concept of *low bidder*, this decision rule is not often used. Another common form of the criterion function is the maximization of the excess of benefits over costs. For an extensive discussion of inappropriate forms of criterion functions, see Hitch and McKean, or McKean (see Bibliography).

Models.   With the establishment of criteria, the next step in the process of choice is to construct a model or models. There is an extensive literature on modeling in the applied economics (operations research; management science; systems analysis) community. A key to modeling is the discovery of variables which affect the values of the criterion function, and the creation of a structure which relates changes in alternatives (as described in terms of these variables) to changes in the criterion function. A model may be a summed column of costs or prices, or it may be a complex parametric engineering, or analytic systems description requiring the use of a computer for evaluation. In the present example, the model might be the sum of the cost per foot of pipeline times the number of feet required; the flow rate and dilution produced by a plant times some cost factors relating those two variables to construction costs; and a series of terms relating the pipeline length, plant flow rate, and dilution to annual operating costs over the life of the plant. Much more complex models are often used for the planning of such engineering-economic systems.

Systems synthesis

During the systems planning process, design and analysis are used to select alternatives. As systems principles and policies are established, organizational and physical elements selected, and planning proceeds, configuration control becomes critically important. It is necessary to keep track of the ongoing plan; it is also necessary to repeatedly check interfaces and interactions between newly added elements and the existing plan. Failure to do this can lead to a plan that is a collection of suboptimizations which fail completely as a coherent whole. Examples of such failure are well known in the physical design field; in planning organizational or policy systems it is far easier to overlook or conceal such failures. Yet we are all familiar with the stereotyped "ineffectual bureaucracy" designed into a feedback loop that keeps itself busy feeding on internally generated work, with no inputs from or outputs to the outside world.

As planning proceeds it is helpful to drop pieces that are completed and interface-checked into a skeleton of the final plan or system. Periodic review by outside observers kept isolated from the day-to-day planning process is also useful.

Implementation planning and programming

As systems synthesis proceeds, a series of special documents is developed for the implementation of the planned system. These include PERT or milestone charts showing the major activities during implementation, their sequencing, timing for key accomplishments, and the *critical path*. This path is the sequence of activities and events that paces the project; a delay in any activity will cause an equivalent delay in completion of the plan if there is no slack at the end. Costs and resources should be associated with the activities in the plan so that potential overruns can be recognized and anticipated by compensation. When plan resources are shared over different activities occurring at different times, a careful resource allocation calculation is necessary to ensure that sequencing is for least cost within time and activity sequence constraints. Personnel and other resource requirements by time period are specified (programmed) in separate planning documents. Time-phased budgets are calculated. Annual or other period activity and budget plans are prepared for the operating life of the system after installation.

Installation, monitoring, and evaluation

The systems installation, monitoring, and evaluation process requires as much control as the systems design. The time-phased resource and milestone schedule for installation and checkout should be used for this purpose. The plan must identify data which will permit evaluation of system performance and suggest improvements, within cost and other criteria established for systems design. Specific responsibilities for installation, data collection, and system monitoring, and periodic evaluation should be established within the systems plan. Time, resource, and cost information for the data collection and evaluation process is necessary. The same quality of analysis should be applied to establishing evaluation criteria and responses to feedback as was applied to the systems design. Such a self-regenerating system will continue to operate as designed for its lifetime, provided resources are budgeted for proper feedback, evaluation, maintenance, and modification.

4. POLICY TECHNIQUES FOR ACHIEVING OBJECTIVES

The preferred technique for guiding systems planning is that of free economic choice. Private markets should not be interfered with unless such action can demonstrably yield more efficient performance. The central criterion here is that of economic efficiency in allocating resources within a systems plan. Economic efficiency requires the use of the least costly techniques available to achieve a desired objective. The quantity and timing of benefits should make the cost of the last increment of production about equal to its value to the consumer. When one of the purposes of a plan is to control or influence the actions of others, a family of direct and indirect control and stimulation techniques is available to the public planner.

Direct control techniques

Direct control techniques include licensing, zoning, contracting, and regulation. The selection of a particular technique or combination must be related to the objectives of the plan in question. The fishing industry is, in most segments, a mature but static or declining one. There is freedom of entry, and many small, inefficient producers exist. Licensing alone would not be an appropriate way of improving the economic efficiency of the industry; while it would work as a means for controlling or limiting the entry of new firms, it would do nothing to increase the efficiency of existing ones, were economic growth the objective.

Zoning is another direct control technique when the public interest requires exclusion of activities from a particular area, protection of activities already being carried out, or stimulation of activity-groupings having interactive or scale economies. The exclusion of industrial hazards from the shoreline near fishing, swimming, or pleasure boating areas, the stimulation of the development of marinas, and the creation of concentrated shore support facilities for mineral extraction or transportation can all be accomplished through zoning of private lands. Zoning alone, of course, will not stimulate economic activity when incentives do not exist for the use of newly opened areas for such activity. It is not as specialized a tool as regulation when physical encroachment is not involved, and it must be used with care. Zoning is often carried out through a forensic process in which the advice of experts is compared with the arguments of parties at interest, and these arguments are usually of a nonquantitative and nonanalytic character. The interface consequences of zoning are not always apparent until well after the act. An all or nothing choice is often necessary. Regulation, on the other hand, permits precise specification of tolerance levels (e.g., of pollutants) and allows fine-tuning of the level of economic activity as well as more gross exclusion of certain activities. The decisions of regulatory bodies are more easily auditable by interested parties when such quantitative standards are involved. Direct cost and benefit calculations can more easily be made by the regulators and the regulatees. Increases in stringency are possible, within technical states of the art, over time.

Contracting is one of the most attractive direct control techniques available since it permits operation through free market mechanisms. In the defense industry the contracting process is well established. Contracting for construction or operation of improved or innovative facilities is beginning to increase in the nondefense sector. The *N.S. Savannah* is one example of capital and technical risk being too high for the private sector to develop and operate a prototype nuclear merchant ship. Similarly, this concept of public support to merchant shipping can be extended to the fishing industry. One suggestion for increasing the efficiency of the fishing industry and obtaining the economic rent for the public's ownership in fisheries is government purchase of excess vessels for operation in the fish protein concentrate program, provided states agree to limit future entry of capital and labor into the fishing industry.

Indirect control techniques

Indirect control techniques include taxation, leasing, and trust funds. Taxation has been mentioned in connection with throw-away soda cans. It is an attractive indirect control technique when a public cost is involved, if assessed to cover all public costs. If the fair cost of container disposal is charged as a manufacturer or purchaser tax, the worth of such cans can be established in the market. The user will then pay for their disposal. User charges are another form of taxation; recovery of the construction costs of marinas or improved port facilities are examples. In public construction the risk is assumed by the public, since the facility is paid for before costs are recovered. The disposable can risk can be placed on the manufacturer by making the tax payable on production before this new waste reaches disposal facilities.

Leasing is another indirect control technique, commonly used for publicly owned lands. The attraction of leasing through a competitive bidding process, with minimum bids fixed after public investigation of probable value, is that the economic rent for use of the public resource accrues to the public. At the same time, a property right is created for the leasor, who can then take capital risks (e.g., constructing and installing drilling apparatus) without the fear that others will exploit parcels he has found productive. A combination of leasing, licensing, and contracting may be the solution to the fishery problem—licensing of existing operators to prevent new entry (as in the New York City taxi industry), contracting to gradually remove inefficient existing producers, and leasing to extract the public value created by limiting the number of operators and increasing the fish available to the remaining operators who share in the fixed total. The minimum bid for leases can gradually be raised, or parcel size offered for lease can gradually be increased to aid in the elimination of inefficient operators. Any dislocation and hardship resulting can be treated separately. There are less costly methods for income maintenance than to continue to support many inefficient producers in their overuse of the public fisheries.

Trust funds represent an indirect control tool used for highways and for uninsured motorists. In the first case, the trust fund was intended as a user charge, collected at the gasoline pump, for motorists. In the second case, which has many parallels in coastal zone conflicts, the uninsured motorist fund permits free market decisions on insurance. Contributions to this fund are used to repay motorists injured by those not insured. In this way the indirect cost imposed on the insured motorist by the uninsured one is placed where it belongs through the mechanism of the fund. A similar device can have wide applicability in the coastal zone. For example, an underwater hazard fund can be created to repay fishermen for damage to nets from man-made structures. Tanker owners could be forced to contribute to pollution fund. Properly created, such a fund could be drawn upon for research or conflict reduction in the subject areas. For example, the cost of marker buoys could be paid out of an underwater hazard fund if analysis shows that use of marker buoys is more efficient than permitting the accidental damage that would otherwise result. On the other hand, it may be less costly to reimburse the occasional fisherman whose nets are damaged, even including the value of his lost catch, if such damage is infrequent enough and buoys are costly enough to install and maintain. In structuring the funds above care must be taken not to reduce the present legal recourse of the parties being protected.

Direct stimulation techniques

Market creation or aggregation, subsidies, and tax shelters are direct stimulation techniques of long standing. One of the most spectacular recent examples of market aggregation is being used to revitalize shipbuilding in the United States. In the past the government has purchased military and subsidized commercial ships in multiple procurements of small lot size, spread over many shipyards. As a result, no one program could justify shipyard capital investment in extensive modernization. Under the new military and merchant marine programs, individual contracts have been awarded for as much as two billion dollars for a series of ships of standard design. On this basis completely new facilities are justified for highly mechanized series production of ships that were formerly constructed from the keel up. Once a market has been aggregated, private enterprise can often do the rest. The government can use its purchasing power similarly in many other market areas for the stimulation of private efficiency, risk-taking, and investment, once scaled markets are created.

Indirect stimulation techniques

Among the indirect stimulation techniques available to public bodies are research and development. When the risk or capital required for R&D in the private sector is too great relative to the size of firms and markets, federal or state support or conduct of R&D can lead to the development of more efficient technology for use by private industry. Two preconditions are that the private sector be unable to undertake such efforts, and that the efforts lead to increased economic efficiency. We have seen that in the fishery industry, improvement in catch technology or increase in the number of fish will not lead to increased efficiency unless freedom of entry is curtailed. In industries with entry limited by capital or technical requirements, but with major advances beyond the R&D capability of individual firms, a case may be made for public planning. The development of jet transport aircraft, 50-knot merchant ships, and undersea mineral exploration and extraction vessels are examples where public benefits result. In the transportation case, the benefits of time savings and increase in intensity of commerce are obtained by the public through market activities. In the mineral case, direct benefits to the public in higher lease bids for offshore exploitation rights can result from the increased value of such properties caused by the more productive technology developed.

5. EXAMPLES

This section contains four brief examples illustrating some of the principles discussed thus far. An analysis of the allocation of additional subsidy funds between oil and mineral extraction shows the basic structure of economic choice and economic efficiency. An illustration of scale economies in size or in production reveals one underlying reason for the development of very large ships; a comparison of size economies under varying constraints sheds further light on the development of large ships and the use (or avoidance) of canals and ports; an analysis of costs and benefits provides a mechanism for considering major port improvements.

The allocation of a subsidy

Suppose it has been determined, through analysis of national priorities or otherwise, that a federal subsidy of, say, C_1 is to be used to stimulate both oil and mineral extraction in such a way that the maximum benefit will accrue to the public from the allocation of these funds. How much of the subsidy should be allocated to each industry?

Production possibilities: public costs. There are many different ways we can allocate the C_1 subsidy (a public cost). If we were to spend it all on stimulating mineral exploration, development, and more efficient extraction, we might obtain a quantity of additional minerals due to the expenditure of C_1. Figure 5 shows this quantity, q_1, as well as the quantity q_2 of additional oil if the subsidy C_1 were spent entirely on oil development. Curve X_1 shows these as well as other combinations of additional oil and minerals obtainable by allocation of the subsidy C_1 in different proportions to oil and on mineral development. At point C, for example, about half the quantity of additional oil and about 80% of the quantity of additional minerals are produced, compared with the amount ob-

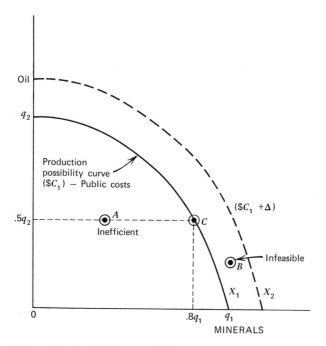

Figure 5.   Production possibility curves (also called production transformation curves).

tained if all the subsidy were allocated to oil, or if, instead, all the subsidy were allocated to minerals. Note that point C does not indicate *how* the subsidy is divided; merely that if enough were allocated to oil to induce $0.5q_2$, the rest of the $\$C_1$ subsidy would be enough to induce about $0.8q_1$ of extra minerals.

Curve X_1 is called a "production possibility curve" or "product transformation curve." It shows combinations of two outputs that may efficiently and feasibly be produced from a fixed total input. Point B is an infeasible point—it represents extra minerals and oil requiring more than $\$C_1$ in total subsidy. Infeasible points lie above and to the right of the production possibility curve. Point A is inefficient. By moving to the right until we reach C we can produce the same quantity of extra oil and more minerals without exceeding our total subsidy. By moving upward, we can produce more extra oil and the same quantity of minerals. In either case, we are better off in terms of quantity produced. Points below and to the left of the curve X_1 and inefficient for a total additional expenditure of $\$C_1$

on oil and mineral stimulation. The production possibility curve X_1 (for a total subsidy of $\$C_1$) forms the boundary between inefficient and infeasible points. We cannot increase one valuable output (oil or minerals) without increasing a valuable input (total subsidy) or decreasing another valuable output. The production possibility curve shown is (as in many economic examples) concave to the origin because of decreasing returns; successively doubling extra expenditures on a commodity produces successively less than double the extra output of that commodity after a given level of production has been reached.

Curve X_2 shows a larger subsidy, $\$C_1 + \Delta$, which stimulates more extra oil and minerals than does $\$C_1$. Similarly, some lower total subsidy than $\$C_1$ would yield a production possibility curve passing through point A. For such a lower subsidy, A would represent an efficient allocation of resources.

The public cost $\$C_1$ can include such other public costs attributable to the extra oil and minerals produced as increased pollution control costs and public waste disposal costs. A more complex calculation would then be needed to produce the constant total public cost curves.

Revenues: benefits. Thus far we have discussed public costs to subsidize the production of additional oil and minerals. Next we examine benefits from extra oil and minerals. These benefits (revenues $R_1, R_2, \cdots$) include additional tax revenues from the extra product and public savings through any lower unit prices caused by the subsidy's effect. If the subsidy program were to benefit oil and mineral producers, revenues should include a measure of their benefits as well (perhaps total profit with subsidy less total profit without, or some measure related to increased return on investment). If the program were to increase the quantity of oil and minerals produced, a measure of the public value of the increase would also be appropriate.

Figure 6 shows public revenues produced from combinations of extra oil and minerals. Curves of successively higher constant total revenue ($R_1, R_2, R_3, \cdots$) are drawn. These public benefit (isorevenue) curves are known as "indifference curves" since (assuming full inclusion of all benefits in R_1) the public should be indifferent to different combinations of oil and minerals on curve R_1, since each combination has the same public value.

Isorevenue curves in many economic cases are convex to the origin since unit prices usually drop as output increases. Succes-

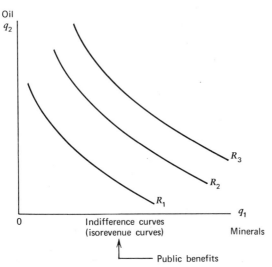

Oil
q_2

0   Indifference curves
         (isorevenue curves)   Minerals

q_1

Public benefits

Figure 6. Benefit curves.

sively doubling extra output of each commodity produces successively less than doubled revenue from that commodity after a
given level of output is reached.

Optimal allocation.   Figure 5 has described the variation of costs
and output; Figure 6 the variation of benefits with outputs. Figure
7 combines the previous figures to show the optimum output mix
for a fixed cost. It is that combination of extra oil and minerals
(output), obtainable from the fixed subsidy $\$C_1$ (input), which
maximizes the public's revenue (benefit). The curve X_1 describing
different production possibilities with fixed subsidy $\$C_1$ is taken
from Figure 5. A family of benefit curves, including R_1, is taken
from Figure 6. Let R_1 be the benefit curve just tangent to curve X_1.
Then the optimal operating point is at this tangent point (*). Any
higher revenue curve (R_A) to the right and above X_1 represents
more than the maximum extra revenue obtainable from any mix of
extra oil and minerals on X_1 (feasible with the budget $\$C_1$). Any
revenue curve $(R_B$ or $R_C)$ to the left and below R_1 represents less
revenue than R_1. The R_1 is the maximum revenue from subsidy $\$C_1$,
however allocated. Furthermore, the only combination of extra oil
and minerals which will produce these maximum benefits R_1 at a
cost no more than $\$C_1$ is q_2^* of extra oil and q_1^* of extra minerals.

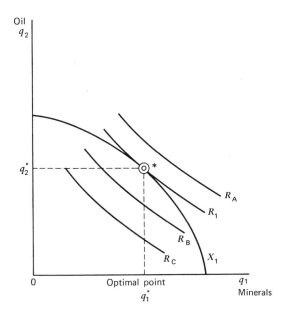

Figure 7. Optimal allocation of a fixed subsidy.

We would therefore plan the allocation of a $\$C_1$ subsidy to oil and mineral stimulation in a way that would produce q_2^* of oil and q_1^* of minerals; the public benefit would be R_1.

If we further require that a subsidy of $\$C_1$ to oil and mineral stimulation will not be applied unless it produces a net benefit to the public, we can compare R_1, the maximum benefit, to $\$C_1$, the public cost in the optimal allocation situation. Unless $\$R_1$ is at least equal to $\$C_1$, we would not subsidize at level $\$C_1$.

Levels of subsidy. We may remove another restriction from our problem definition by freeing the predetermined subsidy level $\$C_1$ to find the best subsidy level (including zero). Let us define the criterion as maximum excess of public benefits over public costs. Figure 8 shows a family of optimal points, each calculated as in Figure 7, for successively higher subsidies, X_0, X_1, X_2, · · ·. The maximum benefits obtainable from each are, respectively, R_0, R_1, and R_2 with increasing mixes of q_1 and q_2. The curve connecting these optimal points is called the "output expansion path." Associated with each point on the output expansion path is a cost, X_i,

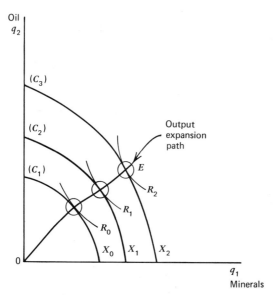

Figure 8.   Alternative optimal allocations.

and a benefit, R_i. Our criterion requires us to find the point where $(R_i - X_i)$ is maximized. If this difference is nowhere positive, the proper subsidy is zero. Otherwise, the point of maximum excess of benefits over costs is the desired operating point, assuming an adequate budget.

Capital budgeting.   When resources are limited and more than two projects are involved, a generalization of the previous analysis, using one of a number of mathematical resource allocation techniques, may be appropriate. Each project can be considered separately and a criterion function calculated.

Next the criterion functions for each project may be compared, using allocation techniques to determine the level of each project to enter the *optimum mix*. These techniques are particularly useful when the pattern of resource requirements, benefits, and total funds available varies over time. If the projects are interdependent, more complex calculations are required, since the shape of criterion functions for the projects are then interdependent.

An extensive literature has grown up in the application of mathematical programming techniques to capital budgeting. Much of this material may be found in the journal *Management Science*.

Large ships

Tankers have recently grown in size from 20,000 to 250,000 deadweight tons and more, presenting many conflicts in the coastal zone. This section describes the economics of such growth. The following section discusses related routing and canal considerations. The chapter concludes with a sketch of an analytic methodology for port and harbor improvement planning.

Figure 9 compares tanker construction costs using two different

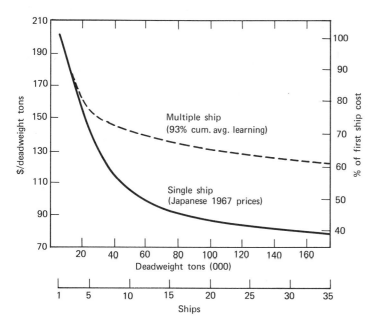

Figure 9. Tanker construction cost—single versus multiple ship.

ways of increasing cargo capacity; more ships of a particular size or a bigger ship. The upper curve shows production economies from producing increased numbers of 5000 deadweight ton ships. The upper X-axis scale shows the total shipping capacity obtained in this way, while the lower X-axis scale shows the number of 5000 deadweight tons equivalent ships needed to obtain this total capacity. The left Y-axis shows the cost per ton of capacity for any total capacity, calculated from values on the right Y-axis, which shows the average cost per ship in each quantity as a percentage of the cost of building only one such ship. The upper (multiple ship) curve assumes 93% cumulative average learning in a good, conventional shipyard. Each time the number of ships doubles, the average cost per ship drops to 93%. The cost per ship for two ships is 93% of the cost of building one ship. If four are built, their average cost is 93% of each of two or (0.93 × 0.93) 86.5% of the first ship cost. The "learning" process reflects labor learning, quantity material discounts, spreading of fixed costs over the production lot, and other factors. It describes an empirically observed effect.

The lower curve shows the decreasing production cost per ton of single ships as they increase in size. The drop in these costs with increased ship size reflects substantial returns to scale; a ship is like a box; and perimeter area and cost increases as the square of length, width (beam), and depth, while volume (capacity) increases as their cube. As a result, the cost of a ton of capacity drops much more rapidly with increased size than with increased number of ships.

Operating costs behave in a similar fashion. The cost of fuel increases much less rapidly with size than with number of ships. Crew size and cost increase very little with increases in ship size, but double as the number of ships doubles. The result of these effects will be seen in the next sections.

Ship size and routing

Ships must satisfy buoyancy, stability, and strength constraints which make the draft (depth) between different designs of the same capacity vary within small limits. Figure 10 shows this relationship. The right Y-axis shows ship size in thousands of deadweight tons, while the lower X-axis shows draft at each size (solid curve). Also shown on the upper X-axis are key ports whose limiting drafts correspond to those on the lower X-axis. The dotted curve shows the cumulative percentage of the 1967 world tanker fleet which can use a given port. About 60% of the world's fleet has draft shallow enough to enter Bordeaux and Ghent. (These ships have draft under about 35 feet; from the solid curve we see that such ships carry less than 50,000 deadweight tons). The remaining 40% of the fleet has draft and size too great for these ports. The Malacca Straits, Puerto La Cruz, and Bantry Bay are deep enough to accommodate all ships in the world fleet in 1969.

What are the economics of ship routing and port use as a function of ship size and draft? Figure 11 shows the total cost per ton

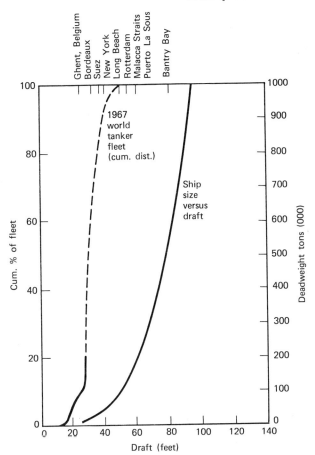

Figure 10. Ship size and draft.

for carrying crude oil (all costs of ship ownership and operation) from the Persian Gulf to Europe, as ship size increases. The curve is discontinuous since certain routes and ports are denied to ships above given drafts (and sizes), whether laden with cargo or returning empty "in ballast" with enough water in their cargo holds for stability.

The first segment of curve A shows decreasing costs per ton with ship size (see previous section on large ships) for tankers carrying oil from Ras Tanura in the Persian Gulf to Rotterdam via the Suez Canal (assuming it is open).*

* When this chapter was written, the Suez Canal had been closed to all shipping since 1967 because of Arab/Israeli, Middle East relations.

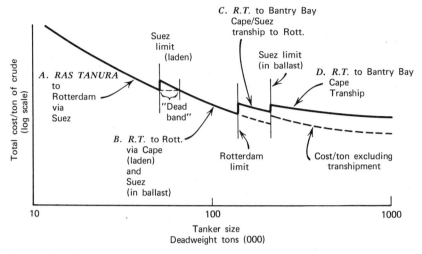

Figure 11. Cost of transport, Persian Gulf to Europe.

The first break point is at the draft limit of the Suez Canal. To the right of that point, the larger ships, laden with oil, must travel around Africa via the Cape; they may return empty (ballasted to a shallower depth with water) via Suez. For ships just larger than the upper Suez limit, costs rise because of the additional voyage time and fuel costs. These ships would be uneconomic to operate, compared with those just to the left of the first break point. Such ships lie in a "dead band" as shown in Figure 11. However economies of scale are enough for still larger ships to travel the longer route at a lower cost per cargo ton than any ship which can use Suez when laden. These ships are to the right of the dead band.

The next break point is reached at the Rotterdam port limit. Curve *C* shows another jump in costs due to the need for transhipment to Rotterdam from Bantry Bay in smaller ships. The final break point is for ships so large that they cannot transit Suez even in ballast. Curve *D* shows such ships traveling from Ras Tanura to the supertanker terminal at Bantry Bay via the Cape both ways, with subsequent transhipment to Rotterdam. No ship, of feasible size, has economies great enough to overcome these transhipment costs compared with costs in curve *B*, Figure 11, at its minimum.

In the absence of port and canal improvement or cost reductions for ships, the least-cost solution is the largest ship on curve *B* (about 120,000 deadweight tons), routed around Africa laden, and returning via Suez.

The dotted curve, which excludes transhipment costs, is a continuation of curve B until the Suez "in ballast" limit is reached. It then jumps because of the higher cost of the return voyage around Africa, but economies of scale soon justify still larger ships as the least-cost solution, assuming enough supply at Ras Tanura and enough demand at the destination to fully utilize such size.

If our final destination is Bantry Bay, or if Rotterdam is improved, least-cost ships are too large for Suez. Since the closing of Suez, larger and larger tankers have been built to obtain economies of scale. Even if Suez were reopened, it would be less costly to continue around Africa with such larger ships. The main use of a reopened, unimproved Suez Canal would seem to be by smaller ships, where their cargo lots are of economic size for a particular set of origins and destinations and for local traffic. An economic basis for port and canal improvement can be derived from Figure 11. Without Rotterdam improvement, the largest economic ship is at the point on the solid curve market "Rotterdam limit." With such improvement, larger ships become more economic. The annual savings to port customers include the difference between the cost per ton at the old limit and the lower cost per ton of the larger ship, multiplied by the annual cargo volume. If these savings exceeded the annualized cost of improvement, such improvement is justified; the costs could be recovered through user charges. The following illustrates such analysis in more detail.

Port and facilities improvement

Figure 12a shows a cost-benefit analysis of improvement to a hypothetical port, with present size limit (D_1), the maximum ship size implied by the port's limiting draft. As we have seen, larger ships have lower costs per ton of cargo carried. The cost differential, multiplied by annual volume of cargo, is equal to the direct benefits obtained by the shippers from increasing port size limits to a specified draft equivalent. These benefits are plotted as "justifiable investment."

The annualized cost of dredging and related physical improvement is also shown (solid line). Assuming full cost recovery through user charges, port improvement is justified up to a draft that can accommodate ships of size D_2, since the increased costs to that point are less than the increased benefits and can be fully recovered. At D_2, no further improvement is warranted on a direct benefit basis since an extra dollar spent on improvement will

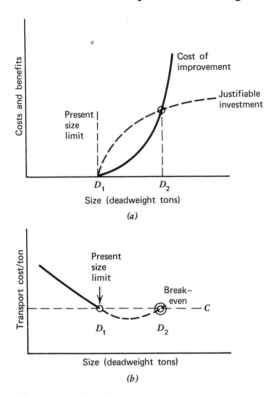

Figure 12. Facilities improvement.

produce less than a dollar of extra benefit. Inclusion of indirect costs and benefits would change the location of D_2, but not the form of analysis.

Figure 12b shows the same analysis from the shipper's point of view. The D_1 are his costs at the present limiting size. As the port is expanded, shipper's costs drop more rapidly than improvement costs. (Shipper's cost includes full charges for port improvement in b.) Up to D_2, shipper's costs are less with improvements than without. When port expansion reaches point D_2, the shipper's new costs including full improvement charges are just equal to the old costs for the unimproved port. This is the break-even, or indifference point for port improvement.

Figure 13 shows a sample calculation for the port of New York. Based on two assumed cargo throughput rates, the shippers benefits, termed justifiable investment, are calculated for various

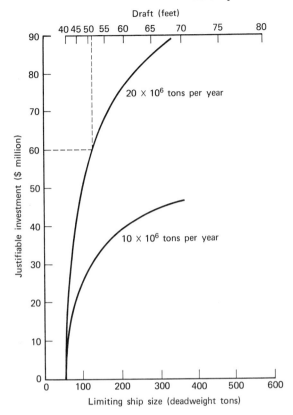

Figure 13. Break even investment, New York.

drafts and implied ship sizes. An engineering calculation of port improvement costs for different depths may be compared with these benefits to find the break-even point. In the example, if 30 million cargo tons per year can be expected at an improved depth of 52 feet, up to $60 million of investment is justified to improve the port to 52 feet.

BIBLIOGRAPHY

Baumol, W. J., *Economic Theory and Operations Analysis*, Prentice-Hall, Englewood Cliffs, N.J., 1965.
Chase, Samuel B. (Ed.), *Problems in Public Expenditure Analysis*, Brookings, Washington, D.C., 1968.
Christ, C. F., *Econometric Models and Methods*, Wiley, New York, 1966.
Hall, A. D., *A Methodology for Systems Engineering*, Van Nostrand, Princeton, N.J., 1962.

Henderson, J. M., and R. E. Quandt, *Microeconomic Theory*, McGraw-Hill, New York, 1958.

Hitch, C., and R. N. McKean, *The Economics of Defense in the Nuclear Age*, Atheneum, New York, 1965.

Johnsen, Erik, *Studies in Multi-Objective Decision Models*, Studentlitteratur, Lund, 1968.

Large, J. P. (Ed.), *Concepts and Procedures of Cost Analysis*, RAND RM-3859-PR, Santa Monica, Calif., 1963.

Litton Systems, Inc., *Oceanborne Shipping: Demand and Technology Forecasts —Part I, Part II*, Clearinghouse PB 179142, 179143, Springfield, Ill., 1968.

Masse, P., *Optimal Investment Decisions: Rules for Action and Criteria for Choice*, Prentice-Hall, Englewood Cliffs, N.J., 1962.

McKean, R. N., *Efficiency in Government Through Systems Analysis*, Wiley, New York, 1958.

National Planning Association, *The Role of Marine Sciences in the Multiple Uses of the Coastal Zone of Lake Erie and Lake Superior*, Clearinghouse PB 185 163, Springfield, Ill., 1969.

Pool, I., *Deterrence as an Influence Process*, M.I.T., Center for International Studies, Paper D/63-3, Cambridge, Mass., 1963.

Resources for the Future, Inc., *Selecting Policies for the Development of Marine Resources*, Clearinghouse PB 180905, Springfield, Ill., 1968.

Wise, Harold F., and Associates, *Intergovernmental Relations and the National Interest in the Coastal Zone of the United States*, Clearinghouse PB 184212, Springfield, Ill., 1969.

CHAPTER 8

Information Systems and Data Requirements: Coastal Development Planning

NORMAN F. SCHNEIDEWIND

The need for vastly improved coastal zone data systems is amply demonstrated by a few of the problems that now beset the coastal zone of the United States: for example, Hurricane Camille, the oil leak off the coast of Santa Barbara, increased coastal waste discharge, destruction of the Great Lakes, loss of coastal recreational areas due to increased pollution, a burgeoning recreational boating population, depressed status of United States commercial fishing and waterborne commerce, significant offshore oil drilling, and new deep draft tankers.

The major applications of coastal zone data systems are the following:

- Coastal weather monitoring and prediction
- Water quality monitoring and control
- Water resources management
- Waste management
- Coastal engineering and construction
- Commercial and sport fisheries prediction services
- Fisheries resource management
- Regulation of fish and game
- Waterborne transportation development and management
- Recreational services
- Coastal zone research
- Coastal zone planning, development, and conservation
- Coastal zone surveys
- Mapping and charting
- Resource exploration and development
- Esthetic enjoyment of the coastal zone

The major functions that must be supported by coastal zone data systems are as follows.

- Research
- Planning
- Development and implementation
- Operations and management

1. DATA REQUIREMENTS

Data requirements for developing and managing the coastal zone may be divided into the following categories:

- Environmental data
- Inventory data
- Statistics

The first category consists of data which describe the physical, chemical, biological, and geological characteristics of the coastal marine environment. In the second category are data which describe the status of marine resources in the coastal zone, for example, number and discharge rate of outfalls along the coast of California. The third category consists of summarizations or aggregations of data in the first two categories. For example, the average of the maximum wave heights at Redondo Beach for July would come under this classification. The three types of data are distinguished because there are major differences in their application to coastal zone problems. These differences result from both the type of user and the manner in which the data are used. In addition, the characteristics of systems for storing and retrieving these data are strongly affected by data category. Third, the response time requirement of the data system employed is largely determined by data category. Some of the characteristics that distinguish the three categories of data are described below in terms of the requirements for data in research, planning, development and implementation, and operations and management.

Research

Research data requirements are primarily for original environmental data. In the chain of events from original data collection to the final production of end data products, data are transformed from discrete parameter observations by processes of interpretation, averaging, merging, summarizing, aggregating, and such, to forms that bear little resemblance to the form of the original data. The scientist is one of the most active collectors of original environmental data, since his need is to understand and discover processes which take place in the marine environment. Although the scientist has a lesser requirement for the other two categories of data, the original data collected by him provide the base from which much of the data in the other two categories are derived. The data collected by the scientist become progressively more refined and are subjected to numerous arithmetic and editing operations in traveling from collector to end user.

Planning

In the planning stage of coastal zone development, the data requirements are primarily for data that describe the number, type, characteristics, and condition of coastal zone resources. Effective planning should begin with and be continuously supported by a complete inventory of existing coastal resources and auxiliary data, such as the following:

- Population
- Facilities
  - Harbors
  - Marinas
  - Aquatic stores
- Users
  - Recreation
  - Transportation
- Natural resources
  - Beaches
  - Parks
  - Animal life
- Equipment
  - Recreational boats
  - Fishing boats
  - Diving gear
- Economic indicators
  - Revenue
  - Costs
- Geography
- Topography
- Physical, chemical, and biological characteristics

- Coastal zone activity
  - Harbor construction
  - Shore stabilization
- Status of coastal zone resources and facilities
  - Beach erosion
  - Storm damage to piers

Development and implementation

In this chapter, development refers to those activities which are necessary to bring a project from conceptualization, which takes place during the planning phase, to fruition. An example is the development of beaches for new activities and the restoration of deteriorated beaches. During the planning phase, the status of state beaches would be assessed, utilizing data from a beach inventory. Such factors as number of beach users; type and frequency of use; projected growth in various types of beach activities; beach physical conditions; types and condition of animal life; suitability of beaches for swimming, boating, fishing, and scuba diving; weather and surf conditions; local ordinances; and costs of development and restoration would be evaluated. As a result of this evaluation, certain beaches would be selected for development and restoration. The development phase begins at this point. Highly specific data are needed on the beaches to be improved, as opposed to the more general statistical data which are adequate for the planning phase. For a beach restoration project, detailed data would be required on sand characteristics, sand, and sediment transport, surf action, weather, physical features, currents, and statistics of beach use.

Operation and management

Once a project is put into operation, it must be managed and/or regulated. For example, after a fishery development program has been planned and the fishery grounds have been stocked, it must be regulated to prevent overfishing and continually monitored in order to obtain the data necessary for effective management. Operating statistics are required in the form of catch/effort data, boat and gear characteristics, ocean environmental data, and weather statistics.

Two characteristics of data requirements, quantity of data and timeliness of response, are summarized for the four phases in Figure 1. The following observations can be made:

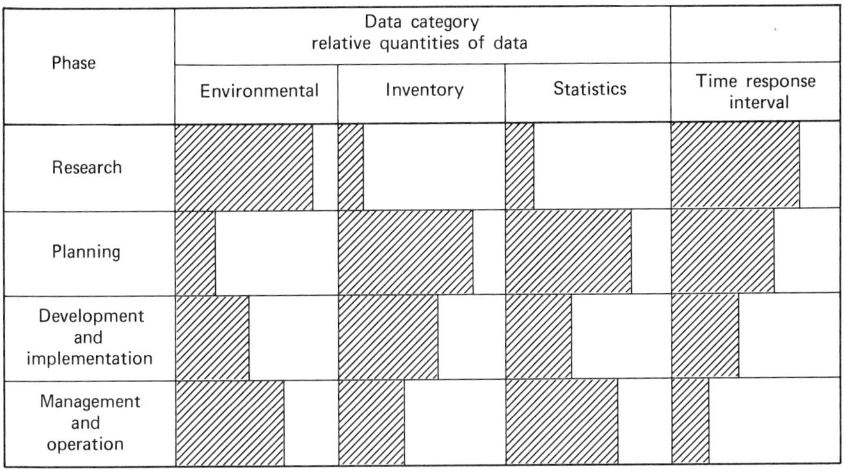

Phase	Data category relative quantities of data			Time response interval
	Environmental	Inventory	Statistics	
Research	▨	▨	▨	▨
Planning	▨	▨	▨	▨
Development and implementation	▨	▨	▨	▨
Management and operation	▨	▨	▨	▨

Figure 1. Relative quantity of data and time response as a function of phase of coastal zone activity.

- In progressing from the research to the later phases, the need for raw environmental data becomes progressively less, until the management and operation phase is reached. At this point the requirement for environmental data increases due to the need to monitor the implemented project (wave action on new breakwater.)
- The requirement for inventory data is greatest during the planning phase.
- Statistical data are important during planning to indicate the condition and uses of the coastal zone. These data are also critical during the management and operation phase for regulation purposes (number of fishing licenses issued) and as input for future planning (beach use statistics after beach restoration.)
- The requirement for timeliness of data collection and retrieval is stringent for management and operation (e.g., weather prediction) and much less critical for the other functions.

2. PLAN FOR A COASTAL ZONE DATA NETWORK

Rationale

To save our coastal environment from total destruction and to preserve and improve those areas which have not yet been adulterated, a national coastal data network is needed. The major purpose of this network is to collect, communicate, process, and disseminate data for the development and management of the coastal zone in such activities as follows.

- Research
- Planning
- Transportation
- Recreation
- Conservation
- Water quality
- Fishing
- Resource exploration

The coastal data network would be developed by the states within the framework of a federally coordinated total national network. The major components of this network are the following:

- Data acquisition at coastal offshore and onshore platforms.
- Data communication from coastal platforms to a centralized data center in each state.
- Data storage, processing, and retrieval at the state data centers.
- Data dissemination from the central data center to local users.

The coastal zone network would in no way infringe on the responsibilities and operations of existing federal military and civilian data networks and data centers. Rather, the coastal network is envisaged as a component of a larger, decentralized national environmental data network, consisting of federal, coastal zone, and state networks, as depicted in Figure 2.

The concept of a national network and its affiliated networks is a plan for data system development and operation rather than an organizing plan which specifies lines of authority for the management of the network. As implemented, there would be no central authority among the federal, coastal, and state networks. The three networks would have equal status. The emphasis would be on the development of communication interfaces within and among networks. The types of interfaces are the following:

- Between and among states (between state networks) where interstate problems occur, such as the common management of data for the restoration of Lake Erie.
- Between a state and the Federal Government (between state

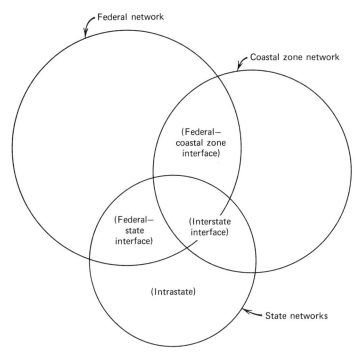

Figure 2. Relationships among the data networks of a national environmental data network.

and federal networks), as in the exchange of water quality data between a state and the Federal Water Pollution Control Administration (FWPCA).

- Between several states and the Federal Government (between the coastal network and the federal network), as in the federally supported development of an interstate region.
- Between levels of government within a state (within a state network) such as the exchange of data between a state water quality control board and regional water quality control boards.

The rationale for this concept of operation is that data communication interfaces should be developed for the exchange of data among federal, state, industrial, and university data sources, to manage better the coastal zone. Many of the existing federal data networks are sources of valuable data to the states. Examples of these data sources are the civilian Weather Bureau Network;

coastal wave data acquisition, telemetry and reduction by the Corps of Engineers; estuarine water quality data collection systems of the FWPCA; and the storage and retrieval of marine data by national data centers, such as the National Oceanographic Data Center and the National Weather Records Center. Water quality data collected by states in interstate waters are an example of a state data source of interest to the Federal Government. Institutions collect much of the research data in the coastal zone which is applicable to water quality, fisheries management, and beach erosion. Private industrial firms are potential sources of coastal engineering data for the states.

Although there are significant problems involved in effectively interfacing the networks, the discussion of these problems is beyond the scope of this chapter. The emphasis in this discussion is on the major components and characteristics required in a coastal zone data system.

The term network does not imply a highly automated system of sensors, data communications, and computers. In many cases, data communication would be by mail and manual processing would be employed.

3. NETWORK SYSTEMS

Data acquisition

A coastal system of sensors and offshore platforms is required for acquiring environmental data for multiple applications. Coastal wave height and direction, surface pressure, humidity, surface water temperature, and wind direction and speed would be acquired for coastal engineering and weather monitoring and prediction applications. In addition, these data would be used in fish location prediction and for coastal transportation operations. Parameters for water quality control such as dissolved oxygen, pH, conductivity, temperature, dissolved chlorides, oxidation-reduction potential, turbidity, and total carbon would also be recorded for water quality applications.

Data communication

Some data and products would be processed by the state data centers prior to their distribution to local and state government users, while other data and products would be obtained directly by the users. An example of the former is the telemetering of estuarine water quality data from several locations to the state data center for storage, analysis, and dissemination to interested parties in a state and to the FWPCA. An example of the latter is the direct access by state research personnel of research reports produced by scientific institutions.

There are several subsystems of the total communication system which should be distinguished. These are the federal, interstate, and intrastate subsystems. The federal subsystem is the existing and planned federal data networks, civilian and military, which are existing and potential sources of data for the coastal environmental network. Examples of these subsystems, certain of which are now incorporated with the National Oceanic and Atmospheric Administration, are the ESSA Weather Bureau Network, the Naval Environmental Data Network, the STORET (FWPCA) system for the collection and processing of interstate water quality data, and the Department of Interior fishery data collection and processing systems. Some federal subsystems are not automated communication and processing operations. Rather, these subsystems provide multiple sources of original data collection, storage, processing, and dissemination; data communication is primarily by mail. An example is the national "network" for the collection of oceanographic data by scientific institutions and federal agencies and the storage, processing, and dissemination of these data by national data centers. With the exception of certain military data, all the federal networks may be tapped at the source of original data collection or after the data have been processed by national or other federal data centers. Environmental data and analyses for prediction purposes, for example, weather forecasting, are routinely available to state agencies through normal channels. Special climatic summaries are available from federal data centers, such as the National Weather Records Center. Sea surface temperature data and analyses are also routinely made available by the Naval Weather Service to the Bureau of Commercial Fisheries on the West Coast for use in predicting fish location. This information is available to coastal zone fishery resource managers and researchers.

Since much of the federal network is supported by large processing facilities and finished data products can be made available to the states, there is no requirement for the states to provide similar services. However, there is a need for creating a more automated interface between state data users and federal data systems. This need arises, for example, in the retrieval of data by a state

from national data centers. Retrieval could be improved by insti-
tuting one or more of the following:

- Providing liaison between the states and the federal centers.
- Installing conventional teletype links between state agencies
  and national centers.
- Installing remote computer terminals at state agencies with
  data communication links to federal centers.
- Providing centralized data analysis and message transmittal
  and receiving centers in the states.

Interstate data communication subsystems exist or are needed
wherever effective management of the coastal zone involves more
than one state. Examples are the management of regional fisheries,
water pollution and control, and weather monitoring and prediction. Since the problems of the coastal zone do not respect state
boundaries, it is obvious that data systems should not be compart-
mentalized according to state boundaries. If a coastal zone network
is to be effective, there must be a free flow of data across state
boundaries and between the coastal states and the Federal Government. Data communication among states could be improved by
standardizing data formats, codes, and communication terminal
equipment for data which are communicated among states. Standardization of computer processing equipment, analysis procedures,
or software in each state would not be necessary. The standardization which is required is at the interface between users in different
political bodies. This approach allows complete freedom for each
state and subordinate political bodies to employ the equipment, processing procedures, and software which is optimum for each state.

Loosely structured intrastate data communication "systems"
exist in such areas as water quality, fisheries management, and
recreational boating regulation. These systems are characterized
by local collection and use of raw data and the submission of statistical data to state authorities. These systems are typically largely
unmechanized and lacking in standardization of data collection
procedures and data formats.

A state is a sufficiently large political unit to warrant some centralization and coordination of data collection and processing procedures, whereas centralization would be impractical for the entire
coastal zone, although common data interfaces should be provided
among states. The large number of county and municipal units
make it wasteful to operate nonstandard data systems for each unit.
This is not to say that a political unit of sufficient size should not

operate a data system. Rather, each local data system should operate according to standard procedures. Some of the measures which can be taken to provide better utilization of data within a state are the following:

- Provide standard procedures for the collection of data: instruments, accuracy, precision, format, codes, and so on.
- Provide standard processing procedures for statistical data which are collected and processed by local units and transmitted to the states, for example, fish catch/effort summaries.
- Provide standard data communication terminal interfaces (where automated systems exist) and standard manual data transmission procedures where manual systems exist.

Data centers

The creation of state coastal zone data centers is needed as a major component of the coastal data network. The purpose of these data centers is to store, process, and retrieve the three categories of data which have been previously described, for both marine and land natural resource data pertaining to the coastal zone. Since geological characteristics are continuous from dry land to submerged areas and some physical and biological characteristics are not distinct at water's edge, it is not desirable to maintain separate land and marine data bases. In addition, a common coordinate indexing system can be employed, if the data are not segregated. Land and marine data would be distinguished by codes in the integrated data base. The indexing system is discussed in greater detail in the following section.

4. DATA STORAGE AND RETRIEVAL DESIGN

The first step is to inventory and classify the available data in the coastal zone. Matrices would be constructed which would indicate the availability of data by geographic area, time of observation or collection, depth and parameter type. The following system of indexing and identifying the data uniquely in space and time could be employed:

> *Lateral*—latitude and longitude (geographic location) 1° Marsden square or arbitrary grid system.
> *Vertical*—depth with respect to the surface of the water. Subcategories of this dimension would be above water surface,

water surface, water column, bottom, and subbottom.
Time—time of data collection or observation.
Parameter type—type(s) of parameters collected.

Each data element would be uniquely identified by lateral, vertical, and time coordinates.

A concurrent activity would be the determination of data needs and an assessment of the criticality of data for coastal zone planning and development. Criticality is determined by ascertaining the effect on planning and development of incomplete or inaccurate data. Highly critical data require highly refined data collection programs. Noncritical data require only gross data collection techniques. Data would be ranked by their criticality, accuracy, and quantity requirements. Next, data availability would be matched with data needs to determine current data deficiencies. Data deficiencies would be described by parameter type, amount, geographic region, depth, and time of data collection. In addition, preprocessing operations, such as code conversion, formating, media conversion, calibration, and quality control, would be specified as part of the data collection and preprocessing programs.

Data bases would be designed to provide several data retrieval modes: time series, synoptic, water column, vertical profiles, horizontal profiles, parameter values for a single point in space and time, and vertical and horizontal contours of constant parameter values. The data management system must be designed so that the efficiency of file maintenance and data retrieval would not depend on data base organization. Data base organization should not be designed to favor a particular application of the data, such as recreation, at the expense of other applications. For this reason, separate data bases for water quality, transportation, fishing, and such, should not be constructed. Rather, a generalized system which integrates all of the data, independently of the application, should be employed.

Coastal zone data bases should be established on the basis of correlating the available data in space (geographic location and depth of observation) and time (time of observation). This would involve the consolidation of data from various data bases into one data base. All the data obtained from a given geographic location (1° square), depth and time would be stored as a unit in the consolidated data base. The resulting data base would be an analog of the coastal zone. Data bases should not be organized by method and instrument of data collection, for example, BT. The method of data collection is important information and should be retained in the data base, but it is not necessary or desirable to organize files on this basis. It would be more useful to employ a data base organization which would permit convenient access to all the data collected at a given location, depth, and time. Also, the data base organization should provide the capability for retrieving the data for all or specified parameters under the following conditions: (1) at or between specified depths, location, and time (water column data and vertical profiles) ; (2) at a specified depth and geographic region and for a constant or variable time of observation (water layer data and horizontal profiles) ; (3) at a specified observation or data collection time, geographic region, and depth(s) (synoptic data) ; (4) at specified locations and depth(s) and chronologically ordered by time of observation (time series data) ; (5) for specified parameter(s) value(s) or range of values, geographic region, depth ranges, and time [surfaces of constant parameter value; e.g., surfaces of constant temperature, or density; a surface of constant parameter value is the same as the traditional contour lines of constant parameter value except that three dimensions are used (depth in addition to latitude and longitude)] ; (6) for a specified value or range of parameter(s) values, depth, and geographic region (contours of constant parameter value in two dimensions; e.g., contours of constant sea surface temperature, surface currents, water temperature or density at a specified depth) ; and (7) for water column properties along a specified track (an assembly of water column properties data for a series of 1° squares along a specified track). Other examples could be cited. These examples serve to illustrate the types of presentation which could be produced. Certain definitions which are relevant to the discussion of data sets as they would be employed in the data storage and retrieval system follow:

- Water column data: sets of data collected in a vertical water column at a given location and time. These data sets would contain all data collected in a particular water column (and bottom and subbottom)—not just Nansen cast data alone. These data sets include more than the traditional ocean station data.
- Synoptic data: sets of data obtained at a specified time or within a specified time interval from several or many locations. The data may be collected from a number of independent platforms and data collection programs.
- Time series data: sets of chronologically ordered data for

specified locations and depths. The data may have been collected by different cruises and over long time intervals.

An important point is that the data storage and retrieval system produces the data assemblies from a diversity of data sources, which vary by cruise, method of data collection, time of collection, and such. These data assemblies may not strictly correspond to ocean station, synoptic, and time series in the sense that these terms are sometimes applied to the *method* of data collection. However, the method of data collection should not govern the methods used for storing and retrieving data. For example, the synoptic data may not be synoptic in the sense of 6-hour ship reports used in a weather forecasting system. Rather, the synoptic data are produced in the data base by assembling and correlating cruise or survey data (where the cruises and surveys may be completely unrelated) which were obtained at approximately the same time from different locations. Similarly, the assembly of time series data may consist of parameter(s) which were collected at the same location, but by different cruises and at different times.

A discussion of a method for storing data which would accomplish the data retrieval properties which have been described follows. The three dimensions (height, radius, and circumference) of disk storage devices (or other three dimensional storage devices) are ideally suited to the implementation of the type of data base organization which has been described. The geometrical coordinates of the disk could correspond to the coordinates of the data as follows:

> Geographical location (1° square)—disk track and record (θ coordinate).
> Depth—disk surface (z coordinate).
> Time of observation or data collection—disk cylinder (γ coordinate).

This scheme is shown in Figure 3. Other mappings between data coordinates and storage device coordinates could be employed. If data are stored in this manner, it is possible to retrieve time series data for various geographic locations and depths; synoptic data for various geographical locations and depths; and all or certain data for a given location, depth, and time. It is possible to retrieve the various data sets concurrently. For example, as the disk rotates under the set of read-write heads (one for each disk surface), cylinders of data retrieved along the θ (location) coordinate for a given γ

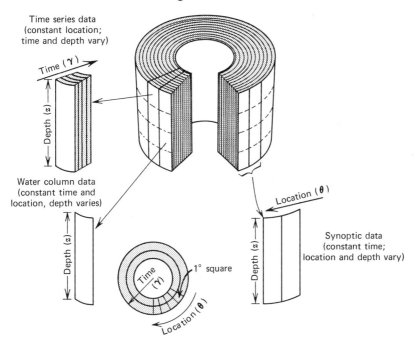

Figure 3. Method of storing coastal zone data on disk storage.

(time) coordinate represent synoptic data; cylinders of data retrieved along the γ (time) coordinate for a given θ (location) coordinate represent time series data; data retrieved along the z (depth) coordinate for given γ (time) and θ (location) coordinates represent water column data; data retrieved along the θ (location) coordinate for a given z depth (coordinate) and γ (time) coordinates represent constant depth horizontal "slices" through the ocean; data retrieved for a given γ, θ, and z represent all the data for a given time, location, and depth. There is no limit (other than disk storage capacity) to the number of synoptic, time series, water column, and single point retrievals which could be accomplished in a single search operation. Of course, time series retrieval will require track switching, and other forms of data retrieval may require track switching if the geographical and time domains of the data to be retrieved are extensive.

The data base organization which is employed will be influenced in part by the user demand for data. If time series data are requested more frequently than water column data, the z coordinate would be used for time and the γ coordinate for depth. Certain difficulties in the data storage scheme should be noted. One is that voids in certain data cells may arise due to large gaps in collected data in terms of location, time, and depth. Second, the number of disk surfaces, tracks, and records will not always correspond to the number of different locations, depths, and observation times used in the storage system. A possible solution to these problems is to leave voids in certain data locations and preserve the integrity of the addressing scheme (e.g., leave room for $1°$ squares for which no data currently exists). This solution would probably be very wasteful of storage space. A better solution would be to pack the data based on locations, depths, and times which are currently represented in the data base; temporarily store new $1°$ square data sets out of sequence on the disk; and periodically reorganize the data base into a completely sequentially addressed system. This can be performed by copying and merging the disk data onto "scratch" disks. An automated directory of data would be used in conjunction with the storage and retrieval of the data. This directory would contain information about the characteristics of the stored data. If data are stored on disk, the directory would contain disk head, track, and record number addresses. If the data are stored on magnetic tape, the directory would contain tape reel number and the location of a given data set relative to other data sets. The purpose of the directory is twofold. First, it serves to provide information to the user and data center concerning the availability and characteristics of stored data, that is, cruise, date, ship track, institutions, and instruments used. Second, the directory provides pointers to the machine locations of classes of data, for example, water column, water layer, synoptic, and time series. Ideally, the directory should be stored on disk. If stored on disk, the directory could be organized with the same coordinate system as used for the data themselves. The directory contains the storage locations of data which are indexed by geographic location, depth, and time. In addition to storage addresses, the directory would contain coded information which indicates the type of data stored. Thus the directory would provide the address or range of addresses of various data sets, after the correspondence (by computer program) between the nature of the data retrieval (location, depth, time, and parameter type) and the computer address has been made. The address information would be inserted in data retrieval routines. The data directory must, of course, be maintained along with the data bases themselves as new data are incorporated in the system.

This type of data organization would also be appropriate for use in conjunction with a "live atlas" presentation. More importantly, it would pull together the data in a fashion which corresponds to the description of the coastal regime. The data storage system would become an analog of the coastal zone not only for the purpose of specific data retrieval, but also for application in modeling. In particular, the system would have direct application to computer graphics. Since the data would be organized as a model of the coastal zone (with rapid access capability), the graphic capability could be applied to portray the types of data presentations described earlier.

5. EXAMPLES OF PROPOSED COASTAL ZONE DATA SYSTEMS

Water quality

The utility of a water quality system for marine data is governed largely by our ability to establish water quality standards which can be employed as reliable indicators of the presence of pollution when the standards are exceeded. In addition, the standards must have such high statistical confidence that legal challenges by waste dischargers can be withstood. A major problem in establishing standards is the difficulty in selecting a set of environmental parameters for measurement which will be valid indicators of the existence of pollution. Second, the frequency and duration of sampling, precision of recording, and density and geographical distribution of sensors must be ascertained to establish the statistical integrity of the measurement. Once the data collection requirements have been established, the data must be obtained. This has proven difficult due to incomplete knowledge of the types of parameters which should be measured and the sampling design which should be employed. The problem is complicated by a highly decentralized system of water quality control in the states and municipalities, each with its own philosophy regarding water quality criteria and pollution control measures. Until these problems are resolved, the usefulness of a water quality data system will be limited. However, it is still important to proceed with the building of a coastal zone water quality data base in parallel with the research which is necessary to better define the criteria for water quality and the associated data requirements.

Since future data requirements are difficult to predict, both in terms of the data to be stored and the questions which will be asked of the data system, it is important to provide great flexibility in the methods utilized for the storage and retrieval of data. The system should be easy to use and should not require the user to either store or retrieve data in rigid computer-oriented formats. The system should also be capable of remote inquiry by a large number of geographically dispersed users. Users should not have to employ complicated data coding forms and mail them to a computer center in order to store or retrieve data. Although numeric coding of data is highly desirable within the computer system in order to achieve economies in storage space and file processing time, free-form formats should be employed for user requests, and data submissions. The retrieval language and input format should be as natural and as computer-independent as the state of the art of information processing technology will permit. With this type of system, the user would not have to be concerned with parameter code numbers, formats of control cards, sequence of control cards, or other detailed information required by the computer but of no interest to the user. A generalized type of retrieval language is highly desirable for the operation of remote inquiry terminals. The cost of providing this flexibility is the cost of resources required for implementing a generalized information storage and retrieval (IS&R) system. This cost is difficult to estimate at the present time due to the uncertainty concerning the plans of computer manufacturers to provide information storage and retrieval systems and languages. These systems have not been standardized as have COBOL and FORTRAN. Many generalized information systems of varying capabilities are available from software firms. Some are primarily file processors and report generators and do not possess sophisticated retrieval capabilities. Others are data management systems with highly sophisticated retrieval capabilities.

Two modes of operation are envisaged which involve the use of remote facilities. One is the remote retrieval and exchange of data by users in the various states and municipalities. The primary need for this type is to provide researchers and water quality officials with direct access to data bases. The value to the researcher is for experimentation in discovering relationships between changes in the environment and the introduction of pollutants. The administrator can use the system as a vehicle for training exercises in pollution monitoring and control or in actual decision situations if data of sufficient quantity and quality are available. Also, the remote inquiry mode of operation can be employed as an experimental system to test the feasibility of this method of operation prior to implementation. The second type of remote operation is one in which data would be telemetered from sensors located in selected estuaries in the coastal zone to state data centers. The primary purpose of this system would be to test the feasibility of the remote acquisition and transmission of water quality data to central storage and processing facilities and the use of these data for continuous monitoring, prediction, and control functions. This system could be gradually augmented in the future to become a vehicle for water quality monitoring, prediction, and control. Since requirements for the collection of water quality data are largely undefined at this time, only gross estimates of an instrumentation and telemetry system can be provided. Eight parameters, such as dissolved oxygen, pH, conductivity, temperature, dissolved chlorides, oxidation-reduction potential, turbidity, and total carbon are assumed to be recorded at each sampling station. Twenty sampling stations per estuary are assumed. If eight parameters (six characters per parameter) from 20 stations are sampled once per minute, 960 characters per minute would be transmitted on TWX or Data Phone facilities to state data centers.

An important adjunct of this system is the development of models for making water quality forecasts. These models would be integrated with the data system so that it may serve as a source of input data for the models and also as a vehicle for model validation and adjustment (improvement of models as more data become available for checking model validity.)

An important facet of water quality activity which has received relatively little attention is the use of economic data and analysis for water quality planning and control. These data consist of such items as the economic and social impact of pollution, water uses, population statistics, and so on. A systematic program for the collection and storage of these data should be started. Much of these data exist in city and county planning files and census files. These files need to be associated with the relevant water quality data.

The water quality data system would be programmed to automatically detect conditions of water quality which are below standards. Of course, water quality standards must first be determined for various areas and stored in the system. The automatic monitoring for below standard water quality can be performed in either the batch processing or on-line mode of operation. Information on industrial waste dischargers and oil spills and leaks (type of discharge, rate of discharge, rate of dispersion, geographical area affected, property damage, etc.) would be included in the system.

Programs would be developed for the analysis of environmental parameters before and after the inception of waste discharge activities to assess the damage done to the environment by pollutants. An analysis of environmental parameters would also be made before and after the inception of waste treatment operations to assess the value of waste treatment operations. The analysis programs and required data would be incorporated in the data system.

Fisheries

Major problems exist with respect to the collection, processing, and reporting of fishery statistics in the coastal zone. These problems are as follows.

- Inadequate funding and data processing equipment.
- Difficulties in obtaining data from commercial fishermen.
- Inconsistencies in data formats.
- Lack of personnel, equipment, and processing procedures in the field for collecting and disseminating statistics.

There are two aspects of fishery statistics:

- Regional reporting of daily and weekly statistics.
- Compilation and reporting of national statistics on an annual basis.

Since there are problems peculiar to each fishery and region, a highly decentralized fishery statistics data collection and data dissemination system are desirable. A description of one segment of this system will illustrate the concept. One location in each region would be designated as the primary receiving and disseminative point for fishery statistics, preseason abundance forecasts, fishery products reports, and fishery advisories. A major fishery is associated with each of the primary locations. Each of the primary locations would be linked by telephone for the communication of digital data to and from other satellite locations. Each satellite facility would collect and disseminate fishery statistics within its area. The processing for each region would be performed at the primary location. Summary statistics and computations would be transmitted over telephone lines to the terminals at satellite locations for ultimate distribution to area processors, distributors, fishermen, universities, and laboratories. Primary locations would be the contact for distributing fish catch/effort data and summaries to state authorities. In addition to statistical information services, the primary locations would provide fishery advisory services and preseason abundance forecasts. The data processing systems at each primary location would be utilized for the preparation of forecasts. The success of these efforts would be highly dependent on the research required to develop relationships between fish migration and behavior with environmental and biological factors. The system would also include sport fishery data collection and processing.

Coastal engineering and weather forecasting

An important requirement for aiding research for the design of coastal structures and beach restoration projects is a wave gauge network along the coasts of the United States, including Hawaii, Alaska, and the Great Lakes. For coastal engineering research and design the system would operate in a nonreal time mode. In addition to its use as a source of historical data for coastal development, such a system would have equal value for coastal weather, wave and surf monitoring, warnings, and forecasts. For this application, the system would operate in real time. The proposed wave data acquisition and processing system would be expanded from a very few stations which currently acquire and telemeter data to approximately 100 stations over the decade. Data would be transmitted over telephone lines to forecast centers and from selected stations to research centers. This could be accomplished by providing voltage controlled subcarrier oscillators for each gauge at each station. The resultant frequency modulated signals are multiplexed and frequency modulate a telephone line carrier. The transmitted signal is demodulated at the receiving end and subcarrier discriminators recover the three original sensor signals from the multiplexed signal. These analog signals are then converted to digital data under the on-line control of an analog to digital (A/D) converter and control unit which receives its commands from digital computers in research and forecast centers. The A/D conversion is controlled by software statements executed in the digital computer. This type of data reduction arrangement provides the capability of remote control of the readout time, frequency, duration, and sampling rate of the analog wave sensors. This arrangement would provide complete control of data acquisition, digitization, and analyses.

The utilization of a national coastal network of wave gauge stations for coastal weather, wave and surf monitoring, and forecasting would significantly improve these functions. Instrumentation for obtaining other parameters, such as wind speed and direction, pressure, air temperature, water temperature, and humidity would be installed at the gauge sites and these data would be telemetered along with wave height and direction to forecast centers. This system would permit the automatic acquisition of instrumented surface and wave observations, detection and reporting of severe waves, and the use of the data in making coastal weather, wave, and surf forecasts. The frequency, duration, and sampling rate of obtaining observations would be under the control of computers in local forecast centers.

The requirements for such a system include the following:

- Computers for local forecast centers.
- Communication equipment for telemetering data to forecast centers.
- Software for data acquisition; spectral analysis; surface observation editing and plotting; and plots and listings for wave statistics, spectral analysis, SST charts, and surface observations.

6. SUMMARY

To summarize, the major requirement for the development of a coastal zone data network is to provide some centralization of storage and processing within each state and to provide interfaces among federal, state, and coastal zone systems so that greater coordination and standardization of data collection and processing may result. The resulting coastal zone network could be characterized as a moderately centralized intrastate system but as a highly decentralized interstate system.

Some of the measures which are needed to develop a coastal zone data network are the following:

- Development and maintenance of an inventory of coastal zone data.
- Establishment of interstate and intrastate data format and transmission standards.
- Establishment in the states of an organizational structure for facilitating the exchange of data among local, state, and federal agencies and the private sector.
- Establishment of a central data center in each state under state control.

- Development of a consistent method for indexing and storing the data.
- Storage of data in a form which is an analog of the coastal zone for the purposes of efficiency of retrieval and the development of coastal zone models.
- Establishment of coastal zone data systems, in such areas as water quality, fisheries, coastal engineering, and weather monitoring and forecasting as part of a larger coastal zone data network.

BIBLIOGRAPHY

Aubert, Eugene J., et al., *A Study of the Feasibility of National Data Buoy System*, Final Report 7485, The Travelers Research Center, Inc., Hartford, Conn., 1967.

Brahtz, John (Ed.), *Ocean Engineering, Goals, Environment, Technology*, Wiley, New York, 1968.

California and The Ocean, A Report By The Resources Agency, December 1966.

California and the World Ocean, conference proceedings: a conference convened by Gov. Edmund G. Brown at the California Museum of Science and Industry, Los Angeles, Calif., January 31–February 1, 1964.

California and Use of the Ocean, University of California, Institute of Marine Resources, La Jolla, Calif., IMR Ref. 65-21, October 1965.

"Federal Plan for MAREP-Marine Environmental Prediction," Interagency Committee on Ocean Exploration and Environmental Services, National Council on Marine Resources and Engineering Development, Washington, D.C., July 1, 1968.

Governor's Advisory Commission on Ocean Resources, Compilation of Recommendations, State Office of Planning, Department of Finance, Sacramento, Calif., January 1965–January 1967, December 20, 1966.

Green, Richard Stedman, Donald Paul Dubois, and Clarence Wilson Tutwiler, "Data Handling Systems in Water Pollution Control," ASCE Water Resources Engineering Conference, Mobile, Ala., March 1965.

Ocean Engineering, Vols. 1–4, National Security Industrial Association, Washington, D.C. 1965.

Operations Research Reports for the National Ocean Survey Program, NSIA/ORI/ESSA, Operations Research, Inc.

Our Nation and the Sea, A Plan for National Action, Report of the Commission on Marine Science, Engineering and Resources, U.S. Government Printing Office, Washington, D.C., January 1969.

Problems of Setting Standards and of Surveillance for Water Quality Control, Publ. 36, State of California Resources Agency, 1967.

Schneidewind, Norman F., et al., *National Data Program for the Marine Environment*, Vol. 1, Phase I, Final Report, System Development Corporation, Santa Monica, Calif., TM (L)-3705/003/00.

Schneidewind, Norman F., et al., *National Data Program for the Marine Environment*, Vol. 1 and 2, Final Report, System Development Corporation, Santa Monica, Calif., TM-4023/005/00.

Storage and Retrieval of Data for Open Water and Land Areas, STORET II, U.S. Dept. of the Interior, Federal Water Pollution Control Administration, Division of Pollution Surveillance.

The Storage and Retrieval of Data for Water Quality Control, U.S. Dept. of the Interior, Federal Water Pollution Control Administration.

A Ten Year Plan For Ocean Exploration, National Council On Marine Resources And Engineering Development, Washington, D.C., July 10, 1968.

CHAPTER 9

Ocean Installations: State of Technology

J. GORDON HAMMER

Much of the discussion in Part 1 of this book is about goals, uses, and conflicts arising in the Coastal Zone. These are examined from a number of viewpoints: social, economic, and political. It is generally concluded that to attain these goals requires a type of management never before necessary. The challenge of meeting these goals, resolving conflicts, and providing the means of physically managing the Coastal Zone must include a major contribution from engineers. Specifically, engineers will be challenged to effect changes in the Coastal Zone, control its environment, and construct major physical systems in the zone. The extent to which they can successfully do this will depend on the state of engineering technology. The objective of this chapter is to examine the available technology, indicate needed progress, and speculate on the future contributions that ocean installations might make to the management of the Coastal Zone.

Physically managing the Coastal Zone implies controlling the sea, preserving the coastline, then altering one or both, along with supporting necessary coastal activity and ultimately providing an extension of normal land-oriented activities into the marine environment. This requires physically constructing in the Coastal Zone, that is, ocean installations. We are concerned with the state of the technology available for doing this. We have reached a logical point in the planning sequence where we must turn from the abstract to the concrete, from ideas to things, and from the ideal to the possible.

The technology for constructing in the Coastal Zone is based on extremely old principles. Many of the kinds of installations used today were in use a thousand or more years ago. There has been a gradual improvement in technology in the sense that larger projects are possible; methods are improved; and the resulting installations are more efficient. Technology is thus advancing in a slow evolutionary way. We do the same kind of things, but we do them better. This kind of technology is our conventional capability. Relatively few demands have been made to challenge this capability on a scale as large, for instance, as the challenge to the aerospace technology to reach the moon. We suspect, however, that this same latent capability is present in the case of ocean installations. It is obvious, however, that mobilization of this tremendous technological potential would require universally popular goals and the necessary political and economic support. The technological barriers are probably the least formidable.

Engineering can limit or remove conflicts between competing uses of the Coastal Zone. Careful planning can permit coexistence of incompatible operations, for example, fishing and petroleum extraction, recreational swimming and boating, and waste disposal. Engineering can also help resolve conflicts arising elsewhere. A current example is the present interest in building airports offshore, a possible way of resolving the problems of land acquisition, nuisance abatement, air corridor safety, and such. It is probable that in the near future the complex problems of urban congestion, environmental pollution, and general population explosion will make utilization of the offshore portion of the Coastal Zone more attractive and more nearly economically competitive.

There is an interrelation between engineering technology and the goals we set for managing the Coastal Zone. The goals determine the technology that is needed; but the available technology helps determine what goals are realistic. To this must be added the time element. Reasonable goals should be based on a realizable schedule, and the probable state of the technology must be forecast so that the goals and the means of achieving them are compatible.

Another important consideration is that the engineer is tampering with a very complex system when he attempts to further a single goal. It is entirely possible that in solving one problem he creates other equally serious problems. His work can easily add to the existing conflicts. A seemingly unrelated engineering project can significantly alter the Coastal Zone. For example, new freeways make the beaches so accessible that major traffic jams bring normal traffic to a halt and even paralyze the operation of emergency vehicles. Often a new freeway will change patterns of residential development so that the original purpose for the freeway becomes a secondary requirement. Large changes in population density can change recreation patterns, overload utilities, and make waste disposal systems inadequate. Often the latter will involve the Coastal Zone. A harbor or marina may alter the normal littoral pattern so that deposited unwanted sand clogs the entrance at the expense of a beach below, which slowly erodes away without replenishment.

In the broadest sense, the Coastal Zone comprises an area that is inland and predominantly a dry environment, an area that is the interface between land and water, and an area seaward that is predominantly a marine environment. The three areas present different problems to the engineer. The best developed technology is that available for the dry land area; the next best is that for the shoreline area; and the least developed is that for the marine environment.

There is an ever-increasing need to use more of the Coastal Zone, moving seaward. The engineering response has been largely to use dry land technology adapted to the semimarine environment. A great challenge to engineers now is to develop technology specifically for constructing durable, efficient structures in the marine environment. This will require the capability for engineering operations in deeper water, cutting loose from dependence on the ocean floor for support, and the development of underwater construction technology.

With considerations like these in mind and realizing that the technology of ocean installations cannot possibly be covered in a few pages, we now turn our attention to our problem: the engineering contribution to management of the Coastal Zone.

1. STATE OF TECHNOLOGY

Our interest is in the kind of engineering support for management of the Coastal Zone that can be provided with ocean installations. Looking at the state of technology, we can single out several important areas for discussion: load determination, analytical procedures, materials science, marine construction techniques, and surveillance and maintenance. While these are areas of significant recent technological progress, they remain a challenge; and it is in these same areas that future progress will have to be made if engineering technology is to be completely responsive to the goals set by planners.

Coastal installations must adequately perform their primary and secondary functions over a reasonable lifetime and at a reasonable cost. Important criteria for such installations are functional adequacy, esthetic acceptability, structural adequacy, durability or long life with minimum maintenance, and overall cost effectiveness.

Most of the significant progress has been made fairly recently, in the past 25 years or so. Although the progress has been in the more conventional technology, there hopefully will be a fallout that will enable the engineering profession to be responsive to nonconventional demands as well.

Load determination

The basic consideration in structural adequacy is what loading the installation will be subjected to in its lifetime. For an installation in the ocean, the most severe loading conditions are almost always caused by wind-generated water waves. These loads can be enormous. For example, the total energy of a wave 10 feet high and 500 feet long in deep water may be as high as a half million foot pounds per linear foot of crest. The alterations brought about in the wave by shallow water place a large part of the wave energy above the level of still water and transport it at a speed approaching that of the wave itself. In the surf zone, pressure readings obtained with dynamometers have been as high as 3 tons per square foot [1]. Wind-generated waves of this sort present an extremely severe loading condition for a coastal installation. Unless these forces can be predicted and provided for, a satisfactory installation cannot be designed.

Coastal installations will have to be constructed in the surf zone, beyond the surf zone but in relatively shallow water, and in deeper water. Water wave characteristics are different in each of these locations, but the problem in general is to relate the loading on an obstacle such as a structure to the shape and motion of the waves. Against a solid surface, such as a wall, loadings can be predicted fairly well from considerations of energy and momentum conservation. Against a smaller obstruction, such as a cylindrical piling, it is also necessary to consider the forces caused by the flow past the obstruction. It is customary to use a rational but approximate relationship that linearly combines a drag force involving a drag coefficient and an inertia force involving a mass coefficient [2]. The drag force is usually considered proportional to the square of the velocity of the water particles. This type of expression is probably more accurate if the flow of water is nearly steady, as might be the case with long, nonbreaking waves. It is, however, a linear approximation to a nonlinear problem. Dean [3] has pointed out that in the problem of wave loadings on piles there are at least four causes of nonlinearity:

1. The nonlinear relationship between the wave profile and the water particle kinematics: particle velocity u and particle acceleration $\dot{u}$.

2. The nonlinear relationship between the drag force and the water particle velocity.

3. The convective nonlinear terms in the water particle acceleration.

4. The nonlinearity resulting from the varying length of submerged members, for example, pilings.

Nevertheless, at present the commonly accepted technique is to base the calculated forces on a linear combination of a term involving the velocity u of the water particles and a term involving the acceleration $\dot{u}$ of the water particles. If the wave profile is estimated using linear wave theory, u and $\dot{u}$ can be obtained. The practice is to calculate the coefficients of drag and mass from experimentally obtained total forces and computed values of u and $\dot{u}$. Since the latter are not accurate, the results for the drag and inertia coefficients are distorted. Dean estimates that the use of linear wave theory to estimate u and $\dot{u}$ for large waves will cause errors in C_d and C_m as large as 42 and 28% (compared to Stokes fifth-order theory). For a nonlinear wave system there is no exact method of transferring water surface displacement to water particle dynamics. The approximate method is to fit a nonlinear wave profile to the measured wave profile and adjust the parameters for a best fit.

The point of the preceding discussion is that it is difficult to calculate loads caused by water waves. It is not completely clear how the loads relate to the kinematics of the water particles; and it is not completely clear how the kinematics of the water particles relate to the wave profile, except under idealized conditions. There is even additional uncertainty as to how the wave form that arrives at the installation relates to the forces out at sea that originally caused it.

The problem of wave motion in a fluid such as water has been of interest to mathematicians for hundreds of years. There are many elaborate wave theories based on different fundamental assumptions [4]. These assumptions include whether linear; wave height relative to depth; whether the depth is shallow, medium, or deep; whether the pressure distribution is hydrostatic; rotationality versus nonrotationality; whether frictional forces are considered; whether the wave is oscillatory or translatory; and whether there is mass transport. Only a few of these theories lead to equations that have exact solutions. The others must be solved by various series approximations or numerical techniques.

None of these theories really tells us what we need to know to predict the loading on a structure. If we had experimental values or parameters to use in the appropriate theory, we could calculate the particle dynamics and try to proceed from there to determine the loads on a structure. However, we would run into the problems described previously.

Probably a more serious limitation in looking at individual wave profiles is that the wave systems are not that orderly and simple. Even if waves are generated in a fairly uniform pattern, they soon become highly complex and far from periodic. This state can best be described as a random process; and although this random nature has been understood for a long time, it was not until recently that ocean waves were considered to be essentially a random process.

The value in treating the problem as a random one is that a highly complex process can be described by a few statistical parameters. If certain assumptions are made, that is, that the waves are random in character and that the height above mean level is a stationary random function, the average wave properties can be related to the energy spectrum for the wave frequency. This kind of representation does much to systemize the chaotic motion of the seas by means of its statistical properties. From a spectrum such as this, one can calculate significant wave height (the mean height of the highest one-third of the waves), period range in which 90% of the energy is found, and other useful statistics. A typical spectrum is shown in Figure 1.

The frequency spectrum can be obtained experimentally from time records of wave heights and narrow-band filtering. It can also be estimated by several empirical relationships using known steady wind velocities at a given height above the sea surface. This has made it possible to make "hindcasts" to estimate the state of the sea that existed during periods when wind or weather data were recorded. Lacking actual wind data, it is possible to calculate a "gradient" wind from pressure contours on weather charts [5].

All of the foregoing offers promise that engineers will be able to estimate the worst sea state at a given location that can be expected to occur during a certain number of years. This can be translated into a significant or design wave, from which loading criteria can

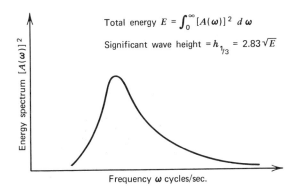

Total energy $E = \int_0^\infty [A(\omega)]^2 \, d\omega$

Significant wave height $= h_{1/3} = 2.83\sqrt{E}$

Frequency ω cycles/sec.

Figure 1. Typical ocean wave energy spectrum.

be formulated. There still remains, however, the problem discussed previously of relating wave particle dynamics to forces on a structure. This is best done by experiment, usually with models.

Wave spectra can be reproduced in large wave tanks for testing model structures or vessels. The Delft Hydraulics Laboratory in the Netherlands has recently constructed a servocontrolled wave generator for their new wind-wave flume. It is equipped with programmed hydraulically driven wave generators. The flumes have a length of 330 feet, a water depth of 3 feet, and a width of 27 and 7 feet. Random waves with frequencies from 0.3 to 3 cycles per second are generated by two separate actuators that permit both translatory and rotational movements. Two input signals can be used: a wave record that has been measured, or a random electronic signal derived from a random-noise generator and filtered by electronic filters according to the energy spectrum required. A very accurate reproduction of an energy spectrum can be produced in the model flume. From this, actual loadings on model structures can be measured and related to actual loads to be expected on the prototype structure.

Analytical procedures

In either design or analysis it is necessary to know the deformations and stresses in a given structure subjected to a specific loading condition. This is especially important in a coastal installation because of the dynamic character of the loads, because the loads are not in the direction of gravity forces, because the ocean

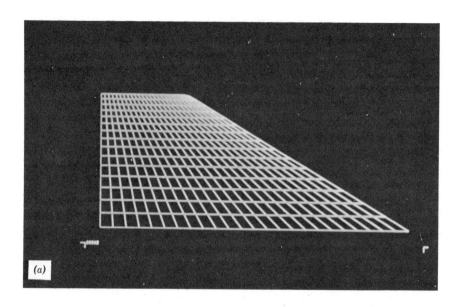

(a)

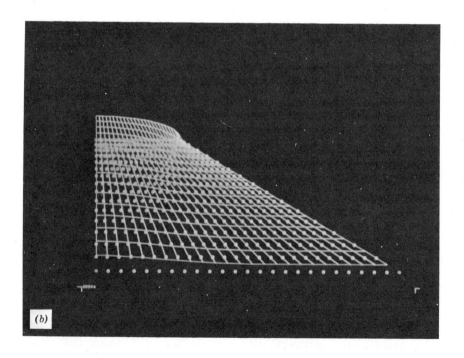

(b)

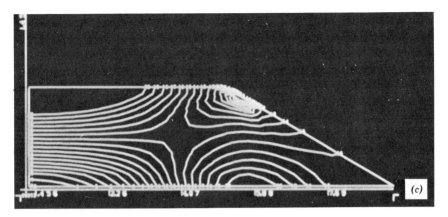

Figure 2. (*a*) Finite element grid for acrylic window. (*b*) Distorted shape under load. (*c*) Stress contours.

is a hostile environment for both construction and maintenance, and because structural failures in a coastal installation are potentially more dangerous to life and property.

The basic techniques for structural analysis are not new, but in the past there have been limitations in the kinds of equations that could be solved and in the time and labor available to do it. Now, however, electronic computation with its great speed has made it possible to obtain satisfactory answers to previously intractable problems by numerical approximations to the classical equations. Moreover, problems can now be solved to any desired degree of accuracy so quickly that it is possible to consider alternative solutions and come up with an optimal one. Computers can provide their answers in graphical form, and in some cases can make actual designs.

Techniques such as the particle-in-cell method and the finite element method have become very popular. The particle-in-cell method employs a combination of LaGrange and Euler formulations so that at successive intervals particles representing the material or fluid under study are traced through a network of fixed zones or cells. At each interval the necessary conditions of equilibrium, energy conservation, and mass and momentum conservation are satisfied. The problem is formulated numerically, and the whole process is tracked by the computer.

In the finite element method the behavior of a real structure is approximated by a mathematical model composed of subregions or elements in which the displacement field is restricted to some linear combination of preselected shape functions. The overall configuration of the model is specified by generalized coordinates associated with the shape functions. At each interval the configuration which minimizes the potential energy is determined. This configuration then can be used to determine the deformations (and stresses) in the individual elements. By careful choice of the size, number, and shape of the elements and by choosing the shape function that accurately represents the property of the material in the structure, it is possible to solve extremely complex stress propagation problems in both two and three dimensions. The principal limitation at present, particularly in three-dimensional problems, is the capacity of the computer used.

Both the particle-in-cell and finite element methods have been used to analyze complex structures subjected to static and dynamic loads. Figure 2 shows a computer solution by the finite element method for the stresses in an acrylic window intended as a viewport in an underwater portion of a structure. The window is shaped like a truncated cone. Because of rotational symmetry, only the cross section need be studied. The grid system shown lies along a principal diameter and extends from the axis of symmetry at the left to the outer edge at the right. Thus if the figure were rotated about its left edge, it would generate the shape of the actual window. The loading would be upward along the bottom surface and uniformly distributed. The window is supported along the inclined edge, which is actually an annular surface in the real window. Figure 2a shows the gridwork chosen. Figure 2b shows the distorted shape as the window is loaded upward uniformly and supported by bearing along its inclined (annular edge). This view is for a particular value of load, and the distorted shape can be translated into local strains in the material making up the window. Figure 2c shows contours having the same value of stress. The particular stress chosen to be calculated is a combination of the principal stresses at each point that satisfies an arbitrary criterion for yielding of the material (von Mises criterion). When this combined stress reaches some critical value for the material in question, yielding will begin. This kind of analysis will predict the adequacy of a structure made of a given material for a given loading condition. Figures 2a, b, and c were all computed and printed automatically by the computer [6].

In addition to the analytical techniques just discussed, techniques are being improved for experimentally analyzing a physical model of a structure or element. Foremost among these is the standard technique of photoelastic analysis, which is not new but is now applied to dynamic loadings and unusual stress conditions. The key to photoelasticity is that certain optically transparent materials have the property of birefringence. If plane polarized light is directed perpendicular to a plate of such a material strained in its own plane, the speed of light transmission varies according to the strain in the material and a fringe pattern is obtained. Figures 3 and 4 show the results of photoelastic analysis of models made of Homolite 100.

Figure 3 shows a section cut from a hollow vessel having the shape of a sphere intersected by a cylinder and resembling a light bulb in general appearance. The vessel was evacuated, sealed, heat treated, and then allowed to cool slowly so that stresses caused by the pressure differential of one atmosphere were locked in. Because

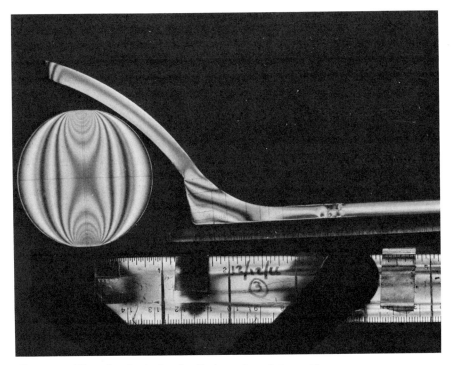

Figure 3.   Photoelastic study of cylinder-sphere intersection.

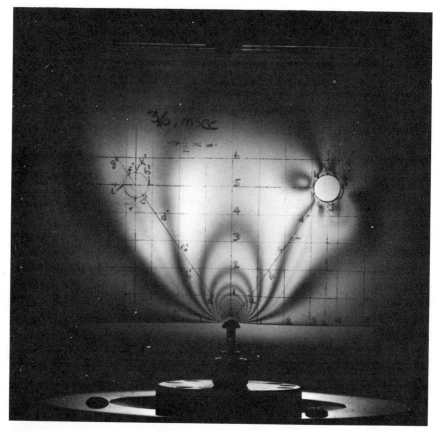

Figure 4. Dynamic photoelastic study of contact stresses.

of symmetry only the thin slice shaped like a question mark was necessary for photoelastic analysis. The round piece is used for fringe calibration. Of particular interest were the concentrations at the intersection of the cylinder with the sphere [7].

Another example of photoelastic analysis is shown in Figure 4. This is a model of a beam that was subjected to a vibrating, point-contact load. The load was applied with a constant frequency, causing a dynamic stress condition in the beam. At the same time a stroboscopic light was used that had a frequency slightly different from that of the load. Consequently, each successive illumination occurred at a slightly different stage of stress development, and a series of pictures was obtained to show the buildup of stress dynamically. In addition to the contact stresses at the point of loading, the stresses around the circular opening were studied [8].

The analyst thus has available to him a number of techniques which include mathematical simulation with a computer, physical simulation by a photoelastic model, scale modeling in wind and wave tanks, and full scale testing of prototypes. The results of specific analyses can be extended to formulate general relationships for analyzing other structures. The prospects for analyzing potential structures for the Coastal Zone seem very encouraging.

Materials science

Equally important to load determination and analytical procedures are the availability of workable, durable, and reasonable-cost construction materials and a knowledge of their basic behavioral properties in the ocean environment. As would be expected, the principal materials used in the Coastal Zone are those used for land installations. Timber, masonry, concrete, steel, and plastics are all finding applications in coastal installations. Timber and masonry have been used for the longest time. Concrete, and particularly prestressed concrete, is proving superior in certain applications. Steel is ideal in many ways and has long been the main material for ship construction. High-strength plastics also display durability, favorable weight, and even transparency.

Untreated timber is particularly susceptible to biodeterioration. This appears to be true in almost any depth of water and has been observed in tests conducted by the Naval Civil Engineering Laboratory on wood specimens at a depth of 6000 feet. In those tests the wood was almost completely destroyed by borers identified as a molluscan type (xylophaya washingtona). With proper treatment, however, timber is a very popular construction material for many kinds of ocean installations. It has a reasonably long life, and because of its comparatively low cost, it can be partially replaced if necessary and still be cost effective.

Masonry has compressive strength, large mass, and is especially suitable for seawalls, groins, breakwaters, and such. It has been used for these purposes for centuries. It is not susceptible to chemical or biological deterioration, and it is fireproof. Concrete has essentially these same qualities. In addition, concrete is easily formed in almost any shape, can be given tensile strength by reinforcement, and can be given balanced strength by prestressing. Admixtures are available for improving certain properties of concrete. Polymer concretes show great promise. Lightweight aggregates can be used to reduce overall weight. Concretes using extremely light plastic or glass aggregate have been proposed to produce a product of comparable density to water itself. If adequate strength properties can also be obtained, it is conceivable that engineers will have a workable concrete that is also buoyant in seawater. Because of its attractive appearance, great durability, geometric flexibility, and relatively low cost, concrete will undoubtedly be a principal construction material in coastal installations in the coming years.

Steel is outstanding from the standpoints of strength, versatility, ease of assembly, and cost. Its principal drawback is that it is highly susceptible to corrosion in underwater uses unless the proper preventative measures are taken. This can usually be accomplished without difficulty in ship construction, where the surface is carefully treated and covered with a protective paint; and the ship is periodically drydocked for scraping and repainting. In the case of a permanent marine structure there is usually no opportunity for that kind of maintenance. In fact, the liner *Queen Mary* is reported to have had some corrosion problems which were discernible after a little more than a year of stationary berthing in Long Beach. This apparently has been controlled by the application of coatings to the hull surface underwater. Steel sheet piling may last only 5 to 7 years without proper corrosion protection. With protection, this can be increased by a factor of about 5.

In order for corrosion to take place, it is necessary to have some galvanic action. An anode, cathode, and electrolyte are needed. The seawater serves very well as the electrolyte. Dissimilar metals can become anode and cathode. However, even a single metal can form anodes if there are irregularities in composition, such as might be caused by stress concentrations, welds, or fabrication. The same metal can provide both anode and cathode if part is in the sandy bottom and part is in the water. The portion acting as the anode is gradually corroded away. If there is wave action to expose the fresh metal underneath the corrosion products, the process can proceed at a rapid rate. Because of this and also because of the presence of a great deal of oxygen in ocean surface spray, the worst area for corrosion of steel sheet piling is the splash zone.

Generally speaking, there are three ways of preventing corrosion. The first way is to provide an anode that is expendable and can be readily replaced at predetermined intervals—the so-called sacrificial anode. For steel structures, an anode of zinc, aluminum, or magnesium would be effective.

The second way is to ensure that all parts of the structure are at the same potential so that there is no anode. Cathodic protection by means of an impressed direct current will do this. Typical voltages for impressed currents are 10 to 24 volts, compared to 0.25 to 0.50 volts for the galvanic systems. The impressed current systems are advantageous when the structure requires long-life protection, as would a coastal installation. However, periodic attention is required for the system.

The third way of preventing corrosion is to remove the electrolyte from the system by coating the anode and cathode. Zinc coatings are effective in accomplishing this. The zinc coating forms its own corrosion products that effectively seal the surface.

Most materials and systems in use today for offshore corrosion control have been developed since 1960. The credit for this development goes principally to the oil industry. Based upon what they have been able to accomplish in protecting large steel structures in the ocean, one can predict that steel will be used in the large and exotic coastal installations of the future. It is likely that such future structures will be a combination of protective coatings with cathodic protection.

The Navy has effectively developed such combined systems for protecting steel water tanks and for protecting steel mooring buoys. In the latter case, the cathodic protection is extended to both the riser chain and ground leads by providing zinc anodes and ensuring electrical conductivity with a steel cable interwoven through the chains and periodically welded to individual links. Thus far, both systems have proved highly successful.

Plastics are used in coastal applications ranging from boats and barges to energy-absorbing fendering systems for docking ships. Plastic coatings are available to protect steel surfaces. Special mastic types can be applied underwater to steel surfaces. Plastics are also used increasingly as structural material. Many of the high-strength materials developed for the aerospace industry will find application in installations for the Coastal Zone.

Marine construction techniques

The uses of modular construction and prefabrication have made construction simpler and more efficient. New methods for connecting structural elements have been developed such as waterproof epoxies that are as strong as the materials that they join. Underwater welding has been improved. The erection of complex, large structures can be scheduled by computer. From the surface, piles can be driven in water of depths as great as 350 feet. Underwater pile drivers are available that require only a connecting hydraulic or electrical cable to the surface for power and control. Individual piles can support loads of several hundred tons. Ocean floor exploratory drilling can be conducted from floating platforms to depths of water of the order of 18,000 feet.

Improvements in construction technology made over the last few years are illustrated in Figure 5, which shows the depth of water versus year for offshore platform construction. Originally platforms were supported by 200 to 300 timber piles of maximum length of around 90 feet. Little knowledge was available as to the forces from the waves. The platforms were not self-sufficient; they were attended by a tender vessel. In the 1950s steel piles were used, the depth of water increased, and the platforms became self-suffi-

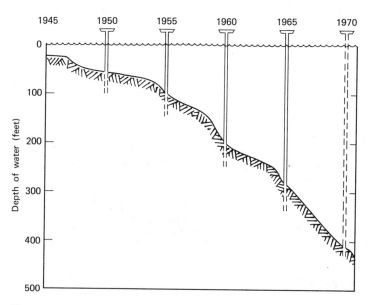

Figure 5.   Depth of water versus year for offshore platform construction.

cient. Steel piles were originally about 12 to 16 inches in diameter and spaced 12 to 15 feet apart. Modern practice is to use larger piles spaced farther apart, eight to ten 30-inch piles at about 30-foot spacing. This reduces the drag forces from water waves, but requires trussed deck spans because of the longer spans. Modern practice also employs a template to position the piles while they are being placed and driven [9].

Bigger piles have meant bigger pile drivers. Total pile lengths are frequently 400 to 600 feet. It is predicted that the template method will eventually be used to depths exceeding 1000 feet. The latest model pile drivers have energies of the order of 100,000 foot-pounds per blow.

Figure 6 illustrates the template method of pile driving. The fixed platforms consist of three parts: template, piles, and hull. The template is fabricated from trussed tubular steel in a shipyard and then towed to sea. On location, the jacket is lifted or launched in the water with its hollow legs upright. The structure is then leveled. Steel piles are driven through the template to the desired depth. The tops of the piles are then welded to the template. Finally, the hull consisting of trussed or plate girders is welded

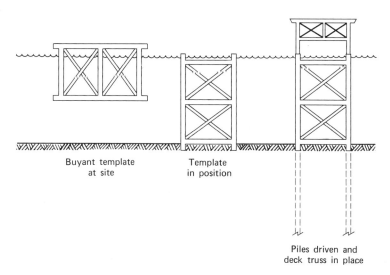

Figure 6. Template method of platform construction.

to the top of the piles. At present, a platform of this type has been designed for installation in water 400 feet deep.

In spite of this kind of progress, much of the construction technology now used in the marine part of the Coastal Zone is simply the dry-land technology adapted to the wetter environment. Extensive construction of ocean installations will require a construction technology unique to that environment. Underwater equipment and tools will be needed and continued development of diver construction techniques are necessary. Better means are needed for testing and determining the characteristics of the soil underlying the water so that adequate structural foundations can be designed.

The Navy has demonstrated in Project Tektite and the *Sealab* experiments that useful construction work can be performed at depths under the water surface. Other tests have shown that site layout can be accomplished underwater using a laser transit instrument and a crew of diver surveyors very much like a dry-land surveying team. The laser transit has been effective for taking readings up to distances of 100 feet. Both boundary surveys and topographical surveys are possible.

However, to have a complete underwater construction capability, engineers must be able to "view" or sense through the water in a manner analogous to the photographic or optical systems commonly used on land. In muddy or murky water optical systems are severely hampered. Suspended particles in the water that have a size equal to and greater than the wavelength of visible light scatter the incident light to produce poor optical transmission. Systems using wavelengths greater than visible light stand a better chance of penetrating. Sound energy having a wavelength greater than about one-tenth of a millimeter will penetrate most turbidity [10].

Systems using longer wavelengths will therefore penetrate longer distances, but usually with the penalty of less resolution. Acoustical systems used at very short ranges can give resolution approaching that of optical means.

Systems employing acoustic wavelengths produce an image either by focusing the acoustic energy or by reconstruction of acoustical wavefronts. Examples of the first method are side scan sonars, fishfinding sonars, and obstacle-avoiding sonars. The second method is holography, in which considerable work is being done. Some of the problems center on how to increase the rate at which holograms can be obtained and displayed. A problem in any acoustic "viewing" system is that certain objects will have the same acoustic impedance as water and will be "invisible." These problems will be solved, however, and eventually a whole range of "viewing" systems will be available, spanning the wavelength range from radar to pure optics.

Experimental acoustic pictures have been taken of models at the Douglas Advanced Research Laboratories in Huntington Beach, Calif. A 6-foot-long model submarine was used as a target and bombarded with sound waves. As the waves broke around the model, a scanning microphone was used to send the sound pattern to an oscilloscope for recording on Polaroid film. A laser light was then projected through the film negative (sonoptogram) to produce an image that revealed some three-dimensional aspects of the model [11].

Surveillance and maintenance

Surveillance and maintenance are particularly important if coastal installations are to perform satisfactorily over a long lifetime in support of human activities. The coastal environment is constantly changing, and the conditions that determine the design criteria for an ocean installation may also change, with possible jeopardy to the installation. Moreover, large portions of coastal installations will be inaccessible for visual inspection. Maintenance or replacement of underwater elements of the installation may be exceedingly difficult, if not impossible. Also, the risks accompanying inadequate inspection and maintenance will be far greater for installations in the ocean than for their counterparts on land. Self-contained systems for detection and fighting fires will be mandatory, because the traditional danger of fire at sea will be ever-present. Large floating installations of the future will require elaborate sensing and control systems to ensure the adequacy of their moorings, or if unmoored, to maintain their station. Position fixes will probably be taken automatically from navigational satellites or from prepositioned energy sources on the ocean floor. These automated systems will be controlled by computers. A high reliability will be required.

Maintenance that is routine for a land installation will require special techniques for the ocean installation. Underwater inspection methods will be needed. Underwater methods for detecting corrosion and chemical and biological deterioration and then for correcting the condition will be necessary. Systems employing cathodic protection will need automatic monitoring and control. Careful controls will be required to limit adverse effects of one coastal installation on its environment and on other systems that share the use of the Coastal Zone.

It will be necessary to detect and control unwanted changes in water channels and harbors in the vicinity of coastal installations. Surveillance methods such as infrared aerial photography will be used to detect changes in turbidity, silting, and chemical and thermal changes in the water. This technique presently uses photos taken from altitudes of about a mile to show the presence of silt by variations in the color reproduced. The contrasting hues from pallid blue to black show variations in infrared reflectivity and suggest differences in water clarity. The greens of trees and other foliage show as red in an infrared photograph. Ultimately, such photographs from high altitudes and space will help detect pollution, silting of harbors and estuaries, and the erosion of valuable coastal lands [11].

Certainly, the five areas of the developing technology just discussed (i.e., load determination, analytical procedures, materials science, marine construction techniques, and surveillance and maintenance) do not comprise all the technological problems. They are a very basic list of essential elements in the construction of ocean installations. One can easily think of other areas that might have been included. However, our purpose in discussing these areas is to get an overview of the present state of technology and the directions it must take. Having done this briefly, we can next look at the functional categories into which ocean installations might be grouped.

2. CATEGORIES OF OCEAN INSTALLATIONS

A particular ocean installation should be thought of as a system or part of a system having some functional purpose. In a general sense most coastal installations, both ancient and modern, would fall into one or more of the following categories:

1. Environment control systems
2. Operational support systems
3. Land reclamation systems
4. Land substitution systems

In the following paragraphs, each of these is explained, typical examples given, and their relevancy to the management of the Coastal Zone discussed.

Environment control systems

This type of installation helps control the sea state, coastal erosion, and damage or pollution to both land and water. Familiar examples are the conventional breakwaters that are used to reduce high sea states to calmer states, thus permitting operation of small craft and protecting the shore line. Other examples are jetties and groins, which prevent unwanted movement and transport of sand. Seawalls protect the shore from waves. Floating barriers of various kinds protect harbor waters from floating debris and other contamination.

As we make greater use of the offshore portion of the Coastal Zone there will be less natural protection, and environmental control systems will become even more important than now. The greatest single problem in moving large-scale operations outward from the shore may be in controlling the seas to permit operation of small support craft and to prevent wave damage to the installation itself. This immediately suggests a need for improved breakwater concepts.

The problem of designing a better breakwater is not easily solved. The enormous energy of water waves must be dissipated in order to reduce the sea state. This can be done by reflecting the waves, causing them to break or become turbulent, allowing them to do work against friction, or introducing an opposing energy.

If the waves are to be reflected, the breakwater must have an enormous mass. This means that it will be supported by the ocean floor, and that there is some limiting depth of water at which a bottom supported breakwater can be economically feasible. For deeper water many types of floating breakwaters have been proposed. Since these do not have the necessary mass to resist movement, the reaction forces must be taken by mooring lines to the ocean floor. The allowable forces in the mooring lines and their anchors place a limitation on this kind of breakwater.

The so-called dynamic breakwaters depend upon introducing motions counter to that of the water particles in the incoming waves. Both pneumatic and hydraulic systems have been proposed. For most applications, however, the power requirements are prohibitive.

Floating breakwaters as a group have an effectiveness that depends very heavily on the relation of their own geometry to the length of the incoming waves. Generally, the longest wave that a floating breakwater will attenuate has a length comparable to the length of the breakwater in the direction of wave travel. This is a very severe requirement for the design of floating breakwaters since the longer waves can be several hundred feet long.

In general, the only type of breakwater that will effectively attenuate a wide band of wave lengths is the massive, bottom-founded type. This kind of breakwater is expensive, normally requires a long time to construct, and has a practical limitation as to depth of water.

A more rapid method that has sometimes been employed to construct massive breakwaters is to float containers to the construction site and then ballast them with sand, rock, or water until they rest on the bottom. The airport constructed at Genoa, Italy in the late 1950s [12] uses a breakwater composed of hollow precast concrete cellular sections, which were floated to the site, filled with dredged material, and lowered to rest on a rubble base on the sea floor in 48 feet of water. Control of the sea during the Normandy landings in World War II was aided by large concrete caissons that were floated, flooded, and sunk to the bottom to act as breakwaters. There have been serious proposals to create peacetime breakwaters by sinking surplus ships in place.

All of these schemes are water depth-limited because the breakwater has to have sufficient height above the waves. There will be some depth of water in every case where it becomes economically infeasible to have a breakwater resting on the ocean floor. One will then have to rely on floating breakwaters with their inherent limitations. Moreover, as floating installations are used farther and farther from shore, the water depth will become too great to permit mooring to the bottom. Large floating installations will be free-floating and probably depend on propulsion systems to maintain their station. Devising independent breakwaters for this kind of installation will be exceedingly difficult since the same conditions that preclude mooring the floating installation will also preclude mooring the floating breakwater. The breakwater will have to take on a different form, and probably be some integral part of the large floating installation.

Operational support systems

These are installations that are incidental to the operation being performed but are necessary for the conduct of it. Beacons and lighthouses are examples of installations that support ocean navigation. Waste treatment and disposal systems, desalination plants, power plants, installations supporting the extraction of marine resources, and scientific installations for oceanographic study are all examples of this category. There are ancient examples. One of the most famous was the lighthouse on Pharos, one of the Ancient Wonders of the World, that survived for nearly fifteen hundred years.

Closer to the present, the Haceta Head Light near Florence, Oregon, has served as a navigational aid since 1894. It projects a beam of a million candlepower that can be seen from 26 miles at sea. Another example is the Freeport Sulphur Company's Caminada mine, which is located about 6 miles off the Louisiana shore in the Gulf of Mexico. The entire mining operation is conducted from a series of pile-supported platforms. Molten sulfur is carried to the mainland by means of a heated, insulated underwater pipeline laid in the Gulf floor [13].

The double-barreled prefabricated tubes for the portion beneath the bay of the Bay Area Rapid Transit System in San Francisco were made and launched at the Bethlehem Steel Yards. They were floated into position near the Bay Bridge and then sunk to align with the sections already on the bottom. They thus became an installation in a system providing operational support to a general transportation system.

Figure 7 shows an elevated causeway being constructed from the shore out into the water. The individual sections are steel orthotropic plate barges approximately 90 by 22 by 5 feet in size. They are normally buoyant and can be floated to the construction site. Circular steel column piles can then be driven through circular spud wells in the barges into the soil underlying the water by a crane-supported diesel pile driver, which is positioned on an adjacent barge. When the piles are driven to the required depth and resistance, the barges are jacked up into position forming an elevated causeway. When the causeway is no longer needed, the barges can be lowered to a floating position and the piles cut. This system is part of a Navy department for *SeaBee* use for rapid port construction.

Another familiar example of an operational support system is the offshore oil drilling platform. Such installations have enabled drillers to sink wells to thousands of feet below the ocean bottom.

Land reclamation systems

These employ coastal installations to recover or create land from the sea. Examples are the dikes in the Netherlands, land fill extensions to airstrips, and artificial islands such as Treasure Island in

Figure 7. Removable causeway.

San Francisco. This kind of installation is very old. The Dutch have been reclaiming land from the ocean since the 13th century.

Polders of dry land are made by putting up dikes to restrain the waters and expose the sea bottom. The dikes themselves are built in the same manner as long narrow strips of landfill. Polders require less fill material than normal landfill and are usually less expensive. Figure 8 is a schematic sketch of a polder system. The Dutch have reclaimed more than 1,600,000 acres of land from the sea since the 1200s. Today they are reclaiming land for about $2000 an acre. The deepest polder constructed so far is near Rotterdam and is about 21 feet below sea level [13].

A current example of such a project has been proposed by the Harza Engineering Corporation of Chicago for the construction of an airport in Lake Michigan. In their report, "An Appraisal of a Lake Michigan Site for Chicago's Third Major Airport," they

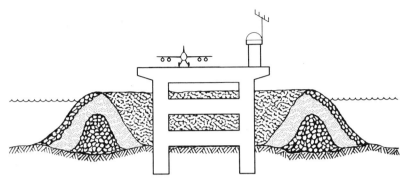

Figure 8.   Sketch of polder system.

conclude that it would be feasible to construct a system of dikes consisting of cores of silty sand, sand and gravel, and quarry stone. After the area became enclosed, it would be dewatered to expose the floor of the lake. Concrete slabs and buildings would then be erected on the lake bed. The dike system would be about 4 miles in diameter. The average water depth would be 35 to 55 feet. The airport would be about 3½ miles from the shore, with access by causeway, tunnel, or water craft [14].

As water depths get greater and other factors enter, it becomes impracticable to construct dikes. It may be more feasible to fill the entire area, raising it to a level above the water. Land filling is the traditional way for building in water, involving simply the displacement of water with other materials. This method is practical in moderately shallow water and when fill material is readily available. The cost of fill material is based on its volume, so the cost of filling increases approximately in direct proportion to the depth of water for large surface areas. Figure 9 shows a typical land fill, with the weight of the buildings carried to underlying rock by caissons. The sides of the island are armored with masonry and stone to resist the abrasive forces of the waves. An artificial island of this type has been built in Lake Huron at Harbor Beach, Michigan, for a Detroit Edison power plant in water ranging in depth from 6 to 20 feet [13].

The Genoa Airport, built in the late 1950s, rests almost entirely on fill land in the water. The airport forms a giant "L" with the short leg connected to the mainland. The main runway was originally constructed to be 6300 feet long, with a provision for lengthening if necessary to 7100 feet. A protective breakwater 9187 feet long

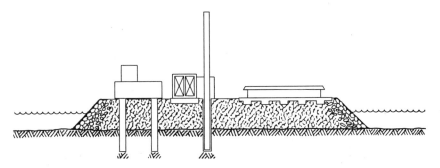

Figure 9. Typical land fill.

parallels the runway and is separated from the runway seawall by a 780 foot ship channel. The seawall is 11,700 feet long. The reclamation was estimated to cost $1.40 a square foot versus about $11.60 for land on the mainland. The total installation replaced about 1.2 million square yards of sea [12].

Land substitution systems

In this category are offshore systems that permit operations customarily conducted on dry land. An artificial land-type environment is created as a substitute. Much of Venice, Italy, is supported on timber piling so that in effect a substitute for land is used for parts of the city. A modern example could be the use of the liner *Queen Mary* as a hotel and convention center, which are normally activities conducted on land.

The large offshore airports considered by many cities are examples of land substitute systems. There have been several schemes proposed for constructing floating cities. There is an interest in constructing floating port facilities. A floating naval base has been proposed. For generations people in some parts of the world have lived on houseboats as a land substitute.

Figure 10 is a sketch of the simplest type of land substitute. Piles of wood, steel, or concrete are used to support large platforms of this type. Piling has the advantage of holding the structure out of the waves so that the forces are reduced to the relatively small loads on the piles themselves. One of the deepest known fixed piling installations is an oil platform in 340 feet of water in the Gulf of Mexico. To provide mobility for offshore exploratory drilling, the

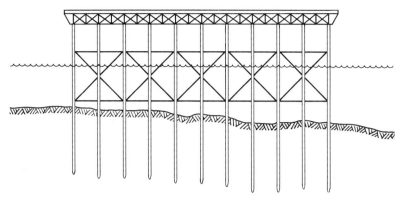

Figure 10. Pile-supported platform.

jack-up platform is commonly used. With the legs withdrawn it is buoyant and can be towed to the site. The legs are then lowered until the bottom mat rests on the ocean floor. The platform can then be jacked up on the legs until the deck is high enough above the waves to permit operations and to reduce the forces of waves on the structure. Figure 11 shows a sketch of a jack-up platform.

Gulf South Research Institute in their report, "A Study of New Orleans Future Airport Requirements 1980–2000," have suggested a pile-supported airport to be constructed in Lake Pontchartrain. It would consist of three levels, each having an area of 735 acres, and be constructed as a reinforced concrete two-way slab system supported on piling. The upper level, which would contain the runway, would rest on a 4-foot-thick slab. The airport would be connected to land with a four-lane expressway plus a rapid transit system [14].

The Pilkington Glass Age Development Committee in England has proposed a city to be built in the sea out of principally non-ferrous materials [15]. The city would be built on concrete stilts and protected by a floating breakwater and a curved wall 180 feet high. The majority of the city's 30,000 inhabitants would live in terraced flats. The floating islands in the central lagoon, which would be artificially heated by waste cooling water, would carry both private and public buildings. The breakwater would be made up of 100-foot-long, 6-foot-diameter plastic bags 90% filled with freshwater so that they remained buoyant in seawater. The main construction materials would be glass and concrete. The city would

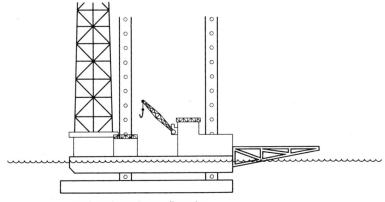

Platform in towing configuration

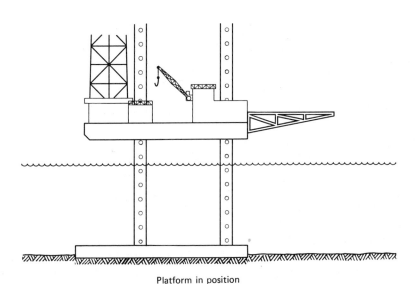

Platform in position

Figure 11. Jack-up platform.

include a desalination plant, 200 bed hospital, two theaters, a museum, and a church. The designers believe such a city will be constructed in 50 years.

Since there is a practical limit to the water depth in which a pile-supported platform can be constructed, planners also are looking at large floating installations. In reasonable depths of water, floating platforms would be kept in position by being moored to the ocean floor. In very deep water, they would maintain their position by some kind of thruster or propulsion system. Concrete has been considered carefully for this application because of its durability and relatively light weight. The possibility of light-weight concretes, even buoyant concretes, makes a very attractive prospect for large floating platforms.

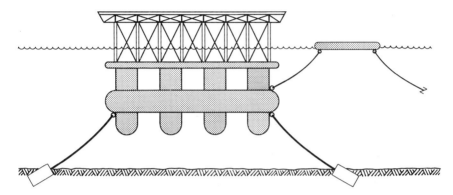

Figure 12.   Floating platform.

One kind of floating structure is shown in Figure 12. The buoyant support is provided by the submerged flotation tanks, which are below the turbulence of the water surface. The fairly open framework of the supporting legs minimizes the wave forces on the structure. A protective floating breakwater of large bags, partially filled with water, is moored around the platform to help protect the structure from waves.

An interesting housing scheme has been designed by R. Buckminster Fuller and the Triton Foundation Inc. under a grant from the Federal Government [13, 16]. Each module or floating neighborhood contains about 1400 apartments and is designed for a population of 5000. This basic 4-acre unit would be built on a steel or concrete platform with prefabricated components placed on it. The unit is designed for depths of water of 28 to 30 feet. Conventional ship anchorage systems may be used if feasible. Elsewhere the designers recommend that the hull of the supporting platform should rest permanently on the seabed. The pad itself would rest on an adjustable hydraulic system.

Three to six of the communities would form a small town. Such a town would accommodate government offices, a medical center, and recreational facilities. The whole complex would have a population of 100,000 persons. Car traffic would be discouraged. Wheeled vehicles would be restricted to a single level in the city complex. Front doors of the dwellings would open on to 18-foot-wide pedestrian-only streets in the air. The designers suggest that the cost of a single dwelling unit could compare favorably with any one of the urban renewal projects now in the United States.

While these concepts just described are in some cases fanciful, they illustrate the serious thinking regarding land substitution systems. Obviously, some of the schemes will not prove economically feasible by present standards, but cost effectiveness is a relative value. Land acquisition and construction costs on land will continue to rise; ocean construction costs should rise at a lesser rate as technology improves. There may be a time when land substitution systems are quite competitive. Moreover, factors other than cost might force the use of land substitution systems. We have already observed the problems of airport construction in congested metropolitan land areas. It could be that solutions will be sought in the waters of the Coastal Zone independently of cost considerations.

3. FUTURE CHALLENGES

At this point we will depart from the constraints of the present and speculate on the future trend of coastal installations. It is well to keep in mind that large installations in the ocean are enormously expensive to construct, and that the reason they are even considered is that they offer a way of easing the pressures and problems that confront us.

Transferring land-oriented activities to the watery portions of the Coastal Zone has the greatest implications for the future. Some of the proposed concepts have already been mentioned; there have been many others. The engineering community and the general public have become so accustomed to attaining "impossible" technological goals that very few proposals are rejected as being unthinkable. The bulk of our national domestic problems seem to be city-oriented, and our cities are concentrated in the Coastal Zone. The possibilities of controlling the environment, meaning both the local seas and the local weather, promise an almost utopian expansion of our work, recreation, and housing activity into the water.

Management of the Coastal Zone in this sense may be still in the future, but the problems that would make this kind of management necessary are already with us.

We can begin by considering further the technology already discussed. Eventually, if this technology proves inadequate, new methods and concepts will have to be found. However, as a start it is logical to look at the presently conceived ways of adapting land-oriented activities to the offshore environment. Specifically, we can look at ocean installations that provide a large stable, stationary surface out in the water. The ways already discussed are creating new land by poldering or filling and creating land substitutes by constructing pile-supported or floating platforms.

Comparative costs

The relative costs of the different ways of creating a large surface area in the water can be predicted in a general way. If the water is quite shallow, fill would be preferred for relatively small surface areas and poldering for large surface areas. Poldering has some practical limit as to the depth of water. As mentioned previously, the deepest polder presently is about 20 feet below the level of the sea. Fill, on the other hand, theoretically can be done in any depth, but the limit is soon reached where the cost of filling will exceed that for constructing a pile-supported platform of the same area. This depth depends upon local conditions and availability of fill material, but it is probably of the order of 20 to 30 feet.

For large-surface areas, pile-supported platforms are more economical than floating platforms except in fairly deep water. This is particularly true if the criterion is imposed that the platform must remain stationary and essentially stable in high seas. On the other hand, in a completely protected area of water a floating platform may be less expensive than a pile-supported one in depths as shallow as 50 feet.

Floating platforms of small surface area (having dimensions less than the wavelengths to be expected) need extra measures to achieve stability. This could mean a cost penalty, and pile-supported platforms would probably be less costly.

For water depths too great for piles, floating platforms would be the only choice. The most extreme design condition would be a large platform in at least several hundred feet of water in an exposed location.

Problems of large floating platforms

Since the discussion at this point is already speculative, it is easy to continue by looking at the ultimate floating system in an exposed environment. We can immediately identify some of the problems in constructing a satisfactory large platform of this type. By "large," we are thinking of something adequate for an airport or small city unit, that is, an area perhaps as large as a half square mile.

Choice of material for construction. The planned lifetime for the installation, the system costs for that lifetime, weight considerations, strength considerations, ease of fabrication, and ease of assembly are all factors that influence the choice of materials. At present, the best materials seem to be steel, reinforced concrete, prestressed concrete, or some combination of these. These are not listed in any order of preference. For any given concept, the feasibility of using different materials would have to be examined; and then costs compared.

Fabrication method. A platform of this size would be difficult to assemble completely in its final ocean location. It would also be difficult to assemble elsewhere and move. The probable answer is to construct modules of some optimum size, deliver them to the installation site, and assemble them there. The optimum size module would have to be determined by considering trade-offs between fabrication, delivery, and assembly costs. Mass production techniques would be needed, and the capacities of steel mills or casting yards, and land transportation and water transportation systems would impose constraints on the choice of the best module size.

Probably the best means of delivery is to make the modules buoyant and stable in the sea with as low a drag as possible so that they can be towed.

Assembly. At some assembly point, probably the final location for the installation, the modules would have to be joined. The technique for positioning the modules, aligning their connections, and securing them, all in open water, will have to be ingenious to say the least. Ideally, most of the equipment for doing this could be part of the modules themselves. The freeboard of the modules could be controlled by flooding hollow compartments so that auxiliary craft and equipment could work on the assembly at reasonable heights above the water.

Structural adequacy. The platform must be designed to have a high reliability of withstanding diverse loadings. These loads include the gravity loads of the installation itself, the buoyant forces that support it, the live loads that will be placed on the platform during its lifetime, the loads from wind and sea, the mooring forces, and any special loading that occurs during delivery and assembly. Particularly important are the live loads during the lifetime of the platform. If the installation were to support a city unit, for example, business and recreation patterns would have to be carefully analyzed so that abnormal loading concentrations could be provided for. Transportation would have to be planned or controlled to avoid adverse load distributions. Since the platform can be designed for only a certain reserve buoyancy, load densities would have to be limited. Any growth of the complex could not be upward, that is, higher buildings; growth would be horizontal by adding modules. It might be feasible to have a provision for leveling or trimming the entire installation by selective ballasting and pumping of buoyancy chambers.

Present construction materials that have the necessary strength are also heavy. To build a structure that has a large reserve buoyancy and at the same time is massive and strong enough to withstand the wave forces, presents a problem in optimization—weight versus strength versus geometry.

Stability. The platform should remain relatively motionless in heavy seas and should remain on station in the proper orientation. If the platform is large enough in plan area, its dimensions will exceed the lengths of most waves. Therefore, pitching, rolling, and yawing will be minimized by the shear size of the installation. Nonrotational horizontal motions, surging, and swaying will probably be limited in a very large installation because the water motion in the ocean crests and troughs will tend to produce canceling forces on the structure. Vertical motion (heaving) might similarly be canceled out in a very large structure that is receiving its buoyant support from both crests and troughs. Extremely long waves such as swells would cause heaving.

Water particle velocities in waves attenuate with depth. The farther that the center of buoyancy is below the water surface the less vertical motion of the structure. This principle has been applied very successfully in research vessels such as *Flip* and *Spar*, both of which can change to a vertical attitude to resemble enormous 300-foot spar buoys. In this position their center of buoyancy is at a depth where very little motion is felt from the water waves at the surface. Vertical motion of *Flip* has proved to be almost negligible even in high seas.

There is another aspect of the vertical motion problem. In addition to limiting the amplitudes of the vertical forces on the structure, it is desirable to avoid a resonant condition between the periodic components of the vertical wave forces and the fundamental period of the structure in heave motion. In the case of *Flip*, it was considered that a fundamental period of about 27 seconds would effectively decouple its motion from the ocean waves containing most of the energy. Typical design spectra for ocean waves have a peak around 16 seconds, and very little energy above 20 seconds.

One concept for a large floating platform is to support a deck by long, hollow tubular legs sealed at the bottom. This would lower the center of buoyancy and lengthen the fundamental period in heave. The period in heave for a sealed, hollow cylinder in a vertical position is approximately 1.1 times the square root of the wetted length in its equilibrium position. If we want a structure with a period of 20 seconds or more, we need vertical legs that are about 400 feet long. This establishes the depth of water needed to float such a structure at somewhat greater than 400 feet. This is an interesting observation since the present limit of water depth for pile-supported installations is about 350 feet. Thus it could turn out that essentially the same tubular-leg structure could be either floated or bottom-supported, depending on the water depth.

It is not necessary, of course, to use vertical cylindrical legs for buoyancy. Other shapes could provide the same buoyancy using a shorter length, but probably at greater cost. Underwater buoyancy tanks could be oriented horizontally, with vertical legs connecting them to the platform above the water. Another possibility would be to have a huge barge-like hull composed of watertight, hollow boxes. Again this would cost more and present problems in construction and assembly. These configurations would probably have a shorter and less desirable period in heave motion; but this problem might be solved by using some kind of damping devices so that resonant oscillations could not build up. Motion could be limited also by applying dynamic resistance. Gyroscopic stabilizers, flywheels, or thrusters might stabilize a relatively small platform. Such a system could be operated only in rough seas to supplement the installation's inherent tendency for stability.

Station keeping. Still another problem is how to maintain an enormous floating structure in the proper location and compass heading. In reasonable water depths with good bottom conditions, conventional moorings might be adequate. In deeper water some propulsion or thrust system would be needed. An attractive possibility is to use some of the energy from the motion of the sea itself to generate a thrust. The proper position of the platform could be determined by reference to preplaced fixed markers or transmitters on the ocean bottom. Station keeping could be automated.

The real difficulties in station keeping may not be in concept but in practicality. The power requirements and cost for precise station keeping can be prohibitive. It could be that an extremely large floating installation could be permitted to wander slightly in position without adverse effect.

Maintenance. As a final problem, the floating installation must be durable and relatively maintenance-free. It must be designed so that all maintenance and repairs can be performed on location without incapacitating the entire installation. When one thinks of the continuous maintenance required for large waterfront structures such as bridges, and the regular preventative maintenance required for ships, it becomes clear what an enormous problem maintaining a permanent floating installation would be.

Baseline concept

Figures 13 through 16 show a possible sequence of construction, delivery, and assembly of a baseline system for a floating structure. The principal construction material is intended to be prestressed concrete. It is a baseline concept because it is as elementary as possible and can be used as a point of departure in planning. It is not necessarily a workable system. It may be structurally feasible. Figure 13 shows the concept. A large rigid platform is supported by long hollow tubular legs sealed at their bottoms. The lower ends of the legs are free; the top ends are so fixed to the platform as to develop full moment resistance. The length of the legs is chosen to give the required buoyancy and to produce an acceptable period in heave motion. In this concept the length has been chosen at 400 feet, which gives an approximate period of 22 seconds. The same period could be obtained with a shorter contoured leg at greater cost.

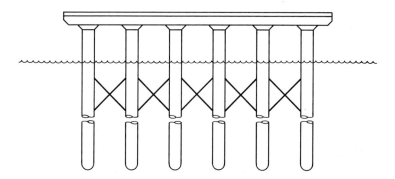

Figure 13.   Baseline concept for large floating platform.

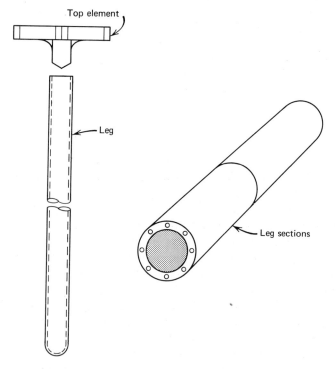

Figure 14.   Details of typical leg.

Figure 14 shows the configuration of a typical leg. At the top of each leg is a moment-resisting element. This rests on top of the leg and provides a moment-resisting connection from the legs to the girder and deck system. Shown are elements having a span of 37.5 feet. The spacer girders also have a span of 37.5 feet so that the leg spacing can be any multiple of 37.5 feet. The legs themselves could be cast in sections. The sections can be joined to form the complete leg by welding steel connection elements or by high-strength epoxy compounds. A minimum amount of spiral reinforcement is needed. The tubular holes permit pretensioning cables to be strung, placing the entire leg in lengthwise precompression.

Figure 15 shows the delivery and placement of the leg section

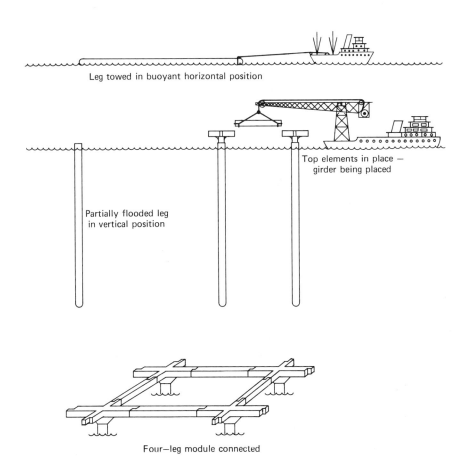

Leg towed in buoyant horizontal position

Top elements in place —
girder being placed

Partially flooded leg
in vertical position

Four—leg module connected

Figure 15. Assembly procedure for module.

and the assembly of the platform module. When the complete leg is formed, both ends would be sealed to make the leg buoyant. The leg would then be launched and towed in a horizontal position to the assembly site. There, part of it would be flooded (between internal bulkheads) so that it could assume a vertical floating position like a spar buoy with the correct amount of freeboard for further assembly. The top element could then be installed by barge crane.

When four legs had been positioned vertically and the top elements placed, the connecting girders would be installed. This would produce a stable floating four-leg module. This process would be continued until the required number was connected. The water ballast in the legs would then be pumped or blown out, causing the structure to rise in the water to its approximate final draft. The deck sections would then be placed.

An alternative method for casting the legs is shown in Figure 16. In this method the concrete would be poured into a vertically

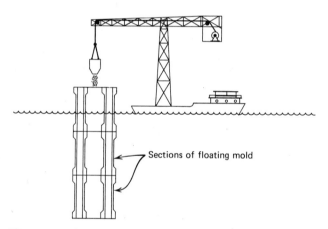

Sections of floating mold

Figure 16.   Alternative procedure for casting legs.

oriented, floating mold. As the cylinder became longer, the mold would be lengthened by adding sections. When the casting was completed, the mold would be sunk and withdrawn from the buoyant cylindrical leg. The end cap and spacer girder elements could be precast on land. A relatively few steel molds of this type would be sufficient for the casting of all the leg sections.

Such a baseline system might be studied in detail to determine its flaws and what modifications might make it feasible. If the general idea continued to show promise, scale models could be tested experimentally in wave basins. Next, large-scale models of modular sections could be evaluated in ocean testing. Finally, consideration could be given to constructing a prototype for actual use. In all probability, the prototype would not resemble this baseline concept too closely. It is reasonable, however, that the construction of a large floating platform is within the present state of the art, and with adequate developmental research, such a platform could be constructed.

4. CONCLUSIONS

We have looked at the role of ocean installations in the management of the Coastal Zone, the state of technology, the kinds of ocean installations, the future challenge of moving land-oriented activities offshore, and an example of how part of the Coastal Zone might be converted to a land substitute.

The report of the Commission on Marine Science, Engineering and Resources [17] discussed some obvious needs for the future if engineering technology is to keep pace with the demands placed upon it. The authors of that report pointed out that research in both basic science and engineering has stepped up considerably in the past 10 years. One estimate is that the level of support for scientific research has doubled during this period. Still, technology for engineering management of the Coastal Zone has not kept pace entirely with the demands of the changing goals. The problems are becoming more difficult and complex, and decisions must often be made on the basis of inadequate technology because there is not sufficient time for specific study and research.

More trained people will be required than currently available. We need a well-informed public who will be aware of the nature of the problems, the alternatives for solution, and the consequences. Engineers need improved criteria for designing fixed coastal installations and improved techniques for determining the properties of the ocean floor. Also they need better determination of wave forces and run-up on shore structures and improved ways for determining design waves and their frequency of occurrence. Further developed undersea construction technology and the application of this to installations in the Coastal Zone are needed. Certain unspoiled areas should be studied and their physical, chemical, and biological characteristics recorded to serve as baseline systems in future years.

The challenges for engineers are not simply to build isolated installations that are more durable, but to make an integrated contribution to a systematic response to the goals. The kind of engineering response where one objective is accomplished without regard to the effects on other systems is no longer acceptable. One must question to what extent he can alter an estuary or structure without destroying one of its uses. How will widening or deepening a channel effect its circulation and sedimentary pattern? In short, engineers must also be concerned with the preservation of balance in ecological systems and must realize that in the final analysis nothing one does is completely independent of other systems and processes.

Effectively designed and economical works to stabilize, protect, and restore coastal lands will always be needed. Beyond that, a technology that enables us to make new and unique contributions to the management of the Coastal Zone is needed.

REFERENCES

1. Blair Kinsman, *Wind Waves*, Prentice-Hall, Englewood Cliffs, N.J., 1965, Chap 1.
2. *Shore Protection Planning and Design*, 3rd ed., Technical Rept. 4, U.S. Army Coastal Engineering Research Center, U.S. Government Printing Office, Washington, D.C., 1966.
3. Robert G. Dean, "Discussion of *Irregular Wave Forces on a Pile*, by W. J. Pierson, Jr., and P. Holmes," *ASCE Journal of Waterways and Harbor Division*, Vol. 92, No. WW4 (November 1966).
4. Bernard Le Méhauté, *An Introduction to Hydrodynamics and Water Waves*, Vol. II, ESSA Technical Report ERL 118-POL 3-1, U.S. Government Printing Office, Washington, D.C., 1969.
5. W. J. Pierson, G. Neumann, and R. W. James, *Practical Methods for Observing and Forecasting Ocean Waves by Means of Wave Spectra and Statistics*, U.S. Navy Hydrographic Office Publ. 603, 1960.
6. M. Snoey and M. Katona, *Structural Design of Conical Acrylic Viewports*, Naval Civil Engineering Laboratory, Technical Report R716, March 1971.
7. S. K. Takahashi and R. Mark, "Photoelastic Analysis of Undersea Structures," *ASCE Journal of the Structural Division*, Proceedings 6440, pp. 317–326, March 1969.
8. S. K. Takahashi, and R. Mark, *Cyclic Impact Studies in Dynamic Photoelasticity*, Naval Civil Engineering Laboratory, Technical Report R632, June 1969.
9. G. C. Lee, "Offshore Structures—Past, Present, Future and Design Considerations," *Offshore*, Vol. 24 (June 5, 1968).
10. D. C. Greene and B. P. Hildebrand, *Applications of Acoustical Holography to Underwater Viewing*, Paper OTC 1096, Offshore Technology Conference, Houston, Tex., May 1969.

11. K. F. Weaver, "Remote Sensing: New Eyes to See the World," *National Geographic*, Vol. 135, No. 1 (January 1969).

12. "Genoa Builds an Airport in the Sea," *Engineering News Record*, Vol. 161 (November 20, 1958), pp. 46–47.

13. W. McQuade, "Urban Expansion Takes to the Water," *Fortune*, September 1969.

14. O. Stephanek, E. Ahlers, and K. E. McKee, "Comparison of Offshore Airport Construction," *1969 Offshore Technology Conference Preprints*, Vol. 2, pp. 465–470.

15. "Self-Sufficient 'Sea City' Proposed," *Oceanology International*, July/August 1968, p. 16.

16. "Cities on the Sea," *Engineering*, Vol. 207, No. 5368 (March 14, 1969).

17. *Our Nation and the Sea, A Plan for National Action*, Report of the Commission on Marine Science, Engineering and Resources, U.S. Government Printing Office, Washington, D.C., January 1969.

CHAPTER 10

Marine Waste Disposal Systems: Alternatives and Consequences

ERMAN A. PEARSON

The public's increasing concern regarding environmental quality, coupled with limited factual information about waste discharge effects and a general lack of awareness of the objectives or performance of conventional waste treatment systems, all contribute to public problems. There is a general belief that all waste treatment systems accomplish the same objectives; that all waste treatment is uniformly good; and that the higher the degree of treatment in any given situation the better the results. Unfortunately, generalizations of such a nature may lead to designs that are conceptually inappropriate and might result in disastrous consequences.

1. THE ESTUARY-COASTAL DISCHARGE DILEMMA

It is well to examine the general estuarine waste disposal problem. Consider a substantial estuarine system with a significant number of individual waste dischargers, both municipal and industrial in character, located around the periphery of the estuary. A fundamental question raised frequently is whether it is preferable to provide at least secondary waste treatment for all municipal effluents and discharge the waste directly to the estuary or whether the wastes should be collected and transported seaward, possibly to the open coast. As one progresses seaward, greater quantities of diluting water are available, and thus it may be possible to provide some lesser degree of treatment at the more seaward location. It should be obvious that such systems could be constructed for essentially equal unit waste management costs (dollars per million gallons handled). That is, the cost increment attributed to the different degrees of treatment could be used for the transport systems carrying the waste flow seaward.

Typical estuarine—coastal waste example

Figure 1 presents an idealized but representative example of the possible choices in estuarine waste management with respect to dis-

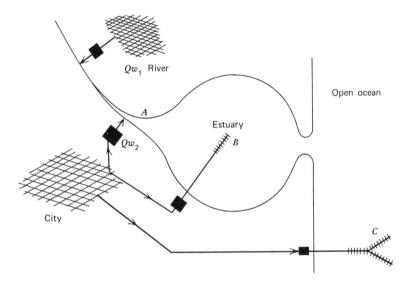

Figure 1. Idealized estuarine-coastal disposal alternatives. Which alternate to choose? and why?

		Landward end of estuary A	Mid-estuary B	Open ocean C
1	Discharge Location			
2	Initial waste dilution (Minimum river flow)	10	30	150
3	Pollutant concentration near source (no treatment)	$\sim C_0/10$	$\sim C_0/30$	$\sim C_0/150$
4	Treatment (assume % removal $\times$ 10^{-2})	Secondary (0.9)	Intermediate (0.75)	Primary (0.33)
5	Pollutant concentration near source	$\sim C_0/100$	$\sim C_0/120$	0.0
6	Treatment (% removal) required for equal pollutant concentrations at all three locations, $C = C_0/150$	93.3	80.0	$\sim C_0/222$

posal location, likely initial waste dilutions attainable, and pollutant concentrations at each location dependent upon the degree of treatment employed. It is of interest to note that the average waste concentrations in the receiving water at the immediate point of discharge are lowest for the case with the least degree of treatment. Similarly, the degree (percentage removal) of treatment required at each of the discharge locations to produce the same pollutant concentration near the source is shown in line 6 of the figure. To achieve a pollutant concentration of $C_0/150$ in the receiving water at three typical locations requires the following degrees of treatment (removal):

Location	Percentage Removal
A—landward end of estuary	93.3
B—midestuary	80.0
C—open ocean	0.0

Two points need to be emphasized. First, other than for disinfection there are no conventional waste treatment processes that remove, on the average, 93.3% of Five-day Biological Oxygen Demand (BOD_5), Chemical Oxygen Demand (COD), suspended solids, nutrients or other significant pollutants; second, for open ocean disposal (average initial dilution of $\geqq 150$) no treatment be required. Generally speaking, a no-treatment system would not be tolerated in California. Thus it would appear from just the standpoint of initial waste concentrations in the environment that the ocean disposal system has substantial advantages. These advantages become particularly important if the ocean disposal system can be built and operated at about equal or lesser costs than either of the estuarial disposal schemes.

Advantages of coastal alternative

1. For the conventional levels of treatment commonly used in California, the coastal alternative produces the lowest pollutant concentrations in the receiving waters.

2. Generally, the coastal discharge location can be selected in an area of noncritical or of lesser significance to the ecology of the area; whereas the estuarine region is one of the most important and critical areas with respect to both the anadromous and marine fishery as well as the local ecology.

3. The residence time of pollutants in the estuary, the critical region, is reduced; hence all effects of pollutants are minimized as a result of by-passing up-stream discharges to the open ocean.

4. If pollutants of unknown character or origin occur, for which the treatment process may be adequate, the coastal system affects substantial reduction in the pollutant concentration by dilution, thereby providing a safeguard to minimize the effects of any changes in the future.

5. With the coastal system, after it has been in operation for some time and if it does not achieve the desired result, it is a simple matter to study the problem and to design and construct additional treatment processes to solve the problem. If the upper estuary complete treatment and disposal system does not perform adequately, what does one do? The cost of increasing the percentage removal of a pollutant from, say, 90 to 98% is very substantial as compared to increasing the removal from 35 to 45%.

6. Considering the upstream (beyond the estuarine region) development of essentially all significant river systems and the inevitability of the advective river water already containing significant concentrations of waste residuals from such upstream development (in the long term, if not at present), it will become necessary to collect all or most of the locally (estuarine region) generated wastes and transport these treated wastes out of the estuarine system. It appears that this will be the most feasible and significant way to reduce the impact of man's activities on the estuarine ecology. At the same time the impact on the coastal region is minimal.

7. The coastal disposal system is less affected by operational difficulties or short-term failures of the treatment system; hence it provides a buffer against substantial transient concentrations of pollutants which might have a harmful effect on the biota.

8. One of the major advantages of the coastal system is its flexibility and economy for adaptation to meet future changes in requirements or to deal with problems either nonexistent or unrecognized at present. That is, water quality criteria are met currently with a minimum of conventional treatment technology and expense. Improvements in treatment methodology can be utilized readily as they become available and are needed as well as new processes which may be necessary to deal with new pollutants or newly discovered pollutant effects.

2. THE OPEN COAST DISPOSAL PROBLEM

The problem of conceptual planning of waste disposal for dischargers located on the open coast is very similar to that facing dischargers located in the estuarine complex. Here the problem is one of determining the optimum combination of waste treatment and dispersion system (outfall-diffuser) that will meet the water quality objectives.

Hypothetical example

Figure 2 shows an idealized set of waste disposal alternatives for a municipality located on the open coast. The alternative analyses are compared for three different dilutions at the immediate point of introducing the waste into the receiving water and for the three conventional levels of treatment which are assumed to remove 90,

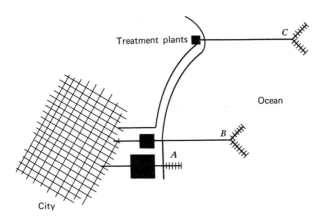

Figure 2. Idealized open coast disposal alternatives.

		A	B	C
1	Discharge Location	A	B	C
2	Initial dilution (at source)	5–20 (10)	60–80 (70)	100–200 (150)
3	Pollutant concentration (at source, conservative, no decay)	$\sim C_0/10$	$\sim C_0/70$	$\sim C/_0150$
4	Treatment (percentage removal)	90	75	50
5	Assumed transport time to shore (decay rate $T_{90} = 4$ hours)	0 hours	12 hours	24 hours
6	Pollutant concentration on beach (conservative, no decay)	$\sim C_0/100$	$\sim C_0/336$	$\sim C_0/450$
7	Pollutant concentration on beach (nonconservative, $T_{90} = 4$ hours)	$\sim C_0/100$	$\sim C_0/10,600$	$\sim C_0/450,000$

75, and 50% of the initial pollutant concentration. The systems are compared on the basis of dilution of the residual pollutants (line 6) and with respect to both dilution and decay. For purposes of somewhat realistic comparison, a bacterial decay rate (T_{90} of 4 hours, $k = 0.58$ per hour) was used which is the usual value employed in design analyses in California. The tremendous advantage of discharging the wastes a considerable distance offshore is obvious considering that the apparent dilutions achieved differ by several orders of magnitude. That is, compare an equivalent dilution of the untreated pollutant concentration, C_0, of $C_0/100$ with $C_0/10,600$ and $C_0/450,000$ for transport (decay) times of 12 and 24 hours, respectively, before the wastes reach the beach from the point of discharge.

Considering the fact that most recently designed marine waste disposal systems in California have been based upon nonconservative pollutants (coliform bacteria), there is little wonder that California practice has led towards longer outfalls and lesser degrees of treatment. For nonconservative materials especially, as well as conventional pollutants for which treatment plants are designed to effect significant ($\leqq 90\%$) removals, the California design practice is both rational and effective.

A documentation of the advantages can be made for deep offshore disposal of waste with only the very specific type of treatment really needed (viz., floatable removal) as compared to high degrees of conventional treatment with nearshore discharge, similar to that presented for the estuary-coastal system. Unfortunately, conventional domestic waste treatment processes (primary and secondary) are not very effective in removing floatables from waste streams. Because floatables rise to the surface, are rapidly transported by the winds, tend to accumulate on surfaces and shorelines, are visible, and tend to present substantial aesthetic and potential health problems, they must be given more attention in design practice. Suitable methods need to be developed to quantitate the amount of floatables both in waste streams and the environment. Treatment processes need to be modified or new methods developed to reduce the concentration of floatables in the waste discharges. Fortunately, current outfall design practice is ideally suited to handle the problem. That is, long outfalls and extensive diffuser systems tend to transport the floatables to discharge locations such that only a small fraction of the floatables return to shoreward points of concern. The extensive diffuser systems dilute the residual floatable materials laterally to levels where they are not offensive and biological decay processes can be most effective oxidizing the materials to innocuous end products.

3. WASTE TREATMENT—SUBMARINE OUTFALL COSTS

To fully appreciate the appropriate role and economic justification of effective submarine outfall dispersion systems, it is necessary to give consideration to the unit costs of waste treatment and the outfall system.

Treatment costs

Table 1 presents a summary of the current approximate unit costs of conventional waste treatment. The costs include all costs, that is, capital (5% interest), operation, and maintenance.

TABLE 1
Approximate Unit Costs of Conventional Waste Treatment
(Capital, Operation, and Maintenance—1970)

Type of Plant	Capacity of Plant (million gallons per day)		
	1	10	100
Primary	125–175	60–80	40–60
(including sludge digestion)	(150)[a]	(70)	(50)
Secondary	250–300	100–200	80–120
(activated sludge)	(275)	(150)	(100)

[a] Dollar values in parentheses represent best estimate.

Inspection of Table 1 reveals that for 10 and 100 million gallons per day treatment plants, the unit cost increment between primary treatment and secondary treatment amounts to about $80 and $50 per million gallons of waste treated, respectively. Conceivably, this incremental unit cost could be spent for construction and operation of an outfall dispersion system that would have the same total unit cost. It is of interest to examine, in a rough-cut fashion, the length of an outfall-dispersion system that could be built for this incremental unit cost.

Typical outfall costs

The costs of outfall construction vary considerably because of differences in surf conditions, hence the cost of the onshore-surf section which must be buried for protection, the length (ratio of offshore to onshore lengths), and depth of discharge as well as the method of construction used. Table 2 presents a reasonable esti-

TABLE 2
Average Unit Construction Costs, Marine Outfall (1970 costs)

Flow (million gallons per day; Accompanying Pipe Sizes Indicated)	Construction costs ($/foot)
10 ($\frac{\Omega}{\mho}$ ~ 24 inches ϕ)	~300
100 ($\frac{\Omega}{\mho}$ ~ 76 inches ϕ)	~500

mate of the average construction cost per foot of length of outfalls of size adequate for the two typical plants of 10 and 100 million gallons per day, capacity.

The values given are in the middle of the range of construction costs (adjusted to 1970 prices) for outfalls built along the Pacific Coast during the past 15 years.

Treatment increment—outfall length

If one assumes that the outfall life is about 40 years, interest at 5%, and computes the unit costs on a $/million gallons–foot of length basis, then the equivalent length of outfall that can be built for the incremental treatment cost can be estimated readily. Reasonable values for the above unit costs and outfall lengths are shown below.

Flow (million gallons per day)	Unit Cost ($/million gallons–foot)	Equivalent Outfall Length (Feet)
10	0.0042	~19,000
100	0.0007	~70,000

The equivalent outfall lengths of 19,000 and 70,000 feet are based upon incremental treatment costs of $80 and $50 per million gallons for the 10 and 100 million gallons per day flows, respectively. The costs above do not include pumping; however, this can be easily included in the analyses as was done by the writer in 1955 [1].

The important point here is that substantial outfall-dispersions systems can be built for the cost difference in the types of treatment cited. This becomes particularly important when one considers the

lack of significant relevancy of secondary waste treatment for open
coast municipal waste disposal.

4. POTENTIAL IMPACT OF REGULATORY ACTION ON LOCAL ENVIRONMENTAL QUALITY

In recent years there has been increasing public pressure to
upgrade waste treatment (convert primary plants to secondary
treatment) without similar support for the construction of larger
dilution-dispersion systems to gain the benefit of reduced waste
concentrations by dilution and decay. In fact, there has been some
general reaction against the latter. Unfortunately, this reaction on
occasion has been encouraged or supported by scientists, regulatory
agencies, as well as by some of those especially interested in designing and building intricate waste treatment processes and plants. All
of this is in accord with the "fuzzy" concept that the more
treatment (conventional type), the better. Consider the fact that
secondary plants essentially only increase the removal of BODs
from about 25 to 85 to 90% and suspended solids from 65 to 90% as
compared to primary treatment. Neither of these parameters are of
any real consequence in open coast waste disposal systems; consequently, it is highly questionable if a policy requiring secondary
waste treatment for *all* waste discharges makes any real sense. In
fact, it may well be adverse and in a substantial way. For example,
if a city near the landward end of an estuary is faced with the
policy and the associated costs of providing secondary treatment
regardless of the location of discharge, it is obvious that there will
be little if any incentive to transport the waste seaward where
greater waste dilutions are possible—to say nothing of transport to
the open coast. Thus the policy will encourage discharging wastes
into the estuary at the point of generation. Larger and larger plants
will be built until the residual waste—that fraction either not
affected or nonremovable by conventional secondary treatment—
will reach a level exceeding the ability of the estuary to assimilate
both the pollutant load in the incoming river flow as well as that not
removed by waste treatment locally. It is well to remember that
there are few if any conventional treatment plants that remove
more than 90% of the pollutants in the waste stream. As the cumulative load builds up ($\sim 10\%$ of a steadily increasing quantity) the
estuary is or will become unduly stressed and what then? Take the
wastes to the open coast after the estuary has been markedly damaged—possibly permanently? Abandon or redesign and rebuild the

existing plants? This does not appear to be a reasonable basis for planning for environmental quality protection, much less for affecting public action by regulatory policies.

REFERENCES

1. E. A. Pearson, *An Investigation of the Efficacy of Submarine Outfall Disposal of Sewage and Sludge*, Publ. 14, California Water Pollution Control Board, 154 pp., 1955.
2. E. A. Pearson, *Marine Waste Disposal*, Vol. 44, Engineering Institute of Canada, pp. 63–68, 1961.
3. C. C. Gunnarson, "Sewage Disposal in Santa Monica Bay, California," *Proceedings of the American Society of Chemical Engineers*, Vol. 124 (1958), pp. 823–851.
4. Kaiser Engineers Consortium, *Final Report, San Francisco Bay Delta Water Quality Management Program*, California Water Resources Control Board, Sacramento, California, 1969.

CHAPTER 11

Marine Transport Systems:
State of Technology

LINCOLN D. CATHERS

Marine transport systems connote different images to people. Most of us would include ships of all types, but how many would also include small submersibles and diver transport devices? Who would normally include a submerged dredge to pump sand to the beach? All of these are considered marine transport systems. For purposes of classification, a marine transport system is defined as a system associated with water and intended to achieve economic, social, or strategic purposes by the movement of people and/or goods with efficiency, safety, and timeliness.

Rather than jumping into the technology for the 1970s, we attempt first to develop the concept of seapower and then establish a background of today's marine transportation industry. The first section discusses some significant marine transport system developments from the hollowed-out log to the modern ocean liner. Seapower, its interrelation with technology, and its relevance today is then developed. The third section documents the conventional marine transport industry of today as we enter the decade of the 1970s. The fourth section consists of some of the most important technological developments for the 1970s. The fifth section briefly discusses special marine transport systems important to opening the resources of the undersea area, especially those of the coastal zone. The chapter concludes with a forecast for the future.

1. HISTORICAL DEVELOPMENT OF MARINE TRANSPORT SYSTEMS

From oars to mechanical propulsion

The history of marine transportation abounds with stories of inventors who succeeded, as well as those who failed, and of outstanding engineering achievements, as well as some fantastic attempts to propel ships through the water. The combined efforts of many sincere and dedicated people have gradually brought us to our present sophisticated stage in marine transportation.

The fundamental principle underlying marine propulsion has not changed through recorded history. The thrust which propels a body through the water is a reaction to the acceleration of a mass of fluid in a direction opposite to the body motion. This thrust is resisted by the hydrodynamic forces generated by the motion of the body through the water.

The same principle applies in hand paddling a log canoe, in the mechanized rotation of a paddle wheel, in the action of a modern screw propeller, and in the ejection of a high-speed water jet into the air. The magnitude of the thrust is proportional to the mass of accelerated fluid and to the rate of acceleration. Although primitive man may not have been aware of these concepts, he had the intelligence to find ways to move more cargo through the water at greater speed and with less effort.

He learned that hollowing out a log both reduced the vehicle's weight without reducing its buoyancy and increased its carrying capacity. Shaping the ends of the hollowed-out log resulted in greater speed for the same amount of expended energy. The fundamental inefficiency of hand propulsion led logically to the use of paddles. By this means, man utilized the mechanical advantage of the lever and the greater propelling power of a wide, flat blade. A double-bladed paddle eased the difficulty of maintaining a straight course while paddling a canoe. The conversion to oars was perhaps the result of early man's attempt to ease the strain on his muscles by supporting the paddle on the gunwale of his boat, pinning it with his hand to form a fulcrum.

Probably the peak efficiency of rowed transport vessels was reached by the Roman triremes. Three banks of oars, pulled by synchronized teams of galley slaves, drove these ships through the water at speeds reputedly up to 6 knots.

It must have been noticed early by paddlers and oarsmen that although they obtained propulsive thrust with the aftwards motion of their blades, they lost ship speed during the forward motion. Although the forward stroke offered a restful interlude, it did not contribute to the propulsion of the vessel. One obvious solution was the sculling stroke used in the Roman triremes. Another solution was a continuous paddling action which could be obtained by using a paddle track or paddle wheel. An ancient Roman bas-relief, reputedly cut in A.D. 527, shows a vessel with three paddle wheels on each side, driven by three pairs of oxen.

In the fifteenth and sixteenth centuries, paddle-driven boats with propulsive power supplied by either animals or human beings were common. Historical accounts do not reveal when it occurred to man that power other than animal or human muscle might be used to propel a vessel through the water.

Ancient writings indicate that in the centuries before and after the birth of Christ, the Greeks built several forms of heat engines which developed motion from the power of steam. Hero's aeolipile, probably built about A.D. 75, was a water-filled, hollowed sphere supported on two bearings above a brazier. Two bent tubes were fastened to the sphere so that when the water was heated, the tubes ejected steam in opposite directions, causing the sphere to rotate like a pinwheel. This and other devices of the time were primarily used as toys and not as a source of mechanical power. In the late sixteenth and early seventeenth centuries serious efforts were undertaken to apply steam to power ships.

These formative centuries of marine propulsion development were highlighted by many brilliant men such as Archimedes, Leonardo da Vinci, and Robert Hooke. These three made many contributions to society, a few of which were directly related to marine transport.

Archimedes served as Chief Scientist to King Hiero of Syracuse. One of his challenging assignments, to determine if a crown ordered by the King were pure gold, led to his discovery of the principle of floatation, which is basic to the design of all marine transport systems. He also invented the forerunner of the screw propeller, namely the screw pump. This device moved water vertically by utilizing a rotating impeller helically wrapped around a shaft and turning in a close-fitting tube.

Leonardo da Vinci is best known for his contributions to art and music. However, he was also a great engineer who anticipated the future of marine transportation systems by over 300 years. In the early 1500s, he sketched a turbine-driven paddle-wheel boat with an intricate gearing system to reduce the high speed of the turbine to the slow speed required for the propeller. It was not until the second half of the nineteenth century that such gear trains were actually employed in marine propulsion systems.

Robert Hooke, one of the great scientific minds of the seventeenth century, is best known for Hooke's Law, which states that within the elastic limit of engineering materials, the mechanical strain is proportional to the applied stress. He is also credited with inventing the horizontal watermill, a device for extracting power from a moving stream; in principle it is essentially identical to the Kersten-Boeing vertical axis propeller "invented" in 1921.

The eighteenth century was an era of great progress. During this period it was proved conclusively that a steam engine-driven propulsion device could move a vessel through the water at a speed greater than that achieved by animal power or sail. Furthermore, it was demonstrated that such schemes were practical and that there was definite promise of commercial advantage in vessels so propelled.

Prior to 1800 almost every ship propulsion device known today had been either suggested or actually tried in full-scale experiments. Of the paddle types the bow-wheel, stern-wheel, submerged-wheels, wheels mounted between twin hulls, and paddle tracks had been tried. Of the screw types, the Archimedian screw was perhaps the most frequently suggested, but screw propellers of relatively modern configurations had been designed.

Surface propellers and airscrews had been built, and single-screw, twin-screw, and triple-screw installations had been recommended by various inventors. Many forms of hydraulic jet propulsion had been proposed, including jets generated by steam pumps, internal paddles, and exploding gases. Various types of gas jets were mentioned, as were a variety of locations on the hull of intake and discharge openings. Ships had been propelled by duck-feet, goose-feet, oscillating umbrella cones, and vibrating boards. Wind and water currents had been harnessed to drive ships through mechanical propulsion systems. Finally, the forces developed in expanding and condensing steam had been put to work to drive propulsive mechanisms.

But with all of this invention, development, and experimentation, there was yet to evolve a mechanically propelled ship which could be termed a commercial success. In spite of the time, effort and dollars invested in propulsion schemes, prior to 1800, no mechanically propelled vessel attracted sufficient cargo or passenger service to reward its inventor financially. Few of the inventors who applied their talents and enthusiasm to the development of marine propulsion realized any more from it than the satisfaction of having contributed to the advancement of science.

However, at the start of the nineteenth century the time was ripe for notable achievements. All of the necessary tools for building a workable steamboat were at hand. Years of experience mainly associated with failures provided a wealth of valuable knowledge to this infant technology. It remained only for someone who had assimilated all of the information regarding past successes and failures to apply this knowledge to the design and construction of a truly practical, mechanically propelled ship.

Paddle wheel versus screw propeller

The beginning of the nineteenth century was the dawn of a new era in developing mechanical methods of ship propulsion. The screw propeller, the paddle wheel, hydraulic jets, and oscillating fins had been used as propulsive mechanisms, and the reciprocating steam engine had been successfully employed as a power source. Inventive minds were being turned to the task of improving ship propulsion devices, and men of vision saw a promising future in the possibilities of driving ships against wind, tide, and current.

The paddle wheel appeared to be the propulsion device most adaptable to the low speed engines of the day. It remained only to improve the engineering and materials of the boiler and engine, and to improve the strength of the hulls to support large concentrations of weight. Once this was accomplished practical self-propulsion of waterborne vehicles became a reality.

As steam machinery became more reliable, and as more confidence in mechanical propulsion was developed, the amount of sail carried by transoceanic vessels gradually decreased. Yet, either as a safety factor, or for additional speed when favorable winds were present, the provisions for sail were never eliminated on ocean-going, paddle wheel steamers.

Although the paddle wheel maintained its supremacy at sea until 1850, it had many severe drawbacks for oceangoing vessels. As paddle wheel ships rolled in a seaway, the alternate immersion of port and starboard wheels would produce imbalanced thrust and make it difficult to keep the ship on course. Heavy weather frequently damaged the paddle wheels or the exposed paddle boxes. The beam of the ship was greatly increased by the paddle wheels, and although the ships had excellent maneuvering characteristics, the wheels were frequently damaged in docking. The large, heavy machinery required to drive the slow turning wheels was both a structural support problem and a problem in providing adequate subdivision for ship integrity in case of damage.

Although paddle wheel driven ships are still in operation, they are well on their way to extinction. By the close of the nineteenth century the seagoing paddle wheel was a thing of the past. Now, as the rivers of the world undergo programs of improvements to increase width and depth and to control the rate of current, the paddle wheel will no longer be required for propulsion on inland rivers.

The paddle wheel filled a distinct gap in technical knowledge during the slow transition from sail to mechanical propulsion. While higher speed marine engines were being developed to drive the more efficient screw propeller, the paddle wheel provided needed experience with mechanical equipment at sea. It gave the public confidence in the marine engineer and fostered the development of the numerous propulsion auxiliaries essential to the operation of a modern seagoing ship.

The paddle wheel will soon be a curio in the museums of the world, but it did its job well, at a time when it was needed the most. The paddle wheel has earned an honored niche in the annals of maritime history.

The transition from paddle wheel propulsion to screw propeller propulsion was a slow process. As an example, the early wooden-hulled ships, fitted with screw propellers, were subject to heavy vibration, and iron hulls were needed to resist the vibratory forces. With shaft and machinery below the waterline, stuffing boxes had to be developed to prevent leakage without damaging the rotating shaft. Thrust bearings were required to transmit the forward force exerted by the propeller to the hull. Higher speed engines had to be developed to realize the inherent efficiency of the screw, and techniques for casting and machining strong, tough metals were needed.

As these many problems were gradually overcome, and as higher speed engines were developed, more and more screw propellers were installed to supplement or replace paddle wheels. The last of the large, seagoing side-wheelers, the *Great Eastern*, was also fitted with a 24-foot diameter, 36-ton screw propeller. The 1600-horsepower screw propeller engine of this mammoth ship turned the propeller at 50 revolutions per minute. Both propeller and engine are good examples of the stage of development reached in ship propulsion by 1858. By modern standards, this propeller was not very efficient. Yet even this crude design must have had an efficiency approaching that of paddle wheels. Although the screw propellers installed in the 1860 era lacked refinement, their performance exceeded that of any other device conceived up to that time. Coupled with the other advantages inherent in underwater screw propulsion, the paddle wheel was gradually rendered obsolete in seagoing ships.

Engineering refinement during the 1900s

With the improvement of marine engines, the design changes in ship hulls and the lessons learned in testing scale models, it was inevitable that there would be progressive changes in the design of screw propellers. In addition, new alloys coupled with improved casting and machining techniques permitted the propeller designer more freedom to design efficient blade sections.

The propellers of 1860 resembled revolving clubs which beat their way through the water. They propelled the ship mainly because they achieved lift by entering the flow with a large angle of attack. Although this form of revolving hydrofoil did produce lift, it also produced a correspondingly large drag; thus the efficiency was low.

During the 1920s and 1930s, the extensive development of airfoils by aircraft designers provided more and more information which was helpful in the improvement of screw-propeller blade sections. Through exhaustive testing in wind tunnels, the characteristics of a wide variety of airfoil sections become known. It was then possible to select blade shapes with maximum lift and minimum drag for a wide range of propeller-design conditions.

During this same period, metallurgical developments came to the aid of the propeller designer. High tensile strength bronzes replaced the steel used in propellers, eliminating the problem of propeller corrosion and the corresponding erosion which destroyed the edge shape and pitted the lifting faces.

Although this era saw the improvement of the screw propeller to a near-optimum efficiency, there were still more changes to be made in blade-section shape. Further increases in power, dictated by the requirement for greater and greater ship speeds, enforced higher thrust loadings on the propeller. With these high loadings, propeller cavitation became an increasingly serious problem.

With the combination of improved theory, model tests, more adaptable power plants, and better hull lines, the screw propeller of today has undergone a series of evolutionary changes. A vivid example of the progress over the last century can be made by comparing the propeller of the *Great Eastern* and a modern single screw supership. Both have propellers of approximately 24 feet, but although the *Great Eastern's* propeller absorbed 1600 horsepower, the modern ship can absorb 25,000 horsepower.

Further increases in the efficiency of the screw propeller may yet be made. However, certainly over the last few years, the percentage increase has been smaller and smaller, indicating a probable approach to optimum. Future improvements are most likely in the ability to absorb higher thrust loadings at greater and greater ship and propeller speeds. Nevertheless, in its present stage of development, the screw propeller is the most universal, efficient, and versatile method of propelling ships which has been devised.

2. SEAPOWER AS A CONCEPT AND A REALITY

What is seapower

Seapower is a term of considerable ambiguity. A military strategist tends to use the term to connote naval dominance of the oceans. Shipping interests, on the other hand, tend to place more importance on a strong national flag merchant marine and perhaps even argue that it is the primary ingredient of seapower. Those who are students of naval and maritime history, especially those who have carefully studied Mahan's writings, consider seapower a combination of naval power, merchant shipping, shipbuilding, and ocean research and development directed toward increased knowledge of the oceans. This understanding of the term recognizes that seapower is a resultant of all forms of ocean activity.

The classical definition is the one stated in Admiral Mahan's 1890 book, *The Influence of Seapower Upon History, 1660–1783*.

Seapower in the broad sense includes not only the military strength afloat that rules the sea or any part of it by force of arms, but also the peaceful commerce and shipping from which alone a military fleet naturally and healthfully springs, and on which its security rests.

In Mahan's subsequent writings he increasingly emphasized the need for a strong Navy to ensure world status as a seapower. This need for naval strength was exclusive of the requirement to protect flag merchant shipping. It constituted a nation's primary capability for projecting its power outward onto the oceans and to the territorial limits of other nations having boundaries on the sea.

It must be recognized that today the close technological similarity that once existed between a naval vessel and a merchant ship has all but disappeared. Naval vessels have nuclear power, missiles, and elaborate electronics; merchant ships have become highly tailored to the special requirements of their particular trade. For example, a super tanker would be useless as a fleet oiler.

In light of the changes, it can be argued that the traditional and perhaps archaic definition of seapower must be modified. For the purpose of the discussion which follows, a shorter and more flexible definition of seapower is proposed:

Seapower is the ability of a nation to project into the oceans, in times of peace, its economic strength; in times of national emergency, its overall defense mobility.

Seapower will be shown to be closely related to activities in the coastal zone. This is the region where ships start their long voyages and unload their cargoes. This is where the Navy returns after overseas operations, and this is one area where industry is moving rapidly in an effort to support our dynamic economy.

Elements of seapower

The sea provides a domain in which national power and continuing political presence may be effectively projected from the nation's coastal zone to the territorial limits of other nations having boundaries on the sea.

According to Mahan, the ability of a nation to use seapower as an element of international influence depends upon the following:

The topography and conformation of the land and water masses is of critical importance. Greatest superiority is accorded to islands, next to peninsulas, then to countries with more limited coast lines, then to isthmuses and with inferiority accorded to nations which have only river access to the sea or which are land locked.

The nature of the coast line is important in terms of its capacity for harbors and access to the major sea routes.

The number of people in the coastal zone must be considered with particular emphasis on people having competence in and an understanding of ocean technology.

The character of the people and their government must be given considerable weight.

Current empirical evidence supports and provides insights into the fundamental truth contained in the hypotheses above. History is too replete with examples (Cuba, Southeast Asia, Lebanon, etc.) to require elaboration of the principle that the sea permits projection of continuing national presence into areas of tension.

Clearly evident is the importance of an island nation to utilize the sea. Thus Mahan foresaw that the island of Malta could provide a strategic balance to the entire Italian peninsula, a theory which was proven during World War II. He identified Cuba as having a similar strategic relationship to the Caribbean. Had his attention been focused on the Pacific, no doubt he would have identified the Japanese islands, Formosa, Guam, and Hawaii as possessing all of the ingredients necessary for effective control of the adjacent seas. His chief example of a domain possessing all of the ingredients necessary to primacy in the use of the sea was the British Isles.

A less obvious corollary of Mahan's teaching is the disadvantage that accrues to the nation having a multiply connected domain to the sea (i.e., two unconnected coasts). Such a nation is faced with the resource burden of maintaining naval vessels and facilities as well as sea commerce on each coast while maintaining effective land defenses across equally disconnected borders.

Inevitably, the mass of people in the interior joins with the defenders of the land boundaries to create an axis of interest away from the use of the sea. So it was that Mahan saw the importance of a canal across the Central American isthmus which when built had the effect of changing the United States from a multiply connected to a singly connected domain. Over 50 years have elapsed since this vital link was established, and its importance to our economy is often overlooked or underestimated.

Recently we have witnessed in the United States a reawakening of the importance of the coastal zone and in particular its use as a terminal for modern ocean shipping. Here the second element of Mahan's thesis is involved. Britain's preeminence as a sea power derived not only from its island entity but from the network of navigable rivers exemplified by the Clyde, Thames, and Tyne. In contrast, Ireland was not similarly blessed and never developed a strong tie with the sea.

To a considerable degree, the United States coastline has the characteristics of Britain on its east and Ireland on its west. On the east, extensive port facilities provided by Boston, New York, Philadelphia, Baltimore, Norfolk, Charleston, and the Gulf ports have been supplemented by inland waterways and extensive estuaries. In 1959 the Saint Lawrence Seaway opened the Great Lakes to modern cargo vessels, reminiscent of when the Erie Canal did a similar job for vessels a century earlier. With the recent emphasis on larger ships, the Seaway may rapidly become obsolete. Improvements in the navigability of the Mississippi extended its connectivity to the sea past Saint Anthony Falls and to its very upper reaches.

With the exception of the Puget Sound area, and to a limited extent San Francisco Bay and San Diego, the West Coast has not been endowed with good harbors and access to the interior. The greatly improved waterway that established Sacramento as a deep-ocean port is important because it opened the interior to the benefits of low cost sea transportation.

It is the third element of Mahan's hypothesis in which the United States is indeed rich. This is the requirement that numbers of people in the vicinity of the sea coast have competence in and an understanding of ocean technology. During the late 1950s and early 1960s the Navy's Polaris Project Office pulled together a team of contractors which performed an outstanding job of placing a workable system of immense complexity to sea in record time. A review of prime and first-tier subcontractors reveals that with but one or two exceptions all were located on the eastern and western seaboard.

Finally, even a partial enumeration of our ocean related activities demonstrates the character of our governments and its people. California is a prime example of a state which has placed priority in education and research highlighting the ocean. Of particular note are the Scripps Institution of Oceanography; the University of California, which has sponsored a series of lectures on the management of the coastal zone; the California Institute of Technology; and Stanford University. Complementing the academic institutions are organizations like the RAND Corporation, General Electric's Tempo, and the Stanford Research Institute.

The U.S. Navy has many centers of excellence in California with shipyards at Mare Island, Hunters Point, and Long Beach; laboratories at China Lake, Corona, Pasadena, San Diego, and Port Hueneme; the Naval Missile Center, Point Mugu; and the Postgraduate School at Monterey. In industry, no major aircraft company has neglected ocean technology. Lockheed, North American, Hughes, Convair, Ryan, and Northrop, to name a few on the West Coast, have substantial experience and competence in the ocean.

California as a state has taken the lead in preparing itself for continued wise and fuller utilization of the oceans. This preparation was vividly outlined in recent testimony by Lieutenant Governor Ed Reinecke before the Congressional Subcommittee on Oceanography of the House Merchant Marine and Fisheries Committee:

California has, for some time, actively supported marine oriented programs. In particular, the State has called for intensive efforts in the field of ocean oriented planning and in the review of existing programs with the intent to provide for the wise use and development of marine resources.

Several State Agencies have been producing single interest plans for fish and wildlife, for shoreline recreation, for small craft harbors etc., and have recently joined with the Interagency Council for Ocean Resources (ICOR) to assist in the preparation of a Comprehensive Ocean Area Plan in which all of California's interests in the ocean area will be represented, differences recognized and reconciled where possible, and integrated programs recommended for implementation.

ICOR was established by order of Governor Reagan, following passage of legislation calling for the preparation of a Comprehensive Ocean Area Plan (COAP), and for the establishment of a new commission made up of representatives of the private sector and State legislators to advise the Governor on marine and coastal matters, including a review of the COAP as it was prepared by ICOR.

ICOR is composed of the five Cabinet Secretaries and myself from the Executive Branch of State Government. It operates to approve development of the Comprehensive Ocean Area Plan which is presently funded by State and Federal planning money ($170,000). The planning team is composed of professionals in resource management and planning with supporting staff. I am chairman of ICOR and thus have a personal interest in the development of all ocean oriented matters.

The new California Advisory Commission on Marine and Coastal Resources continued the activities of the former non-statutory Governor's Commission on Coastal Resources, but because it is now funded and charged with specific responsibilities by law, it has become much stronger and more influential in reviewing and guiding California's marine and coastal activities. It is funded by State money.

Governor Reagan has also taken a first step towards the establishment of a Coastal Zone Authority, by calling for a reorganization of State Government which was approved by our legislature this year, and which would provide for an enlargement of the responsibilities of the Department of Harbors and Watercraft to include other marine matters. This new Department, named *Navigation and Ocean Development,* would also be charged with implementing the COAP.

California is alert to the national developments, and is ready to work with the Federal Government in facilitating the coordination of the activities of National Ocean and Atmospheric Administration (NOAA) with California, and looks forward to Federal legislation which will provide for such coordination.

Seapower in the 1970s

To understand seapower in the 1970s, it is useful to carefully examine two important developments which occurred since the end of World War II which are profoundly affecting our utilization of the oceans. Also a basic understanding of some of the major technological constraints is useful when projections are attempted.

The first major development is political in nature and involves the rapid increase in the number of new nations since World War II. Africa offers a striking example. On V-J Day ten nations held control of that vast land area. Today there are over 40 independent nations in the "dark continent." These new nations, underdeveloped economically, socially, and politically, are prime targets for aggressive nations. It must be recognized that the sea is the main avenue of approach to these countries.

The second major development is also political. The United States now has more commitments, in more places, with more nations, and involving more people than any nation in history. The United States is committed to the defense of some 60 nations, either by treaty or by other agreements. The great majority of these nations border on the oceans of the world. In short, the United States has moved irreversibly away from isolation. Events today and in the future, halfway around the globe, will profoundly affect our own national life. Most significant in the trend from isolationism is the amount of United States business overseas and the rapid growth of United States sea trade to over 400 million tons annually.

There is a fundamental constraint upon technology, well known to the naval architect, called the "power law." Simply, it states that to a first-order approximation, the horsepower to propel a vessel is proportional to the cube of the speed. Therefore, to double the speed of a given vessel an excess of eight times more horsepower must be applied. However, even from a military point of view, if speeds of 60 knots were obtained, the transit time of a major task force from one world theatre to another would still be measured in days. The transit speed of ships has the curious effect of making credible national intent in a particular conflict theatre and precludes misinterpretation of naval deployment as bluff or feint. This "message content" of sea deployment is too often dismissed in projections of national requirements, although never overlooked in periods of international tension.

The second fundamental constraint of technology is the ability of coastal zone engineering to keep pace with the requirements imposed by new marine transport systems. Larger and faster ships are also capital intensive ships. They make money only if they are fully utilized. They work well until they enter the coastal zone where they must unload and reload. The superships with drafts up to 70 or 80 feet cannot enter today's harbors. The high-speed container ship must rely on special terminal facilities for turning around in a matter of 24 hours or less so that it can fulfill its commitment to a guaranteed schedule.

For the super ships massive dredging is necessary, or provision must be made to transfer cargoes out from the coastline where depths are sufficient. The local features of the coastline dictate the more rational approach. For handling superships, California with its rapid drop off in depth along much of the coastline has a built-in advantage over, say, the Gulf of Mexico, where literally tens or hundreds of miles of dredging would be required to provide a 70-foot channel.

Superships have also made the Panama and Suez Canal obsolete. Truly massive engineering undertakings would be required to upgrade them or to build new canals in these locations. The epic voyage of the *Manhattan* may result in a reassessment of the need for a new canal across Panama.

The Arctic is perhaps the ultimate challenge to the coastal engineer. In this region of frozen tundra and ice covered waters, it is even difficult to define the coastal zone. The extraction of resources and the utilization of this region as a major shipping route will necessitate the installation and operation of many support facilities.

3. CONVENTIONAL MARINE TRANSPORT TODAY

Background

When the Merchant Marine Act became law nearly 35 years ago, American foreign trade consisted primarily of the higher-value general cargo transported by conventional freighters. Today the trade pattern has been drastically altered; 85% is now dry or liquid bulk cargo and only 15% is general cargo. Imports of strategic ores and petroleum products are steadily increasing, as are exports of agricultural surpluses in bulk shipload lots. Because less than one third of United States merchant ships are bulk carriers, Americans have had to rely more and more upon foreign-flag ships to carry these commodities.

The United States merchant marine is a small industry playing a large role in national and international affairs. Because of its importance to the nation's commerce, defense, and international prestige, American shipping has been assisted by the Federal Government since 1789. Direct and indirect subsidies now approximate $400 million per year; the Federal Government provides most of the industry's cargoes, monitors its labor relations, regulates its rates, guarantees its credit, trains its officers, and looks after the health and safety of its employees. However, instead of building a strong and expanding merchant marine, these efforts have created friction between subsidized and nonsubsidized firms and in some respects have weakened the industry.

The problems besetting the merchant marine are both economic and political in origin. For more than 100 years American seafaring wages and ship construction costs have been higher than those of other nations. Some form of U.S. Government assistance has been necessary to attract private investment and to persuade American entrepreneurs to register their ships under the United States flag. However, the regulations that were imposed to safeguard the government's interests in the national flag fleet have created additional problems for subsidized operators. An even more serious result of the subsidy program has been to make United States merchant shipping dependent on political support for survival. To many Americans, it is unthinkable that the United States should not have a functioning, healthy merchant marine.

Although aid to the United States merchant service has a long history, direct subsidies were not provided until the Great Depression. The Merchant Marine Act of 1936 provided the first systematic peacetime formulation of the U.S. Government's maritime program and sought to provide aid on a sound, long-term basis. It authorized payment of operating and construction subsidies to companies that used United States built and manned vessels to provide essential services on routes designated by the newly established Maritime Commission. The subsidies were designed to place United States shipowners on a parity with foreign competitors—generally by compensating them for differentials in cost. World War II interrupted the fledgling Commission's plans for orderly reconstruction and engulfed industry with new demands.

United States shipping emerged from the war with approximately 60% of the world's merchant tonnage, compared to 13% before the war. The number of companies engaged in overseas operations had tripled, and seamen's wages were approximately double their prewar level. The war also disrupted patterns of trade; upset international economic relationships; and altered the structure, composition, and financial status of the United States maritime industry. The U.S. Government's stake in merchant shipping increased greatly. The merchant marine became "America's fourth arm of defense." These developments gave maritime activities a new orientation, shifting interest from commercial objectives to defense requirements.

The material which follows is an attempt to establish a better image of the character of the merchant marine—or at least to provide some clues to that character—although the scope of the subject is truly encyclopedic. To understand the present and the plan for the future, one has no recourse but to consult the past.

U.S. Merchant Marine Act of 1936

The 1936 Merchant Marine Act is still the basis for present-day U.S. Government aid policies and programs. Its Declaration of Policy states:

SECTION 101. It is necessary for the national defense and development of its foreign and domestic commerce that the United States shall have a merchant marine (a) sufficient to carry its domestic water-borne commerce and a substantial portion of the water-borne export and import foreign commerce of the United States and to provide shipping service on all routes essential for maintaining the flow of such domestic and foreign water-borne commerce at all times, (b) capable of serving as a naval and military auxiliary in time of war or national emergency, (c) owned and operated under the United States flag by citizens of the United States insofar as may be practicable, and (d) composed of the best-equipped, safest, and most suitable types of vessels, constructed in the United States and manned with a trained and efficient citizen personnel. It is hereby declared to be the policy of the United States to foster the development and encourage the maintenance of such a merchant marine.

This act established direct subsidies for shipping government cargoes and to make up the difference between American and foreign shipping costs. It created the U.S. Maritime Commission, which was empowered to administer the subsidy features of the act, to construct ships, and to charter them to private companies for operation.

The power of the Commission was detailed to include authority to contract as may be necessary to carry out its authorized activities (46 U.S.C. 1117); purchase or acquisition of vessels constructed in the United States as may be necessary to establish, maintain, improve, or effect replacements upon a service route or line in the foreign commerce of the United States (Section 1125); requiring the payment of minimum wages, and such, on vessels operated under operating-differential subsidy agreements (Sections 1131–1132); granting construction-differential subsidies (Sections 1151–1152); limiting the profit of shipbuilders in the construction of vessels under subsidies; granting operating-differential subsidies on vessels used in an essential trade of the United States (Sections 1171–1182) ; selecting steamship lines to operate on routes essential to the defense of the United States (Section 1195) ; requiring that no operating-differential subsidy operator operate any foreign-flag vessel in competition with any American-flag service (Section 1223) ; requiring United States crews on United States ships (Section 1241) ; requisitioning, in time of emergency, the title to or use of vessels owned by citizens of the United States (Section 1242).

Several other acts which followed had important policy implications. The Transportation Act, 1940, transferred the power to regulate waterborne intercoastal commerce from the Maritime Commission to the Interstate Commerce Commission. The Merchant Ship Sales Act, 1946, gave the Commission authority to dispose of surplus war-built merchant ships and to establish a National Defense Reserve Fleet, readily available for security needs but frozen for commercial use. The Fishing Vessels Construction Assistance Act provided a subsidy assistance program to correct inequities in the construction costs of fishing vessels.

Over the past 15 years, maritime policy has been subject to an almost continual national debate. The Congressional intent of the 1936 Act was that a "substantial portion" of United States foreign waterborne commerce must be carried in United States flag bottoms. Today, with less than 7% of this commerce being carried by United States flag ships, a reappraisal of how much must be so carried to serve national interests is indicated. The 1936 Act also stipulated that if a "substantial portion" were not being carried, the U.S. Government should then authorize and direct the construction of such new vessels in American shipyards as would be required to carry out the objectives of the act. But in the words of Senator Magnuson: "There appears to be a total disregard on the part of administration after administration of any responsibility or statutory duty to implement and administer existing law in the maritime field." Hence the Senator would "adjust the language of the law in such a manner that this administration—or any subsequent administrations will be unable to frustrate the clear intent of Congress."*

"The need to revitalize the maritime industry," said Alan S. Boyd, former Secretary of Transportation, "is a paradox. We are

---

* From the statement of Senator Warren Magnuson before the Subcommittee on Merchant Marine and Fisheries, Committee on Commerce, U.S. Senate, April 13, 1967.

faced with an industry which many describe as dying because of a lack of Federal support . . . and . . . its continued decline would be a tragic blow to our military and economic strength as well as to our national prestige . . . but . . . the only solution to our maritime problem is one that will fully protect every single interest and meet the demands of every single group."†

This is, in effect, the maritime policy problem of today and for the past 15 years as well. By trying to "protect" all interests, the industry has lost much of its incentive for innovation and competition. The policy to protect the longshoremen's or seamen's jobs hinders the development of automation in ships and shipyards, the streamlining of ship's crews and the introduction of efficient cargo handling gear and techniques. Similarly, the policy of full financial protection for the United States shipbuilder has tended to stagnate shipyard development.

In addition, there is a level of federal subsidy beyond which the public interest is not served. What public resources the U.S. Government will actually devote to achieve long-term economic stability is a major question. The past uncertainty about support has undermined the confidence of American labor and management and has tended to make policy decisions *ad hoc*.

The national interest requires a readily available fleet of merchant ships in support of national defense. The focus of debate has been on interpretation of what ships are or are not readily available, whether United States flag ships or what foreign flag ships under effective United States control. Furthermore, the changing world political and military environment and changes in the very character of sea transportation systems have invalidated many statutory assumptions of the 1936 Act. New technology is one of the major contributors to the rapidly changing character of ocean transportation.

The Merchant Marine today

The world's merchant fleet, comprised of vessels of 1000 gross tons and over and totaling over 19,000 ships with a combined carrying capacity in excess of 260 million deadweight tons, is increasing at a rate of 6 to 8% per year. The distribution of this total tonnage as of 1967 was as follows:

† From the statement of Honorable Alan S. Boyd, Secretary of Transportation, before the Subcommittee on Merchant Marine and Fisheries, Committee on Commerce, U.S. Senate, May 1, 1967.

Freighters	36%
Combination (passenger-cargo)	2
Bulk carriers	20
Tankers	42
	100

The annual growth rate of tonnage of the various ship types is markedly different, as shown by the following:

Freighters	Constant
Combination	−5%
Bulk carriers	+20 to 25
Tankers	+8 to 10

Replacement and modernization programs have resulted in a strong worldwide shipbuilding program dominated by Japan, Sweden, England, and Germany. For example, as of June 30, 1967, there were 2120 ships worldwide totaling over 58 million tons on order or under construction. The average size of the tankers on order was 66,000 tons and of bulk carriers, 38,000 tons. The freighters on order averaged 8000 tons, with the largest 23,000 tons deadweight.

Although freighters have not kept pace with the rapid growth of the bulk carrier and tanker fleets, they are nevertheless becoming more efficient. This is brought about by wider use of new concepts such as the transport of cargo in containers. Many container ships are already in operation, and many more are on order or are under construction. These ships have a big advantage over conventional freighters in that they spend much less time in port loading and unloading. The United States is the leader in this field and owns the largest fleet of container ships in the world, but foreign competition is increasing rapidly.

The United States percentage of the world's ships is relatively small. As of September 30, 1967, the United States had 975 active oceangoing ships in the privately owned United States flag merchant fleet: 27 passenger-cargo, 614 freighters, 57 bulk carriers, and 277 tankers. In addition, there were 1070 U.S. Government-owned merchant ships, of which 1008 are in the National Defense Reserve Fleet; they are mothballed ships in excess of 25 years of age and in relatively poor condition.

The United States flag merchant fleet ships across the board are somewhat older than the average for the world fleet. United States freighters average 19 years; the world average age is 16 years.

United States tankers average 17 years; the world average is 11 years. United States bulk carriers average 22 years; the world average is 11 years. Quite obviously, most of the United States flag fleet is obsolete.

In addition to the United States flag merchant fleet, many foreign-flag ships are owned by foreign affiliates of United States companies. Most of these ships are under the Liberian or Panamanian flag. Some are considered under effective United States control to the extent that they would, by contract agreement, be readily available for United States use in time of national emergency. As of June 30, 1967, the so-called flag-of-convenience ships under "effective U.S. control" were estimated at 466 ships, 110 Panamanian, 10 Honduran, and 346 Liberian.

In 1967 domestic shipping moved approximately 135 million short tons between United States ports, while United States foreign export–import trade represented 430 million tons. However, of this total, United States flag ships carried less than 7%; yet as recently as 1947, United States flag ships carried 57% of the total.

The Soviet challenge

Soviet merchant seapower is an accomplished fact. Its merchant marine ranks sixth or seventh on a deadweight tonnage basis among maritime nations and consists of an increasing number of well-designed, technically advanced, fast oceangoing freighters, bulk carriers, tankers, and passenger ships.

The USSR regards its merchant marine as an essential element of its national economy and, according to Jane's *Fight Ships*, a vital factor in national defense. The Soviet merchant marine is a planned fleet. Ships are added to the fleet on the basis of planned needs and in keeping with goals established for increased national production of industrial, agricultural, and petroleum products and for expansion of economic and commercial ties.

As a result of this emphasis one of the great national assets of the USSR is its fleet of 1345 merchant ships totaling 9.6 million deadweight tons. A relatively youthful and balanced merchant marine comprising all types of ships, it is the product of a consistent national maritime policy. The rise of the Soviet fleet has been rapid. In less than 20 years, its tonnage increased 3.5 times and its average age decreased from 22 years to 14 years.

Net additions to the fleet were relatively small between 1946 and 1955, averaging only 50,000 deadweight tons annually. It was not until 1960 that the USSR gave impetus to its plans to build a strong, modern, and competitive merchant marine. By 1960 the fleet had almost doubled its 1946 tonnage. However, it was still a merchant marine of contrasts, for the average ages of some segments of the fleet, such as bulk carriers and tankers, were 8 and 8.4 years, respectively, while those of freighters and passenger ships were 20.6 and 27.9 years, respectively. The closing of the Suez Canal in 1956 pointed up Russia's need for bulk carriers and tankers.

The expansion during the next 5 years was spectacular. The fleet practically doubled in tonnage, 4.9 million deadweight tons in 1960 to 9.6 million tons in 1965. Between 1960 and 1965 freighters increased by a net of 321 ships and 2.3 million deadweight tons. The increase in the number and tonnage of tankers reflected the rise in oil production and the need for tanker facilities to service the widespread areas of the USSR and its foreign markets.

From the viewpoint of national defense, the Soviet merchant marine is readily adaptable as an important arm of the Navy. It has many timber carriers, for example, that can readily be converted to missile carriers, and its new passenger ships are readily convertible to troop transports. Although its large, modern fishing fleet is not considered part of the merchant marine, it can serve as an important defense adjunct by becoming a fleet of minesweepers, and it does serve as observation posts for the USSR just outside the territorial waters of many non-Communist nations. There can be no doubt that economic and political exigencies are motivating factors in the expansion of Soviet maritime interests.

Coincident with the growth of Soviet shipping is the realization by the USSR that new ideas of management and planning in ship operations are essential if Soviet shipping is to achieve economic progress and to compete with ships of the larger maritime nations. There appear to be tentative steps toward decentralization of fleets and a recognition of the need for certain "capitalistic" criteria for fleet operations.

The fact that the Soviet fleet has increased tremendously in size in a relatively short time has been a source of concern to many of the major maritime nations. It is a huge state-controlled enterprise to which substantial allocations of national resources are made, not only for ship acquisitions but for the construction and improvement of ship repair facilities, ports, research, and development and for maritime personnel training facilities.

Although the USSR is still a "user" of shipping services, albeit not to the same extent as the United States, it is understandable why some of the "supplier" nations are uneasy about the long-term trend of Soviet shipping. The Soviets have recently chartered some of their ships to western countries, and their advertised intent is to increase this operation, especially during the winter and spring seasons when many Soviet shipping lines are relatively inactive. The Russians have also carried cargo between non-Communist ports at attractive rates on return voyages to earn foreign exchange rather than sail in ballast.

The announced plans clearly outline the future. The Soviets plan to double their merchant marine, with a target of 20 million deadweight tons by 1980, a figure well in excess of the present United States tonnage of less than 15 million deadweight tons.

Since World War II, the United States has kept a sizable portion of her Navy in being. During most of this period we have been able to assume essentially undisputed control of the world's oceans and largely by virtual default of all other naval powers. Today this control must be viewed with question. A second Navy, that of the Soviets, has emerged which has a composition strikingly dissimilar to that of the United States.

The Soviet Navy is predominantly one of submarines (over 350 in operation) and missile-equipped surface ships. A large force of operational nuclear-powered submarines plus a new construction program for such submarines indicates to most United States strategists that the Soviets intend a prolonged antishipping strategy for any major conventional war at sea.

The threat of Soviet seapower is much greater than that posed by her merchant ship growth and her naval forces. In "Report on the Soviets and the Seas," a report of the Congressional Delegation to Poland and the Soviet Union, August 4, 1966, the Congressmen who participated said:

Since World War II, the Russians have realized that knowledge of the oceans' secrets would be mandatory if the Red goal of world naval, economic and maritime superiority was to be achieved . . . Highly directed Soviet planning in oceanography is one of the reasons for their present progress. It was our impression that these are their major goals:

- Rapid and efficient conversion of the results of basic oceanographic research into economic development.
- World respect for Soviet scientific achievements.
- Gaining leverage with the international scientific community and making use of the accomplishments of foreign oceanography.

- International political leverage as a result of assisting nations to establish their own oceanographic programs.

The Congressmen noted that the Soviets have over 200 oceanographic and hydrographic vessels at work and about 9000 oceanographers and technicians compared to our 3000. Their edge in fisheries is also significant: a catch of 5.6 million tons of fish in 1965 compared to 2.3 million tons for United States fishermen. In the same year, the Soviets planned a 50% expansion of their catch by 1970, and it appears that this has been a realistic planning goal.

In summary, the Soviet's seapower threat is four-pronged: oceanographic, fisheries, merchant marine, and naval forces. The total of their strength in each of these areas is Soviet power at sea which can increasingly challenge our free use of the seas in peace and war. Admiral J. S. McCain, Jr., a former Commander in Chief, U.S. Naval Forces Europe, said in a recent speech:

Russia is quick to realize what the western world is equally quick to forget, namely, the increasing importance of the oceans to the entire human race.

Cost of shipping operations

To understand the motivation for new technology, it is necessary to have a general knowledge of the breakdown of costs for typical shipping operations. The costs associated with the five major stages of a typical shipment from the United States to a foreign market break down as follows:

Inland (United States)	14%
Port (United States)	36
Sea	25
Port (foreign)	18
Inland (foreign)	7
	100%

Note that only 25% of the shipping cost is associated with the sea voyage, that over 50% is associated with port costs, that the costs for United States port services and inland transportation about double that of foreign countries. Ship delay time is charged to port costs. Inland costs do not include any packaging charges.

Following is a typical percentage distribution of the costs associated with the at-sea transportation portion:

Ship operation and housekeeping	34%
Maintenance and repair, labor	11
Maintenance supplies	4
Repairs ashore	10
Amortization	17
Fuel	16
Insurance	8
	100%

It can be seen that these costs are roughly half labor and half materials, services or amortization. Maintenance and repair make up about 25% of the total.

During the United States in-port phase, the following would be a typical breakdown of the costs:

Cargo handling	56%
Port charges	14
Breakage fees	3
Crew	14
Amortization	10
Insurance	3
	100%

These percentages would be typical for a conventional "break-bulk" cargo ship. Obviously the percentages would change considerably for, say, a tanker or a bulk carrier.

The items which reflect high labor costs, namely cargo handling and ship operation, provide the major stimulus to the modern capital intensive ships. These new ships are faster and larger and are provided with improved cargo handling features. As a result the labor cost is a smaller percentage of the total.

From a total systems viewpoint, the port is critical. There over half the costs accumulate. The size and capability of a port should be matched to the vessels it services. If the facilities are too limited, ships are forced to wait to unload. If the facilities are overbuilt, ships usually can come immediately to the discharge point, but under most traffic conditions many facilities remain unused. Of course, distribution of ship arrivals is important to efficient matching of ship and shore facilities.

Shipbuilding trends

Today United States built vessels cost roughly twice the prevailing world market price. The reasons for this uncompetitive stance are complex and intertwined. United States shipbuilders themselves tend to blame the high cost of labor. United States shipyard workers are paid about two-thirds more than even the well-paid Swedes; yet the heavily mechanized Swedish yards compete vigorously with Japan, even though Swedish laborers earn more than twice as much as the Japanese.

Part of the problem stems from the U.S. Government attempt to support a geographically dispersed industry by parceling out Navy and subsidized merchant ship orders among many yards. Government policy has kept the builders out of bankruptcy, but it has provided little incentive to modernize. Regardless of the causes, the United States builders usually get orders only for Navy vessels and merchant ships that have to be built domestically to qualify for federal subsidies.

Study of United States shipbuilding leads to some broad generalizations and to specific recommendations in regard to prospects for reducing costs and improving the prospects for the industry. Merchant shipbuilding must compete in an international market where the high hourly labor cost, characteristic of the American economy, is a crucial handicap. But only a casual survey of the industrial scene reveals that shipbuilding suffers a further serious handicap in comparison with most other United States industries. A stable production situation characteristic of more prosperous industries has not been attained in peacetime shipbuilding. The record shows that in the past few years the number of United States flag merchant ships constructed annually has been relatively small and ship construction programs have been uncertain and variable in character. Naval shipbuilding has been larger in volume, but it has also been subject to wide fluctuations in the years since World War II. Furthermore, until recently postwar policies did not encourage the authorization, funding or procurement of naval ships on a multiple unit basis.

In this environment, it is not surprising that postwar shipbuilding management has not been aggressive. Capital outlays for new shipyard facilities and equipment have been relatively low in comparison with other industries, although they are definitely increasing at the present time. Shipbuilding in the United States has a lower level of output per man-hour expended than most other industries, indicative of its labor intensiveness.

By contrast it is interesting to note that during World War II the results of multiple ship construction in the United States were outstanding in terms of output and cumulative cost reduction. In fact, many of the foreign yards based their present techniques on United States experience in those days.

The conclusion is inescapable that with an adequate program of ship construction over a period of years, shipyard management could again concentrate on methods to improve production efficiency and could afford to invest more money in new facilities with the expectation of recovery over a reasonable period of time. Furthermore, the higher the level of production of ships in individual yards, the lower will be the resulting costs, even though a true mass production level cannot ever be attained.

Recent attempts at multiple ship procurement have been successful. Avondale Shipyards, Inc., received contracts for nine high-endurance Coast Guard cutters and 27 Navy destroyer escorts. These contracts have enabled Avondale to become the first American shipyard since World War II to build enough of the same class of vessels to justify a full production line assembly. Avondale's president, Henry Zac Carter, thinks that this building concept could be the salvation of the American shipbuilding industry if it were carried through on other contracts for both commercial and military vessels. Furthermore, he believes that if the continuity of multiple ship procurement contracts is maintained and if the number of orders is commensurate with the actual needs of our merchant fleets, our domestic yards would soon compete with any shipyards in the world.

Other groups are not quite as optimistic as Carter. In a recent study conducted by the Center for Maritime Studies, located at Webb Institute of Naval Architecture, it was estimated that under a long-range, multiple ship program, it should be possible with available knowledge and techniques to reduce the construction differential subsidy from 50 to 55% to 25 to 30%. Further reductions might be obtainable, but only through more drastic measures growing out of an aggressive research and development program.

The study concluded that aggressive steps are needed to revitalize both the shipbuilding industry and the environment in which it operates. Steps recommended for making the United States shipbuilding industry more efficient and thus for improving its future prospects are summarized below:

1. Stabilize production in shipbuilding. This requires firm construction programs for a reasonable number of ships over periods of several years.

2. Build ships in quantity. The number of vessels of similar design to be built in each participating yard(s) should be as large as practicable with minimum differences to different owners.

3. Make capital improvements designed to reduce costs. The nature and extent of investments that would be optimum under stable production conditions in individual United States shipyards could be determined for different sized programs.

4. Design for production. This requires time at the beginning of every program for careful ship design and production planning, with associated simplification of structure and outfitting, modular construction and standardization of components.

5. Continue to upgrade shipyard management techniques. There should be continuing improvement in industrial engineering, production planning control systems, and cost accounting systems.

6. Pursue research and development programs. These should be aimed at improved ship design and building techniques for easier and more economical production. They require cooperation among industry, labor, and the U.S. Government in obtaining adoption of the new techniques developed.

Thus the problem of improving United States shipbuilding prospects does not have a single simple solution. Intensive efforts will be required over a period of years to establish a favorable environment for the industry and to develop optimum production methods in relation to United States wage rate patterns, standards of living, and industrial standards. And these methods must be dynamic, changing, and evolving with the times. Most would conclude that shipbuilding in the United States cannot become fully competitive with foreign industry even under favorable conditions. However, the differential can be greatly reduced.

An editorial in the December 1969 issue of *Fortune* Magazine indicates that the Nixon administration intends to make substantial efforts to improve the situation:

American shipyards have come to resemble nothing so much as those captive artisans in the Williamsburg restoration, who can be seen in quaint buildings at work on spinning wheels and anvils. To keep all of the country's twenty-seven shipyards in business, Navy work has been spread around; the average commercial order since World War II in-

volved only 3.4 ships per contract until the past couple of years . . .
American yards have been encouraged to assume the role of custom
contractors and have been positively discouraged from investing the
enormous amounts of capital necessary to modernize and achieve the
economies of large-scale production.

The Nixon Administration has now proposed a new $3.8-billion pro-
gram to revise and modernize the industry. If Congress approves, thirty
new ships a year, mainly general cargo vessels, will be built over the next
decade. Builders will receive their subsidies directly, but the maximum
subsidy will be reduced from the current 55 percent to 45 percent of cost
in fiscal 1971 and to 35 percent by 1976. The plan specifies "multi-year"
procurement contracts for large groups of ships, and calls for the shipyards to work out designs in order to take advantage of efficient construction methods.

Not everyone in the industry is delighted, however. There is no question that the time-honored practice of dividing all shipbuilding among all
yards has kept many marginal businesses in operation at the taxpayers'
expense. Multiple procurement is all but certain to make the big bigger
and kill off the small and inefficient.

Marine transportation in support of fundamental national interests

Today and for the foreseeable future, the marine transportation
industry will be essential to the well-being of the United States.
The viability of the national economy depends to large extent upon
a steady growth in world trade. National defense continues to rely
heavily on shipping and shipbuilding to ensure adequate military
response for all sorts of contingencies. Marine transportation and
trade help to maintain satisfactory political relationships between
the United States and its NATO and other Free World allies, which
include most of the maritime powers of the world.

With a steadily declining percentage of United States foreign
sea trade carried in ships flying the United States flag, the United
States is at a major decision point. The question which faces this
nation is whether national defense and economic interests can be
met despite a steadily diminishing United States flag merchant
fleet.

The basic issues in regard to national defense are whether sufficient merchant ships are or will be available to meet the planned
for military contingencies, whether a shipyard capacity will be
available to meet the demands of ship repair and new construction
in time of war or national emergency and whether a sufficiently
large base of personnel skilled in ship operations and in ship-

building are available to provide for the necessary expansion of the Navy and its supporting elements in time of war.

On the side of a relatively small merchant marine, it is argued that the contingencies of the next two decades in which the United States may be involved will be like Vietnam, limited, conventional, and not between major powers. For such wars there appears to be a ready availability of Free World shipping.

As to the availability of a shipbuilding capability to meet wartime needs, the very nature of the expected wars denies a requirement for an extensive national commercial shipbuilding industry or even any additional military construction. The wars of liberation, not considered a national emergency, do not require rapid expansion of the shipbuilding industry, and all-out nuclear exchange infers an almost total destruction of any shipbuilding base, no matter what its size. The argument for a large United States shipbuilding base to meet United States needs in time of war is lessened by the compensating skills and technology developed by the extensive aerospace industry.

The arguments advanced on the other side in favor of a large United States flag merchant shipping and shipbuilding mobilization base assert the unpredictable nature of the wars of today and in the future. Thus, although the role of airlift is recognized, it is argued that a sealift capability must provide the huge tonnages required to support modern military operations.

The difficulty in predicting war needs is evident from past history. Not until the Spring of 1967 were shipping demands to South Vietnam met despite continued attempts to charter free world shipping along with a large-scale reactivation of merchant ships from the National Defense Reserve Fleet. Looking further back, the prices for chartered shipping more than doubled during the Korean and Suez crises. In World War II, the assumption that a fleet adequate to carry United States peacetime commerce was also adequate for war proved seriously in error.

United States owned "flags of convenience" by agreement are requisitionable for "national emergencies." A war like Vietnam does not qualify; yet defense planning considers such limited wars of greatest likelihood for the near future. Thus it is argued, for the probable contingencies of the next two decades, such shipping cannot be responsive to defense needs.

Reliance on the merchant fleets of the maritime allies of the United States, considered tenuous, involves certain risk in defense planning. Even if such ships were readily available, the military needs for "over the beach" capability, compartmentation on troop transports, at-sea transfer capability for tankers and general cargo handling under varied conditions, could not be adequately met.

Furthermore, the trend toward automation and specialization in the United States merchant fleet jeopardizes the total national capability to redeploy and expand the merchant fleet rapidly for defense needs.

The basic issue of the United States sea transportation industry is economic, centering around whether the industry can compete and whether benefits from expanding it through U.S. Government subsidy and preferential treatment outweigh the penalties.

At the root of the problem is the high standard of living enjoyed by citizens of the United States and its associated higher cost of labor. The wages of American merchant seamen are three to five times greater than those of foreign seamen. Similarly, labor costs contribute to shipbuilding costs far in excess of material costs for the same ship built abroad. The problem is compounded because United States flag ship firms are required to buy costly United States built ships to carry either domestic trade or preferential overseas U.S. Government cargo. Under these circumstances, it is argued that, maintaining a competitive position for foreign trade requires that United States shipping firms receive operating subsidies and construction subsidies. Similarly, United States flag tramp ships must depend on U.S. Government preference cargoes.

The need for subsidies appears high in an economic environment in which the major portion of United States world trade can economically be carried in foreign bottoms. As partial justification for incurring these costs, it is argued that shipping rates to United States shippers would probably increase without a substantial United States flag fleet.

The political value of merchant ships flying the United States flag should be considered in assessing the cost of a subsidy program designed to ensure a substantial flag presence on the oceans of the world. The American flag on the sterns of ships carrying United States foreign aid cargoes emphasizes American friendship for foreign countries. Additionally, an argument can be made for the availability of American flag ships and those of her allies to carry the developing trade of many newly emerging nations, if only to preclude their total dependency on the Soviet block for shipping services. Finally, it is politically advantageous and stabilizing to the free world to create close economic ties with new nations through waterborne trade relationships.

The arguments pro and con on the national role of the United States maritime industry have been briefly presented both to show the dilemma created for policymakers by this industry and to provide a basis for judgment as to the direction which the United States industry should be taking. A more liberal maritime policy with a well-defined annual United States merchant ship construction program is now being debated in Congress; if passed, it will be a first step toward stemming the present decline of the industry.

4. TECHNOLOGY FOR THE 1970s

During the last 15 years, the development of ocean transportation has been dramatic. For California it has been particularly important since the state bounds on the world's largest body of water. To put this progress in perspective, one can visualize a world globe focusing on the Western Hemisphere—the continents of North and South America. To the east the Atlantic Ocean insulates the Western Hemisphere from Europe; to the west the great Pacific Ocean lies between the United States and the Orient. To visualize the effective change that has taken place in ocean transportation in just 15 years, one can merely move the continents together so that the distance between them is one-quarter of the distance of 15 years ago. That is a strange looking world, but that is the world as it exists in terms of bulk transportation costs over water.

What has brought about this great revolution in ocean transportation? There are several related factors. There has been a great increase in the size of carriers. Tankers have grown about ten times the size of 15 years ago, and bulk carriers have grown six to eight times. There are obvious economies and efficiencies that come with increased size. In an attempt to support these superships, there has been the initial development of supporting facilities required for loading and discharging cargoes.

There has been a continued improvement of hull structure, cargo handling, propulsion, and automation. Nuclear power appears only a few years away from practical and economic utilization. We have seen the introduction of the combination carrier, ships that can carry radically different cargoes, enabling them to earn revenue a larger percentage of the time.

Much has been done to change the form in which bulk material moves. For example, iron ore concentrate has been delivered in a slurry form from Peru to Oregon. It is essentially handled as oil. Improvements in the movements of cargo from ships to shore facilities is going to have a revolutionary impact on the industrial and economic development of California.

We have a world of shrinking oceans. California is on the great Pacific Ocean, a body of water that is rapidly assuming the character of a pond in terms of ocean transportation costs. This fact is going to have a great influence on the state's industrial development.

What price distance—Superships

Distance is becoming a less and less meaningful variable in commercial or military operations. The theory that military strength or economic usefulness declines linearly with distance has often been stated, but it has never been true, and the technology that is now upon us makes it even less true.

Sea transportation has always been a bargain, and it promises to be an even bigger one. The problem is not one of distance but rather of what is encountered at either end of the voyage. Terminal facilities have been a common problem for both our military and civilian sea transportation systems.

It was rather common until recently to talk of the comparative disadvantage to the United States in fighting 8000 or 10,000 miles from home against an adversary whose home base is near the scene of conflict. Although these dramatic long-haul distances catch the headlines, neither in current nor in past technology do they determine the matter of comparative disadvantage. Studies have documented the logistic support difficulties at present levels of technology in several areas of possible nonnuclear conflict—in Thailand, in the Himalayas, in Iran, in Lebanon, and in the actual Korean conflict.

The most striking fact displayed is that the capacity for long-distance lift (sea transportation) massively exceeds that for short-distance lift inside the theatre. Bottlenecks inside the theatre are largely determined by local factors such as climate, terrain, harbors, port unloading facilities, railroads, and roads.

In commercial sea transportation systems utilization of superships has completely revised the economics of transporting low-value commodities like crude oil. The economics of a supertanker are difficult to grasp. A tanker with a capacity of 150,000 deadweight tons can move crude oil 5000 miles at $1.69 per ton compared to $7.29 per ton for a 10,000-ton tanker. Construction costs decrease with increasing tanker size from $220 per ton at 20,000 deadweight tons to less than $70 per ton at 300,000 tons. Operating costs also decrease, particularly with increased automation. By way of comparison, the *Tokyo Maru,* a recently constructed tanker of about 135,000 deadweight tons operates with a crew of 29, although earlier tankers of 50,000 tons often employed 35 or more.

During the 1970s the Japanese will be constructing 500,000-ton tankers, roughly ten times the size of the largest tankers available during the 1956 Suez crisis. As a result of such changes, not only are distances around gateways like the Suez cheaper than they were, but because of the limitations of the gateways themselves, the voyage around may be more economical than the direct route. Suez as presently configured is limited to fully loaded tankers of less than 70,000 deadweight tons.

An interesting comparison can be made on the costs to ship bulk cargo to Los Angeles from Australia and from inland California. Assuming that a 130,000-ton bulk carrier is used on the 6300-nautical mile sea route from Brisbane to Los Angeles and rail is used on the California land route, the ship transportation costs are approximately 0.03 cents per ton mile, and the rail transportation costs are approximately 1.0 cent per mile or 30 times greater. Based on this differential, shipping the bulk cargo 200 land miles costs as much as shipping it 6300 sea miles.

Special bulk cargo ships are now beginning to appear. For example, a new low-cost system for ocean transportation of iron ore has been announced by Marcona Corporation, San Francisco. This system may well completely revolutionize the economics of shipping raw materials such as iron ore.

The system, named Marconaflo, was successfully demonstrated last summer when 4000 long tons of Marcona superconcentrate iron ore was shipped from Peru to Portland, Oregon. The system permits loading and discharging of iron ores and other mineral concentrates in slurry form and makes it possible to transport these materials in large, high-economy tankers rather than in traditional bulk carriers. An important element of the system is the method of slurrying cargo after it has hardened or compacted in the ship's hold.

Large tankers can now make deliveries anywhere in the world, lie offshore in deep water, and pump slurrified cargo into a pipeline; they no longer need rely on conventional port facilities that often cannot handle the big economical bulk carriers. Handling costs of loading and discharging iron ore concentrates can be reduced by as much as 90% from the cost of conventional ship unloading systems. This reduction is made possible in part by the minimal facilities required for pipeline loading and discharging.

Despite the changing dimension of seapower, its importance in the Mahan sense should not be overlooked. Today 40 of the 50 largest cities in the United States have thriving port activities located either close to or within easy water access to the sea. These port cities have developed on waterways which were sufficiently deep to allow the movement of great tonnages of commodities to the doorstep of thriving industries. For two-thirds of this century these 40 locales have been called deep-water ports.

For the last quarter of this century, only a few of these ports will provide sufficient depth off their piers (even with extensive dredging) to handle superships designed as an integral part of competitive basic industries. The importance of the need for ports with deep draft capability is vividly illustrated by the Japanese success in producing steel at lower cost than United States industries.

With Japanese steel mills newly located adjacent to pier areas for the off-loading of ore ships (drawing up to 57 feet), the savings in transportation costs are sufficient to provide a major cost difference helping to offset the more efficient United States steel production operations. The cost of loading ore into freight cars and the additional freight costs in transhipping by rail, although less than 1 cent per ton mile, creates a substantially greater cost.

A new type of "regionalism" or economic grouping of countries because of low-cost sea transportation is thus developing. Superships will continue to cut the cost of distance and will force more economic dependence between nations.

What price port time—container ships

Clear understanding of the term containerization is necessary before discussing container ships. "Containerization" is a means by which goods are transported within large, uniform containers or boxes that can be interchanged and conveniently carried by and transferred between different modes of transportation. The container is large enough to require mechanical handling and is without wheels. Of standard shape and dimension, it has standard fittings for handling and securing to the various carriers. The goods carried in the container may be packages of assorted or uniform sizes and shapes; they may be a large single item; or they may be bulk or liquid commodities, refrigerated stores, or even cattle.

It is recognized that the answer to the problem of improved transportation of general cargoes does not necessarily lie in faster ships, or even primarily in "better" ships. It requires improved systems for the distribution of manufactured or processed goods, systems in which ships play an important part. The broader problem includes consideration of the form in which goods are shipped, the location of warehouses, the method of land transportation used, the marine terminals, and even the paperwork involved in ordering, shipping, and custom clearance of goods. Helping to solve this problem is where containers enter the picture.

The shift from "break bulk" cargo to containerized cargo has been dramatic. Presently there are over 178 United States flag merchant ships with a single-trip capacity of more than 45,000 containers, mostly of the 20-foot by 8-foot size. This tremendous container capacity includes full container ships and ships with an assigned partial container capability. All ships can carry containers either in their holds or on deck, but the figures here only include those ships with special container facilities.

The following figures were based on a summary prepared by the Office of Government Aid, Division of Trade Studies, Maritime Administration, and updated to June 1, 1969: there were in the United States merchant fleet 17 new container ships and 67 vessels converted to full container ships. Of this group, 38 ships without cargo gear for handling the containers depend completely upon shore facilities for loading and unloading. There were also 94 ships with partial container capacity.

Table 1 which appeared in the June 15, 1969, issue of the *Maritime Reporter* indicates the extent of container operations. The list of ships with partial container capacity includes only those for which special provision has been made for carrying containers.

The container assists in many transportation functions, including the packaging of goods at the initial point of shipment, environmental protection during the entire trip, simplified documentation, easier handling, and flexibility and potential for scheduling on a total systems basis. These benefits are not without problems. Labor unions have objected; custom inspections have had to be modified; high capital investments have had to be financed; lack of standardization has confused everyone; and difficult technical decisions have been required.

Containerization today is being labeled an affliction by many in the traditional ocean transportation business, some going as far as naming the affliction "containeritis." The traditional ocean carrier

TABLE 1
United States Flag Ship Container Operations
as of June 1, 1969

Full Container Ships

Owner	No. of Ships Conv.	New	Total	Total Container Capacity	Container Size-Std. (feet)
Alaska Steamship Co.	2	0	2	352	$24 \times 8 \times 8.5$
Amer. Export Isbrandtsen Line	6	3	9	6,112	$20 \times 8 \times 8$
Amer. President Lines	2	0	2	756	$20 \times 8 \times 8$
Containership					
Chartering Service, Inc.	3	0	3	1,080	$35 \times 8 \times 8.5$
Containship, Inc.	0	2	2	156[a]	$17 \times 8 \times 8$
				54[a]	$35 \times 8 \times 8$
Donmac Corporation	5	0	5	1,130	$35 \times 8 \times 8.5$
Hudson Waterways Corps.	9	0	9	1,709	$40 \times 8 \times 8.5$
Litton Industries Leasing Corp.					
(Operated by Sea-Land)	19	0	19	6,990	$35 \times 8 \times 8.5$
Madison Transportation Co.	1	0	1	332	$35 \times 8 \times 8.5$
Matson Navigation Co.	9	1	10	4,218[a]	$24 \times 8 \times 8.5$
Monterey Transportation Co.	1	0	1	360	$35 \times 8 \times 8.5$
Moore-McCormack Lines	0	1	1	800[a]	$20 \times 8 \times 8$
Pacific Far East Line	1	0	1	400	$20 \times 8 \times 8$
Sea-Land Service, Inc.	5	0	5	1,628	$35 \times 8 \times 8.5$
Seatrain Line, Inc.	2	4	6	NA[a]	NA
United States Lines	2	6	8	7,774	$20 \times 8 \times 8$
Totals	67	17	84	33,851	

Partial Container Capacity

Owner	No. of Ships	Total Container Capacity	Container Size-Std. (feet)
Amer. Mail Line	8	1,415	$20 \times 8 \times 8$
Amer. President Lines	8	929	$20 \times 8 \times 8$
Farrell Lines	5	910	$20 \times 8 \times 8$
Grace Lines	10	1,528	$20 \times 8 \times 8$
Highland Steamship Corp.	1	18[a]	$40 \times 8 \times 8$
Hudson Waterways Corp.	1	NA[a]	NA
Matson Navigation Co.	5	490	$24 \times 8 \times 8.5$
Moore-McCormack Lines	11	2,706	$20 \times 8 \times 8$
Motorships of Delaware, Inc.	1	6[a]	NA
Pacific Far East Line	14	1,303	$20 \times 8 \times 8$
States Steamship Co.	9	1,338	$20 \times 8 \times 8$
Sun Leasing Co.	1	260[a]	$40 \times 8 \times 8$
Sunexport Holding Corp.	1	NA[a]	NA
Union Carbide Corp.	2	384	$30 \times 8 \times 8$
United States Lines	17	724	$20 \times 8 \times 8$
Totals	94	12,011	
Grand Totals	178	45,862	

[a] Has capacity for roll-on/roll-off vehicles or railroad cars. NA—either not applicable or not available.

sees the character of the investment changing radically from a preponderance in ship hardware to one biased toward containers. As far as the ocean carrier is concerned, the value of containerization is limited to what it can do in the port-to-port cycle, providing quick turnaround for his vessels and security for cargoes from damage and pilferage.

The mere existence of a large number of containers, whether standardized and interchangeable, will not in and by itself bring about or even lead to a true integration of our transportation system if the technology is merely superimposed on the present, fragmented transportation system and national transportation regulatory philosophy.

What has been proposed is to look at the container as a vehicle of transportation in itself—as opposed to a form of packing that is now largely thought of—thus constituting an entirely new mode of transportation on a par with the present modes: the truck, train, ship, or airplane. The unique feature of this new mode is that it is physically capable of moving on land, on sea, or in the air and therefore requires a new approach to trade and commerce regulation that now applies to the other modes separately.

One proposal is to introduce a new identity, namely the "transmodalist." Whatever he is called, he will have the responsibility for providing a container at some point for loading; he will make necessary arrangements for all modes of transport to destination; and he will have responsibility for discharge of the container and delivery of its contents to the consignee.

What does the application of containers mean to future ship trends? By 1975, it has been estimated that about 50% of our general cargo will be containerized. The point-to-point delivery time by this integrated transportation system will be appreciably less than that of present "break bulk" systems. This more rapid delivery time is accomplished by high speed vessels and specially designed container handling cranes at the docks.

In his transportation message to Congress on March 2, 1966, President Johnson called for a study of high-speed, large-capacity ships, devoted primarily to transporting preloaded containers of varying types between the major ports of the world. The vessel used in the study was a conventional displacement ship which carried 1200 20-foot containers at speeds up to 25 knots. The ship was a conservative design whose performance and operating costs were well known. That the ship would be operated with a crew of 32 men was assumed. It was further assumed that the containers were filled by the manufacturer and delivered to the pier at the manufacturer's expense. Consequently, the only cargo handling expense charged to the ship was that required to load and discharge the containers at pier side.

The study provided assurance that United States flag ships could be designed, constructed, and operated at a profit without subsidy in the North Atlantic trade. The conclusion was based on the assumption that the present and future freight rates would be between 40 and 80 cents per cubic foot. Specifically, the study showed that if the ship were operated at full capacity on a round trip voyage the break-even freight rate would be 23 cents per cubic foot.

Another way of looking at this capital intensive system is to look at the break-even number of containers assuming unsubsidized operations and charging the prevailing conference rate of 80 cents per cubic foot. The break-even point would be between 20 and 25% capacity or only about 240 to 300 containers out of a possible 1200.

The problem becomes more complex if one postulates general rate reductions due to more efficient ships and if one includes low-cost foreign built ships. Even with these factors, the study showed that American ships can be built and operated profitably on some trade routes by Americans, without the need for construction differential subsidy or operating differential subsidy. The results were surprising, in fact, startling.

What price speed—nuclear ships

At present there are strong differences of opinion regarding the prospects of nuclear power for merchant ships. In the mid-1950s the *NS Savannah* was built and served as a visible demonstration of our nation's advanced technology. She is not economically competitive in any sense of the word with today's modern conventional ships. However, her reactor technology, at least 15 years old, no longer provides a meaningful comparison. The attractiveness of nuclear power as a source of propulsion power for merchant ships lies not in its novelty but in the way it can respond to the recent trends in United States flag shipping.

During the 1930s, a speed of 8 to 10 knots was conventional for American merchant ships. Merchant ships built during World War II generally were designed for 12 to 16 knots. It is important to note that these vessels still comprise approximately 75% of our fleet. Postwar ships were built to cruise at about 18 knots, and those becoming operational today generally average 20 to 24 knots.

This substantial increase in speed was in direct response to the requests of shippers seeking to minimize the length of time goods are in transit, in large measure to expedite payments from their customers. Consequently, even faster ships are considered by ship operators. Vessels with a cruising speed in excess of 30 knots most assuredly will attract business from even the express ships of today.

The major problem with high-speed ships is their consumption of fuel. Fuel requirements increase, as a rule of thumb, by the square of the speed. Thus greater amounts of fuel must be carried at the expense of cargo space. Also, high-speed ships are generally much more sleek in design resulting in a less efficient cargo space layout.

The amount of fuel used by the *Savannah* to cross the Atlantic is equal in volume to a clenched fist. By contrast, a conventionally powered ship of similar size would require about 430 tons of fuel oil for the same voyage. In its $6\frac{1}{2}$ years of operation before refueling, the *Savannah* consumed only 119 pounds of U-235 enriched uranium oxide fuel. There is little disagreement that the best way to achieve high speed without excessive intrusion upon carrying capacity is through nuclear power. The argument arises over the projected economics of nuclear propulsion.

The construction cost of a nuclear ship exceeds that of a conventional ship by 25 to 50%. No one will argue that fact, but, problems arise in making comparisons. Many would argue that comparing the two is similar to comparing today's jets and yesterday's propeller craft. The jets are much more expensive, but their increased speed and high utilization make them a much more efficient revenue producer.

Many studies have been made comparing the economics of a nuclear ship with a fossil-fuel ship. Generally speaking, they indicate that second-generation nuclear ships would be an economic toss-up with conventional ships. If optimistic figures are used for nuclear power, nuclear ships have a slight economic edge. With less optimistic figures, nuclear ships appear to be slightly less economical than conventional ships.

However, advocates of nuclear power will argue that given the experience in design, fabrication, and construction of the second-generation ships, the third generation of nuclear vessels definitely will be economically superior.

In 1968, a study was conducted for the U.S. Maritime Administration (MARAD) by General Dynamics Corporation in which nuclear and fossil-fueled 30-knot container ships were compared. They were designed to service the route from the East Coast through the Panama Canal and to the Far East. Table 2 summarizes the characteristics of these two vessels.

TABLE 2
30-Knot Container Ships

Characteristics	Nuclear	Conventional
Length, overall	871 feet	871 feet
Beam, maximum	104 feet	104 feet
Depth	61 feet	61 feet
Containers $(8 \times 8 \times 20)$	1,532	1,556
Crew	40	40
Normal SHP	100,000	116,000
Displacement, light	22,236 tons	18,967 tons
Crew and stores	420 tons	400 tons
Fuel	NA	10,636 tons
70% utilization		
Containers	11,690 tons	11,872 tons
Displacement	34,346 tons	41,875 tons
Draft	27 feet 7 inches	32 feet 0 inches
Speed	30.5 knots	30.3 knots
100% utilization		
Containers	16,700 tons	16,960 tons
Displacement	39,356 tons	46,963 tons
Draft	30 feet 7 inches	34 feet 9 inches
Speed	29.7 knots	29.3 knots

The study concluded that the total construction cost would be $61.9 million for three nuclear ships vice $43.0 million for three conventionally powered ships. Annual operating costs, not including fuel costs, for the three ships were estimated at $16.2 million for the nuclear ships and $15.0 million for the conventional ships. The economic issue became cloudy when subsidy payments were included. Suffice it to say, the nuclear ship would be able to obtain higher subsidies and the construction and operating costs to the owner-operator would be essentially a toss-up.

Essentially, the argument involves two issues: is a 30-knot ship needed and if so is nuclear power the best way to proceed? Most shippers would agree that a 30-knot ship would be economical in some segments of our world trade. Proponents of nuclear power argue that nuclear-powered ships would guarantee more reliable schedules because it would be easier to build in a power margin to compensate for foul weather or port delays. They also argue that United States shipyards would benefit because these high technology ships would be beyond the capability of most foreign yards.

Although there are divergent views on future costs, it is clear that the manning, maintenance, and initial construction costs of nuclear ships will continue to be higher. For example, a 25,000-shaft horsepower nuclear plant costs about $4 million, as opposed to $1 million for a conventional plant. The margin of difference lessens as 100,000-shaft horsepower is approached; the nuclear plant costs about $7 million compared with $3.5 million for the conventional.

The hope for nuclear power lies in the projected drop in nuclear fuel costs and an associated increase in the cost of fuel oil. The present nuclear fuel cost is somewhat less than fuel oil. In the 1968 MARAD study the estimated per ship annual operating expenses, not including fuel, for the conventional ship and the nuclear ship were 5.0 million and 5.4 million, respectively. Equal costs (operating plus fuel) occur with nuclear fuel priced at 2.5 mils and fuel oil priced at 3.1 mils per shaft horsepower hour. The present fuel oil price of $1.90 per barrel equates to the 3.1 mils figure. If fuel oil prices increase or if nuclear fuel prices decrease, the economic edge will shift to the high speed nuclear ship vice the conventionally powered ship.

What price the environment—arctic ships

This year witnessed a $30 million gamble by Humble Oil and Refining Company to evaluate the technical feasibility of a super icebreaking tanker ramming her way 4500 miles north and west through the Northwest Passage to the potentially prolific oil province in Prudhoe Bay, Alaska.

Clearly the principal objective of the voyage was to prove that oil could be transported through the ice-covered sea to East Coast markets, but the undertaking has much broader and long-range implications. Few ocean-related undertakings had so much riding on its success.

The reconfiguration of the *Manhattan* was a marvel of marine technology in itself. The vessel chosen for conversion was a 945-foot, 142,500-ton supertanker, the largest commercial tanker carrying the United States flag. The ship was leased from Seatrain Lines, Inc., in January 1969 and was to be ready in time for a summer start.

The vessel was cut into sections to speed the "jumboizing" which added 9000 tons and 65 feet. Because of the press of time the task was divided among four shipyards. Sun Shipbuilding and Drydock strengthened the vessel internally and added a double skin to the stern section. Alabama Drydock did similar work on the midbody and Newport News Shipbuilding and Drydock on the forward section. Bath Iron Works built the new ice-breaking bow. When the "jumboizing" and modification were completed, the sections were shipped to Sun Shipbuilding at Chester, Pennsylvania, where they were welded together and final testing was accomplished.

Model tests had indicated that the *Manhattan*'s new bow was capable of increasing the icebreaking capabilities as much as 40 to 60% over conventional icebreaker bow designs. The bow works on the "down-breaking" principle; it moves into the ice at an 18-degree angle and increases to the more conventional 30-degree angle before the extended bow breaks the ice. The new bow also has a maximum width 16 feet wider than the remainder of the ship. This feature leaves more free water along the hull sides and reduces ice friction.

The ship as reconfigured was lengthened to 1005 feet and widened to 148 feet. New high-strength propellers and shafts, external protectors for the propellers and rudders and an external sloping ice belt along the sides were installed. A specially constructed heliport was installed so that scouting missions could provide information on the ice ahead.

Why the big push to evaluate an ice breaking tanker? Simply stated, to bring crude oil to the East Coast by ice breaking tanker has been estimated to save 60 cents a barrel over the next least costly method. This represents many hundreds of millions of dollars of shipping costs per year.

Oil companies will need new ships to transport oil through the Northwest Passage. This is domestic trade and United States flag ships must be utilized. Construction of these ships would bolster the United States shipbuilding industry. Humble alone has projected needs for six 250,000-deadweight ton vessels by 1975, with the fleet growing to perhaps 25 or 30 by 1980. Humble's need represents an expansion of our present tanker capacity by 250%. Each of the tankers will cost perhaps $50 million.

Easy access to arctic oil has many national security aspects. Besides providing substantial increases to our reserves, it would allow us to aid our Western European allies in case of a fuel emergency. The distance from Alaska by ship is roughly the same to London as to New York.

A proven Northwest Passage translates into a new international trade route which in turn will have a marked influence on world trade patterns. The passage means a shorter, more direct route between Europe and the Far East. The present mileage from London to Tokyo is about 16,700 miles if the Suez Canal is by-passed, 8600 if it is used. The distance using the Northwest Passage is less than 8000 miles. Furthermore, using the Suez Canal limits vessel size to approximately 70,000 tons. It is interesting to note that a point on the northern shore of Banks Island (500 miles east of Prudhoe Bay) is essentially equidistant from New York, London, and Tokyo, approximately 4000 miles.

Perhaps the biggest winner in the opening to this route will be the mining companies. There is a great wealth of both base and precious metals located above the Arctic Circle which would become economically important once access is established.

This mineral industry is a sleeping giant. For example, exploratory drilling has identified the fabled Mary River iron ore deposits on Baffin Island. The ore appears of sufficient quality that it can be fed directly into steel plant furnaces. Other minerals present in abundance are tungsten, lead, zinc, nickel, and copper. These rich deposits have lain dormant mainly because the present shipping season is only about 6 weeks long.

It must be recognized that if the Northwest Passage is opened, business, government and educational institutions will be confronted overnight with great opportunities as well as with equally great problems and responsibilities. This need has been recognized by President Nixon, who has announced that the U.S. Government would be stepping up its arctic activity in an effort to be better prepared to provide the needed service functions (weather and ice forecasting, safety, communications, inspections, etc.) which are clearly U.S. Government responsibilities.

5. SPECIAL MARINE TRANSPORT SYSTEMS

Submersibles

Small submersibles are not new; in fact they date back at least to the Revolutionary War era. During the war David Bushnell designed and built a small submersible to attack British Men-of-War. His submersible was hand propelled, and its method of attack was to come up underneath the enemy warship, drill a hole into the hull and attach an explosive charge. The only problem was the ordnance system. Bushnell was unable to drill through the copper sheathing and consequently could not attach the charge.

The last decade has seen a rapid development in the number and variety of submersibles. With few exceptions the vehicles have had a limited depth capability when compared to the maximum depth of the ocean, almost 7 miles. In general their design depths have been in the 2000- to 8000-foot range.

A notable exception to this depth limitation was the French *Trieste* which in 1961 descended to the bottom of the Marianas Trench, the deepest known location in the oceans, to a depth of 35,800 feet. This submersible could best be described as a vertical elevator because it had virtually no horizontal mobility. The small pressure sphere for the two operators was located below a huge tank of gasoline, which in effect made the vehicle an undersea balloon.

Most of the small submersibles built during the last decade have been designed to carry out specialized marine transport tasks. The Cousteau *Saucer* and the Woods Hole *Alvin* have been used primarily to carry scientists and engineers into the actual ocean environment. The *Star III* built by General Dynamics Corporation, has performed the very specialized transportation task of supporting underwater archeology in the Aegean Sea.

The *Ben Franklin* designed by Jacques Piccard and built by Grumman Aircraft Corporation, supported a crew of scientists on a 2000-mile drift in the Gulf Stream from Florida to the Canadian Maritime Provinces.

The Lockheed *Deep Quest* has supported many underwater operations, but the best known is probably its recovery of the flight recorders from two aircraft which fell into the sea shortly after takeoff from Los Angeles International Airport.

The U.S. Navy has been an active participant in submersible development. The *Deep Submergence Rescue Vehicle* (*DSRV*), constructed at Lockheed Missiles and Space Company, was launched in early 1970. When operational, this vehicle and others like it will be able to transport trapped sailors from a downed submarine to safety. The rescue system can be supported either by a nuclear "mother" submarine or from an *Auxiliary Submarine Rescue Ship* (*ASR*).

The recently commissioned *Nuclear Research Submersible* (*NR-1*) is a marked departure from previous submersibles which have had severely limited endurances. She is designed to operate submerged for a period of 30 days. This figure represents the endurance of the crew rather than of the vehicle.

During the 1970s two very interesting submersibles will become operational. One is the U.S. Navy's *Deep Submergence Search Vehicle* (*DSSV*), which will carry a crew of three or four to 20,000 feet to conduct search and recovery operations for up to 30 hours. In contrast to the *Trieste* the *DSSV* will be much more than a vertical elevator.

The most imaginative submersible is one being built by the Oceanic Foundation in Hawaii called *Deep Voyager*. It also is a 20,000-foot vehicle, but it has two unique features. The pressure capsules are massive glass, and propulsion will be obtained by gliding with wings. By ballasting heavy on the surface, it will fly down at a nine-degree angle and a speed of about 6 knots until it reaches the ocean bottom. At that point it will blow ballast and become light and glide up. Fifty such cycles of 50 miles each will cover the 2500 miles from Hawaii to California.

Man-in-the-sea systems

The last decade has seen rapid development of advanced diving techniques and equipments. Many systems utilize the concept of saturated diving advanced by George Bond in the 1950s. Man is exposed to the high pressure environment for extended periods, and the gases absorbed in his body tissues reach an equilibrium condition with the surrounding hyperbaric environment. He is not returned to normal atmospheric conditions after each diving operation but is supported either in an undersea habitat or is returned to the surface in a pressure capsule and transferred to a surface chamber maintained at a pressure equal to the diver's operating depth.

These advanced diving systems are rapidly moving from mere experimental undertakings to practical and presumably cost-competitive systems. Several companies are developing undersea oil recovery systems utilizing divers for at least some of the operations requiring the presence and decision-making capability of man.

The depth capability of advanced diving systems is closely related to the 600- to 1000-foot depths of the coastal zone. Diving to depths of 400 to 600 feet is a relatively routine commercial operation. Extensive experimentation under controlled laboratory conditions has been conducted to depths in excess of 1000 feet.

This coming decade will probably see the operational depth extended to encompass all coastal zone depths and perhaps even deeper, with projections ranging from 1200 to 2000 feet.

Submerged dredge

One very serious problem associated with the coastal zone is the loss of sand from selected beaches. This situation is often aggravated and accelerated by man's activities. For example, the regulation of a river's flow by dams reduces the sediment and sand transported during periods of high runoff. The installation of coastal structures often has the effect of blocking the flow of sand parallel to the shoreline.

Fort Pierce, Florida is a community which has lost sand from its beaches. It recently contracted with Ocean Science and Engineering to pump offshore sand to the beach at 94 cents per cubic yard. Such a contract might have gone completely unnoticed except that OSE plans to use a submerged dredge rather than a conventional surface dredge.

The dredge is mounted in tracks and moves from the beach into the water using an umbilical to provide electricity for the machinery and breathing air for the diver-operators. At the front of the vehicle is a 30-foot swing ladder equipped with a rotary cutting head. Sand is pumped through a submerged pipeline directly to shore.

Adaptions or modifications of this system may find application in the coastal zone for tasks such as offshore mining or burying underwater pipelines.

6. FORECAST FOR THE FUTURE

The vast majority of goods in intercontinental trade will continue to be carried by displacement ships with only about 1% of world trade going by air. Waterborne commerce passing through United States ports is expected to increase at least 5% per year. During the last decade, world seaborne trade has increased in excess of 7% per year. At only 5.5% per year, seaborne trade during the next 20 years would triple from its present 2250 million long tons to 6750 million long tons.

In contrast to the shipping volume, the total number of ships sailing the oceans will probably decrease about 15%. The total world ship tonnage will more than double during the next 20 years. Supertankers of great draft and tonnage (up to 500,000 tons per ship) will steadily replace the present inventory of ships. The draft of these giant tankers will be 70 to 80 feet when fully loaded, creating new problems of channel dredging or necessitating off-shore loading and unloading facilities. An ever growing proportion of cargo will be handled in bulk and by specialized ships, with most manufactured goods and consumer commodities carried in containers. The concentration of bulk and containerized cargoes in a smaller number of much larger ships will cause most freight to flow through fewer ports.

Most world sea commerce will have traffic lanes involving only 1% of the ocean's surface, but congestion in the entrances to a diminishing number of ports will require traffic control systems to keep every ship in the area under close surveillance. Massive amounts of potentially hazardous cargo carried by these ships coupled with the poor maneuverability characteristic of these ships accentuate this problem.

The present United States shipbuilding industry with its Vietnam war impetus will dominate the short-term outlook. Greatly improved shipbuilding techniques seem to be on the near horizon. The Department of Defense has taken a creative lead in ship procurement practices by its planned multiship buys. Modernization and automation of present shipyards is indicated with larger shipyards developing and many of the smaller shipyards closing because of their inability to obtain contracts of sufficient size and time span to finance modernization.

The evolving integrated systems approach to transportation with corporations devising total transportation systems to meet their specific needs should provide the impetus to change sea transportation from a labor intensive business to a capital intensive business. The entry of the aerospace industry into this area will lend additional impetus. It will take large amounts of capital to place total systems into operation, but the overall savings will make the systems approach cost effective. In the process, sea transportation will become more efficient with the ships spending more hours at sea. This translates into more effectiveness out of personnel for the cost of their labor.

The shift to a total systems approach, with much wider use of containerization and highly efficient bulk cargo handling systems, will have far reaching effects on many activities in the coastal zone, including the following:

- Reduced longshoreman requirements per unit of cargo handled.
- Need for a simplified bill of lading and consignment of cargo.

- Reduction in the number of ports required, but a marked improvement in their cargo handling facilities.
- Relocation of ports to areas remote from city centers with the release of valuable waterfront real estate to more people-oriented purposes.

The limited war requirements for foreign shipping indicate a continuing need for several hundred United States-controlled merchant ships. These needs are over and above military auxiliaries, Military Sea Transportation Service (MSTS) ships and our expanding airlift capability. The increasingly specific design of ships to fit most efficiently into a total systems approach to transportation (tankers for only one product, cargo ships without handling gear, etc.) will make merchant ships under United States control less flexible for responding to military contingencies.

The increasing size of ships, automation with reduced crews, and the added premium for reliable service will create a rapid growth in requirements for worldwide, accurate, long-term weather forecasts. Ship routing based upon environmental predictions will be extended worldwide. The technology of the 1970's will decrease transport costs significantly, especially long distance costs. Larger payload vehicles both on the sea and in the air will greatly reduce costs per ton mile. These vast improvements in long distance transport will intensify cultural and economic contacts.

The common denominator for the future is change. This change will be responsive to many factors, some of which are listed below:

- New technology: computers; cargo handling; nuclear.
- New problems: pollution; congestion; conflicting use.
- New needs: raw materials; ports; data and services.
- New economics: superships; interest rates; labor costs.
- New competition: airplanes; pipelines; trucks.
- New money: aerospace; conglomerates; government.

Assuming that the present trends continue for the next two decades, certain fallouts can be conjectured which should benefit other developing marine programs. In the coastal area, harbor congestion and pollution of major ports should decrease markedly with better traffic control, increased use of offshore loading, and unloading facilities, and major relocation of port facilities to areas well removed from the port city's center of cultural and business activity. The salutory effect on the city dweller's enjoyment of his coastal or estuarine environment should be greatly enhanced.

BIBLIOGRAPHY

Bannerman, Graeme C., "Multi-Year Ship Procurement and Other Ship Acquisition Concepts," *Journal of ASNE*, December 1967.

Chabot, Paul L., "Choosing the Route Through the Ice," *Ocean Industry*, August 1969.

"Changing Patterns in U.S. Trade and Shipping Capacity," U.S. Department of Commerce/Maritime Administration, December 1964.

Culver, John A., *Ships of the U.S. Merchant Fleet*, Dennison Press, Weymouth, Mass., 1969.

Frosch, Robert A., "The Emerging Shape of Policies for the Acquisition of Major Systems," *SNAME Journal of Marine Technology*, July 1969.

The Future of American Merchant Shipping, Brookings Research Report 54, The Brookings Institution, Washington, D.C., 1966.

Hamren, Fred A., "Makai Range Habitat Readied," *Undersea Technology*, February 1969.

Henry, James J., and Henry J. Karsch, "Container Ships," *Transactions of SNAME*, 1966.

Hood, Edwin, and Nathan Sonenshein, "An Objective Look at Shipbuilding in the United States," *Transactions of SNAME Diamond Jubilee Meeting*, June 18–21, 1968.

Kesterman, Frank, "Nuclear Merchant Ship Economics—A Twenty Year Forecast," *Naval Engineers Journal*, April 1969.

"Lockheed's Subsea Cellar System," *Ocean Industry*, August 1969.

Mahan, Alfred Thayer, *The Influence of Sea Power upon History 1600–1783*, American Century Series, Hill and Wang, New York, 1966.

Maritime Subsidies, U.S. Department of Commerce/Maritime Administration, 1969.

Marx, Hans, "The United States Merchant Marine 1789–1903," *United States Naval Institute Proceedings*, Vol. 89, Nos. 8, 10, and 12 (1963).

Merchant Fleets of the World, U.S. Department of Commerce/Maritime Administration, Report 560-20, July 10, 1968.

Metropolitan Transportation—1980, The Port of New York Authority, 1963.

Niblock, Robert W., "The Manhattan's Mission: To Open the Northwest Passage," *Undersea Technology*, July 1969.

"Northwest Passage—What it Could Mean," *Ocean Industry*, July 1969.

"The Problem of the United States Merchant Marine," Encyclopedia Britannica Library Research Service, 1969.

Proceedings of the Symposium on Marine Resources Development in the Western Region, University of Southern California, Los Angeles, February 2, 1968.

Pryor, Taylor A., "Commercial Test Ranges," *Oceanology International*, July/August 1969.

The Soviet Merchant Marine, U.S. Department of Commerce/Maritime Administration, 1967.

"A Statistical Analysis of the Worlds Merchant Fleets," U.S. Department of Commerce/Maritime Administration, December 1967.

Taggart, Robert, *Marine Propulsion: Principles and Evolution*, Gulf Publishing Company, Houston, Tex., 1969.

Will, John M., "Are Nuclear Ships the Answer?" *Oceanology International,* July/August 1969.

Wohlstetter, Albert, "Illusions of Distance," *Foreign Affairs,* January 1969.

"Woods Hole Conference in Maritime Research and Development," U.S. Department of Commerce/Maritime Administration, July 1969.

Zeien, Charles, "Ship Procurement—Isn't there a Better Way?" *SNAME Journal of Marine Technology,* July 1967.

INDEX

solving, 253
conflicts, examples of, 124
  resolution of, 193
  theory of, 119
conservation, definition, 40, 149
  minimum standard, 41, 46
  planning (management criteria), 6
  problems of, 157
construction maintenance, 263
  techniques, 259
container ships, 314, 329
  30-knot, 335
continental borderland, 154
continental shelf, exploitation of, 29
contracting, direct control technique,
  204
controlling the environment, 274
controls, contracting, 204
  direct, 203
  indirect, 204
  policy, 203
  statutory, 153
  zoning, 203
corrosion, 258
cost-benefit structuring, 197
cost estimation, process of, 199
costs, "life-cycle cost structure," 197
criterion functions, 200

data, criticality of, 232
  synoptic, 233
  time series, 233
  water column, 233
data acquisition, 228
data base, organization of, 232, 235
data centers, 231
data communication, 228
data network, 225
data requirements, coastal zone management, 222
data retrieval, system design, 231
data storage, system design, 231, 234
data systems, applications of, 221
decision-making, 73
Deep Sea Drilling Project, 25
demographic projections, socioeconomic trends, 81
desalination, 67
design criteria, engineering, 23
destructive organisms, 56

detergents, 51
developing nations, ocean resources,
  32
development of information systems,
  224
dikes, 268
disarmament, ocean bottom, 31
dispersants, 54
domestic sewage, 49
dredge, submerged, 341
dredging, sand, 60, 70

earthquake, effect of (deep ocean
  structures), 23
education, factor in productivity, 89
electrical engineering (ocean technology), 22
electromagnetic spectrum, element of
  environment, 116
embayed coasts, 4
emulsifiers, oil spills, 54
energy, daily oil-equivalent, 151
  tidal, 160
energy resource production, 151
engineering design criteria, 23
engineering structures, coastal zone, 4
engineering technology, relation to
  management goals, 246
environment, coastal zone, 116
  control of, 274
  management of (total approach), 74
environmental control systems, 265
environmental data, 222
environmental parameters, planning, 3
environmental pollution, industrial
  waste, 11
estuaries, habitats (breeding grounds),
  6
estuarine pollution, 33
estuarine waste, 286
eutrophication, 50
evaluative planning, 15
extractive resources, inorganic materials, 54
extractive use, ocean resources, 8

ferromanganese nodules, 71
fish consumption, per capita, 44
fisheries, data system, 240
flags of convenience, 324

DATE DUE

MAR 02	